ROAD TO REFERENDUM

THE OFFICIAL COMPANION TO THE MAJOR NEW TELEVISION SERIES

IAIN MACWHIRTER

Road To Referendum
978-1908885210
Iain Macwhirter
First Published 2013
Published by Cargo Publishing
SC376700
© Iain Macwhirter 2013

Printed & Bound in Scotland by Bell & Bain
Cover design and typeset by Craig Lamont
www.cargopublishing.com

Also available as:

Kindle Ebook
EPUB Ebook

To Chrissie - if she'd only known

CONTENTS

PREFACE

×

THIS BOOK began life as an accompaniment to a television series, *Road to Referendum*, which traces the extraordinary changes in Scottish politics in the past fifty years as we have gone from being at the very heart of the Union to facing a referendum on independence. However, the road is rather longer travelled than that. The wars of independence in the Middle Ages, when Scotland first asserted its independence and defined itself as a nation, are clearly where the story of Scottish Nationalism really begins.

But this isn't intended to be a history book and I have only included sketches of key periods in Scottish history to the extent that they make sense of what is happening in the present. For example, the current arguments about whether Scotland was extinguished by the Treaty of Union clearly require some understanding of how and why Scotland relinquished its political autonomy in 1707. Similarly, the Darien colonial adventure in 1699 is important mainly because of the way it is used to this day as shorthand for either English perfidy or Scotland's economic inadequacy.

As a journalist, I venture onto the minefield of Scottish history with trepidation and my accounts will no doubt be contested by scholars. But I have tried to write this for a wider audience than just Scots and I have tried to provide an introduction for people not acquainted with Scottish politics and who have only a vague notion of what has been happening here and cannot be expected to know or care much about the Caledonian Antisyzygy or the 57 varieties of Devolution Max.

Chapters 7 to 12 cover broadly the territory of the TV documentaries, and I am indebted to STV, not just for the opportunity to present a three-part series which was long overdue, but also for being able to draw directly on many of the interviews in the programmes and to the Herald & Times Group for making the project happen. This is not a recapitulation of a television script and these chapters cover very much more ground than a television programme ever could. All opinions expressed in this book are mine alone and should not be taken as in any way reflecting the views of STV or the Herald & Times Group.

This book in part represents my own attempts to come to terms with the astonishing growth in Scottish national identity during my lifetime. I was born in Margaret Thatcher's constituency in London and brought up in Edinburgh, where I was completely deaf to the appeal of Scottish Nationalism, even though my mother became a prominent member of the SNP. I spent half of my professional life as a journalist in London, mainly in Westminster, and the rest in Scotland, latterly at Holyrood, where I have been continually surprised by the rapidity of political change in Scotland. I have a great affection for Scotland; I feel I understand its confusion over its identity, and its uncertainty over what, if anything, it still means to be a part of Great Britain.

I am not a member of the Scottish National Party and many Nationalists will find my portrayal of the movement at times unsympathetic. Labour politicians will assume, as they generally do, that I'm a closet "Nat". Both sides now accept that Scotland could become a viably independent country. At time of writing, there is no firm evidence yet that the Scottish people want to go to the trouble of detaching themselves from the United Kingdom, a country in which they feel at home, even as they depart from it politically. Geography is destiny and Scotland and England are condemned to coexist on this small island off the coast of Europe and live in each other's worlds. But it would be a great mistake to assume that Scots will remain within the UK come what may – it will have to change to survive.

Like Robert the Bruce, the excommunicated Scottish king who defeated the English at Bannockburn in 1314 despite having spent most of his life fighting for England, the Scots will only sue for independence once they have explored every other conceivable option, and when they have established beyond doubt that it is in their material interest so to do. That moment may never come. But in the meantime, the constitutional relationships between the constituent parts of this extraordinary island will undergo a process of permanent renegotiation. If you halve the distance between two points, and then keep on halving it, you go forward – but you never arrive.

CHAPTER ONE
INTRODUCTION

×

I ' V E N E V E R been much interested in the Edinburgh Military Tattoo. Sitting in the rain watching pipe bands marching up and down is not my idea of an enjoyable evening, though more than 200,000 people pay to see it every year during the Edinburgh Festival. So, it was with some surprise that I received an invitation to accompany the First Minister of Scotland to the Royal Box for the 2007 Military Tattoo. How could I refuse?

Alex Salmond had only just been installed as First Minister of Scotland after the first election victory by the Scottish National Party in its 80-year history. I don't know what the Brigadiers and Lieutenant Colonels made of him, but Salmond certainly seemed to find it all hilarious, sitting in for the Queen on her own portable 'throne' playing with the light that flashed every time he had to rise to take the salute from some regiment of foot. I wasn't quite so comfortable, sitting next to Michael Martin, the Speaker of the House of Commons, who a few years previously had reported me to the Sergeant at Arms in Westminster for an article I had written on MPs' expenses.

As a journalist who has witnessed the career of Alex Salmond for a quarter of a century, I've been used to surprises – but this was positively surreal. Here was the former leftist who had once been expelled from the SNP for being a republican socialist, now sitting at the heart of the Scottish establishment – assuming such a thing exists. The leader of the Scottish National Party leading the 10,000-strong Tattoo audience in a rendition of *God Save the Queen*. Hugh MacDiarmid, the Marxist poet who co-founded the National Party of Scotland, would be turning in his grave, along with Queen Victoria and James Keir Hardie.

After the salutes, the flutes of champagne arrived and Salmond staked his ground – wherever there is attention, the First Minister will always be at the centre of it. "I can see you're getting to like this," I remarked. "You'll be wanting to start a war next."

"Sadly, no," he replied. "Unlike Tony Blair I can't launch any invasions. Though I'm told I have a navy – a couple of fisheries protection vessels – so maybe I could start a new cod war." A couple of Lt Colonels laughed uneasily. Salmond looked around the circle of suits with that wide-eyed look of his that seems to say: "You may think I'm a jumped-up politician, but I just don't care."

Who was laughing at whom, I wondered. Was Salmond sending up the British Empire? Thumbing his nose at the Great Britain whose imperial past was being celebrated out there on the esplanade of Edinburgh Castle? Or was this some kind of post-Nationalist gesture of conciliation to the UK, like his promise to keep the Queen as head of state of an independent Scotland? Perhaps he had simply been adopted as a new regimental mascot, to be humoured and tolerated by the UK because, as First Minister of Scotland, he was all office and no power? I don't even know if he knew himself. Salmond doesn't go in for too much self-examination. So long as he is winning elections, he doesn't care what anyone thinks.

There have been many equally surreal moments in the past hectic six years as Salmond took his party from relative obscurity, seized power in the Scottish Parliament that was supposed to kill off the SNP and went on to challenge the very existence of the United Kingdom. It was a very Scottish coup. He rose to power in a Scottish Parliament that had become almost a national disgrace in its early years, riven with financial scandal, resignation and petty factionalism. He won a landslide election in 2011 by being more Labour than Labour. Before the Unionists had realised what was happening, he had scheduled a referendum on independence to be held in the autumn of 2014. The date was set, the clock was ticking.

IT'S A MYSTERY

Here's the mystery. How did Scotland go from being a willing and enthusiastic partner in the Union with England to a referendum on independence within the space of little more than a generation? In the 1950s and early 1960s, Scottish Nationalism was the preserve of the lunatic fringe; a motley crew of eccentrics who spent their time blowing up pillar boxes and stealing the Coronation Stone from Westminster Abbey. It was the Monster Raving Loony Party of its day, the only difference being that it didn't attract as many votes.

The Scottish National Party barely registered in general elections until the 1970s. And yet today, under Alex Salmond, the SNP commands the political landscape of Scotland, having achieved what most political commentators, this one included, said was impossible – an absolute majority in a parliament elected on a form of proportional representation. 2011 was Labour's worst defeat in Scotland since 1931. Scots are now preparing to vote in a referendum that could lead to the extinction, after 300 years, of one of the most successful political unions in history, which once commanded an Empire encompassing a quarter of the planet.

How did we get here? What went wrong with the Union? Where did this Nationalism come from? Are Scots only kidding? Do they really want to leave the United Kingdom, withdraw from Westminster and set up an independent state? Or is all this just an elaborate exercise in political theatre, designed to leverage Scotland's position within a union the Scots have no intention of abandoning? As we interviewed most of the key players in the Scottish debate of the past three decades for the STV television series, questions wouldn't go away: they just got bigger.

The rise of Scottish Nationalism doesn't fit any of the standard historical templates. This hasn't been a struggle for national liberation – not even the most Anglophobic Nationalist seriously argues that Scotland is an oppressed country. Scotland's colonial grievances, if such exist, date back 700 years to medieval times. Scots are experts at holding a grudge, but not even the chippiest could remain so outraged at King Edward's theft of a block of sandstone in 1296 that they would consider it grounds for political divorce today.

For the past 300 years, Scots have been largely content with their role as junior partners in the Union with England, which allowed the Scottish middle classes access to imperial markets, jobs and gave the all-powerful Scottish Kirk the right to evangelise the heathen in the British colonies. The Act of Union in 1707, when the bankrupt Scottish nobility was "bought and sold for English gold", as Robert Burns put it, were certainly unpopular at the time, and there were riots across Scotland at the loss of the Scottish Parliament – even though the vast majority of Scots had no rights to vote in it. The new English taxes, like the Malt Tax, weren't appreciated either. But these grievances were largely assuaged after 1750 as

Introduction

Scotland's economy boomed as never before thanks to the commercial advantages of access to the British Empire. Some might say that the Scots were bought and sold for imperial gold.

In the last battle fought on British soil, when the Young Pretender, Bonnie Prince Charlie, met the Duke of Cumberland at Culloden outside Inverness in 1746, there were almost as many Scots fighting on the "English" Hanoverian side, as were in the ranks of Catholic Jacobite clansmen. Lowland Scotland wanted nothing to do with the crazed Highlanders and their tartan absolutism. The increasingly Anglicised middle classes of Glasgow were too busy founding the great 18th-century tobacco and slave-trading houses, organising colonial plantations and seeking promotion in the British Army.

The intellectuals of Edinburgh, such as David Hume, one of Europe's pre-eminent philosophers and self-styled "North Briton", were at the time of the Jacobite uprisings struggling to free themselves from dogmatism and religious obscurantism. Adam Smith, the founding father of modern economics, regarded the Union with England, however emotionally regrettable, as unarguably the best way of bringing Scotland into the age of reason and to increase the wealth of the nation. If you'd suggested to any of these gentlemen that they should throw their lot in with the ludicrous Young Pretender, they'd have regurgitated their claret in disbelief.

After the defeat of the Jacobites at Culloden, many of the rebellious Highland soldiers – at least those who had escaped the Duke of Cumberland's execution squads – found their way into the British Army and became the shock troops of the emerging British Empire. After the Seven Years War, Pitt the Elder celebrated the military achievements of the former clansmen, who seemed to be completely unafraid of death. An extraordinary transformation took place as the vanquished became the conquerors during the expansion of the Pax Britannica: the Highland tribes took to slaughtering the tribes of America, India, Africa. In this bloody endeavour, Scots began to take pride in Great Britain and flattered themselves that the British Empire, the best bits anyway, was also a Scottish Empire. Scotland was no longer a state, but it remained a nation, contained within a nation, contained within an Empire. A Russian doll of cultural allegiances.

Scottish identity didn't disappear – in fact it flourished in the early years of the 19th century thanks to the romantic movement and the novels of Sir Walter Scott, who used the mystique of the Highlander to reinvent Scottish identity in a synthetic tartan guise. The *Waverley* novels recast Jacobites history as heroic fiction. Lowland Scots loved this valiant new self-image, borrowed from the Highland clan culture they had brutally obliterated in the previous century. The cult of the medieval patriot, Sir William Wallace, who had fought against the English was revived.

But the Scottish middle classes didn't see any need – even in the great age of Nationalism in the 19th century – for this identity to be expressed politically or as a demand for statehood. In fact, Scots loved the Union and the British Empire so much that they vigorously opposed Irish Home Rule after the turn of the 20th century in case the departure of Ireland weakened it. This was registered in their electoral support for the Scottish Unionist Party, the most successful party in 20th century Scotland, which was created out of a merger of Tory and Liberal Unionists who opposed Gladstone's Irish Home Rule bills. The Union in the party name was not the 1707 one between Scotland and England, but the 1801 Union between Great Britain and Ireland. Scots were so dedicated to Unionism that they defined their politics by it.

There were some modest proposals for Scottish home rule in the wake of the Irish question at the turn of the 19th century. Winston Churchill even suggested a form of federalism but no one took him very seriously, and though devolution bills were proposed they never went the parliamentary distance. Labour toyed with a Scottish Assembly after the First World War, but decided that there was little demand for home rule as the rise in working-class industrial politics seemed to make national boundaries irrelevant, an archaic obstacle in the way of socialist internationalism.

However, through the era of Red Clydeside and the Great Depression after 1931, Scots voted in very large numbers for the Scottish Unionist Party in general elections. This is one of the great paradoxes of a country that is supposed to be a Labour nation; dedicated to Robert Burns's egalitarianism, Keir Hardie and the veneration of the common man. For most of the 20th century, the common man voted Tory Unionist in Scotland. As recently as the 1955 General Election, the Scottish Unionists (they didn't call themselves "Conservative" until 1965) gained a majority of seats and a majority of votes – the only party in Scottish electoral history to achieve this electoral double. Not even the SNP managed that in their 2011 landslide in the Scottish Parliament elections. This support for Unionism expressed not just support for the idea of Great Britain and the Empire among Scots of all classes. It had a profound religious significance too – particularly among working-class Protestants in west central Scotland. Voting Unionist was a way of affirming Presbyterianism and opposing the Church of Rome – the origins of the sectarianism that scars Scotland today.

Political Scottish Nationalism is a very recent phenomenon. So recent that it is hard to believe that it can be for real. The National Party of Scotland, forerunner of the SNP, didn't come into existence until 1928 and for the next 40 years Scottish Nationalists spent most of their time arguing with each other. The Scottish National Party that emerged from a merger of the NPS and the smaller, Scottish Party (which proposed dominion status for Scotland like Canada or Australia) in 1934 was more like a sect than a political party. Its attempt to ignite the Nationalist passions that had led to the Irish Civil War in the 1920s was anathema to the vast majority of Scots. As was the SNP campaign to make Scotland neutral in the Second World War, a policy which led to the vilification of the SNP's wartime leaders, Douglas Young and Arthur Donaldson, as Nazi sympathisers – which they weren't. It didn't help that the Nationalist poet, Hugh MacDiarmid, a founder member of the NPS, had been given to quoting the Nazi-supporting Wyndham Lewis on the virtues of "Blutesgefuel"[1] in the early 1930s. Christopher Murray Grieve, to use the real name of the journalist from Montrose, was a brilliant modernist poet, though he was ideologically promiscuous – rather like the SNP, which couldn't decide whether it was of the Left or the Right, so tried both.

The SNP achieved a short-lived triumph at a by-election in Motherwell in 1945, but only because none of the mainstream parties were standing during the wartime electoral truce. Labour won it back in its 1945 landslide. Thereafter, Scots returned to their support of the Unionist Right. The Nationalists were nowhere in the 1950s. The historian and former SNP chairman, the late James Halliday, famously said that he thought the SNP only had 150 members in the whole of Scotland. The National Covenant, which in 1950 attracted two million signatories for a devolved Scottish Assembly, was not a Nationalist project as such, but the brainchild of John MacCormick, a Scots lawyer who had left the Scottish National Party during the war.

It wasn't until the mid-1960s, after Labour had finally ended Conservative hegemony in Scotland, that the SNP emerged as a significant political force. In 1967, the SNP gained its first proper parliamentary seat when another Scottish lawyer, Winnie Ewing, won the Hamilton by-election – one of Labour's safest Scottish seats. But even this looked like a protest vote, a flash in the Caledonian pan. Mrs Ewing promptly lost it again in the 1970 General Election. The SNP won a raft of eleven seats in October 1974, following the discovery of oil in the North Sea and then lost all but two of them in 1979 when they withdrew support from the Westminster Labour government and precipitated the General Election that brought in the Nationalist Nemesis – Margaret Thatcher. "Turkeys voting for an early Christmas," as the Labour Prime Minister James Callaghan described it.

Yet now, in 2011, those SNP turkeys command the Scottish Parliament – the very institution that Labour's Shadow Scottish Secretary, George Robertson, had confidently predicted would "kill Nationalism stone-dead". Of course, some say this is all an illusion, a bigger flash in a bigger pan. Most Labour MPs think the SNP is still just a protest organisation and that Labour remains the true "national" party of Scotland as is clear from its continued dominance in UK general elections. They call the Scottish Nationalists "Tartan Tories", who have bribed the Scottish voters with "Salmond freebies" such as free prescriptions, free university tuition, free elderly care – what Alex Salmond calls the "social wage". There is an obvious contradiction here that Labour has been unable to resolve: namely that this party they call "Tory" is considerably to the Left of the Labour Party in Scotland. But Labour is adamant that Alex Salmond, the charismatic if rotund leader of the SNP, is not really committed to progressive policies and has only assumed this leftist agenda – the "something for nothing society" as the Scottish Labour leader, Johann Lamont now calls it – in order to dupe Scots into voting Nationalist and tearing Scotland out of the Union with England.

This argument that the SNP are "faux" Labour probably made sense until May 2007 when the SNP under Salmond won its first victory in the Holyrood elections. Now that the SNP has been in government for six years and has had an opportunity to demonstrate what it can do the protest theory has lost credibility. Scottish voters were impressed with Alex Salmond's dynamic minority administration after 2007, which used the powers of the Scottish Parliament to much greater effect than the seemingly lacklustre Liberal-Labour coalitions which had managed the early years of devolution. Labour can no longer console itself with the belief that the Nationalists will crumble under the burden of government. Indeed, Labour was left, in April 2011, borrowing policies from the SNP's election manifesto as it saw its support evaporate across Scotland. Labour still thought of the SNP as a tartan joke, a "pretendy" political party. But Scottish voters now had sufficient confidence in the Nationalists to elect them by an overwhelming majority in 2011 in Holyrood.

However, they only did so secure in the knowledge that a vote for the SNP did not necessarily mean a vote for independence, because the SNP had promised a referendum before any attempt to negotiate departure from the British state. The old SNP doctrine that a Scottish majority in a general election – any general election – was enough to justify secession and to trigger independence negotiations was abandoned by Alex Salmond in 2000, much to the dismay of fundamentalist Nationalists such as Jim Sillars, a former Labour MP and the First Minister's deadly rival. In a sense, the SNP made itself electable by sidelining its key policy of constitutional separation and by concentrating on running the devolved Scottish Parliament on its own terms. It succeeded by making Labour's devolution work.

So, where does that leave us? Clearly, devolution has not "dished the Nats" as the Labour Party hoped it would. It appears instead to have turbocharged Scottish Nationalism, in the Scottish Parliament at least. Labour assumed that the Scots, in gratitude for their Parliament, would allow Labour to rule in perpetuity. Was Scotland not a Labour country? Well, the truth is that it wasn't: Labour had only recently replaced the Tories as the "national" party of Scotland in the 1960s. And while a million Scots still voted Labour in 2010, Labour's hold on Scottish domestic politics was fragile, disguised by tactical voting in general elections against the Tories which inflated Labour's vote. Labour started to go into decline at the end of the 20th century in Scotland not long after it took over from the Tories who, with Margaret Thatcher, had made themselves unelectable in Scotland.

The rise of the SNP in Holyrood was on the backs of the two main Unionist parties, and Alex Salmond has been aware that he was riding two horses – appealing not just to social democrats but to refugees from the old Scottish Unionist Party. He steered those difficult steeds extremely well, after 1999, but only because he was not riding them to independence – at least not right away. The SNP landslide in the Scottish parliamentary election of 2011 was clearly a turning point for Scotland – though in which direction remains unclear. The Scottish voters were not voting for independence because of the "double-lock" on independence. But Scots surprised themselves by the strength of their support for the SNP in 2011. The Nationalist landslide raised the question of independence in a form with which the Scottish voters are unfamiliar: as a practical possibility. By lending their support so massively to a party of independence, the Scottish people began to realise that they may have crossed a kind of Rubicon.

It certainly sent a message to Westminster that it could no longer ignore – a demand for a referendum on separation. The Independence Referendum of 18th September 2014 will be the first real threat to the continuation of the Union since 1746. It really is that long since there has been any significant opposition to Scotland's membership of the UK. In the immediate aftermath of the 2011 General Election, it looked for a while as if the Conservative Prime Minister, David Cameron, might listen to his Tory backbench and refuse to allow Scotland the right to hold a referendum on independence, as the Nationalists had pledged in their election manifesto. After all, it was argued, should England not have its say, too, on the vital matter of whether Great Britain should be consigned to the knacker's yard? The Scottish Parliament had no formal powers to stage a binding referendum on independence since the constitution is one of the powers reserved to Westminster. Constitutional authorities, such as Professor Robert Hazell of the Constitution Unit and University College London, advised that there should not be any binding referendum until the terms of any Scottish disengagement from the UK had been finalised and the people of Scotland had an opportunity to see what they were voting for. But Cameron realised what many Tory MPs did not: that denying a referendum to Scots would only play into the hands of the Nationalists, who would complain that London was imposing a veto on the democratic aspirations of the Scottish people.

And so, in the Edinburgh Agreement of 15th October 2012, the UK Government took the extraordinary step of legitimising a ballot that could lead to the extinction of the United Kingdom. It will be a simple choice, without any second options or half-way houses, as the SNP leader, Alex Salmond, had initially proposed. Scots will be asked a deceptively simple question: "Should Scotland be an independent country?" Some Unionists objected that it was a leading question, however, they couldn't argue with its brevity. Some have styled it the shortest suicide note in history.

The Unionists are confident it will be rejected; if it isn't that independence will spell doom for Scotland as the country is ejected from the European Union, is blackballed by the Bank of England, denied use of the pound sterling, and left an impoverished and threadbare statelet ignored by history and struggling under the weight of its debts. The Yes Scotland campaign reply is that such negative Unionist "scaremongering" is baseless and that Scotland will join a community of prosperous Nordic nations, such as Denmark, Norway and Finland, and will use its oil wealth for the benefit of its people. Many Scottish voters are genuinely unsure about the nature even of the choice they have to make and are frustrated at what they see as an unwillingness on the part of Unionists and Nationalists to give them the information they need to make a choice.

David Cameron's gamble is that the Nationalists will not be able to translate their electoral support in the devolved Holyrood Parliament into a vote to leave the United Kingdom. So far Cameron's luck has held, and, according to the opinion polls, Scots are still opposed to leaving the United Kingdom by about two to one. But whether this commitment to the Union will endure until September 2014 remains, as BBC reporters like to say, to be seen. The majority of Scots[2] say they want the Scottish Parliament to have greater powers within the United Kingdom. This option, sometimes called Devolution Max or Devolution Plus, will appear nowhere on the ballot paper. The danger for Cameron is that many supporters of this essentially federalist option may feel disenfranchised in the referendum and lend their votes to the Yes campaign. We know that Scots want a stronger parliament within the UK, with most economic powers devolved, but that isn't on offer. What we don't know is whether they will decide to back the SNP as the means of achieving it.

This book is an attempt to explain why Scottish Nationalism emerged so suddenly from the ruins of a social democratic Scotland. I start by taking a closer look at the SNP, a paradoxical party that isn't Nationalist in the traditional sense and isn't even particularly Scottish, in that it doesn't base its appeal on any sense of ethnic or racial exclusivity. I make no apologies, however, for reviewing the founding myths of Scottish Nationalism in the Middle Ages. The history of Wallace, Bruce and the Wars of Independence tell us nothing about how Scots are likely to vote in the 2014 referendum, but they do tell us a lot about how many ordinary Scots think of themselves.

The Scots gave up their parliament and political identity in 1707 after the disastrous Darien episode, but that failed colonial venture was only part of the story. Scotland was exhausted by the chaos of the 17th-century conflicts between Church and State which had brought war, occupation, persecution and impoverishment. After the Union, the all-powerful Kirk largely occupied the space left by the state, and Scotland became a country where politics, if it happened at all, tended to happen in church. Unlike in Ireland, there was no significant political Nationalist movement in Scotland in the 19th century. Instead, there was a synthetic tartanism largely invented by the Victorians after the romantic novels of Sir Walter Scott.

The Scottish middle classes saw Empire as a joint enterprise, in which Scotland provided the moral conscience as well as the military manpower. Scotland's greatest Victorian celebrity and the ultimate "lad o' pairts", the missionary/explorer David Livingstone, embodied that Scottish ideal of progressive colonialism. He fought slavery and transportation in Central Africa, even as the people of his birthplace were being enslaved in the cotton mills or transported through the Highland Clearances to Canada and New Zealand. The other side of Scottish Presbyterian culture was the Rev Thomas Chalmers, who led the Free Kirk after the Disruption in 1843. A social reactionary who launched a clerical revolution, Chalmers is almost forgotten today, but was one of the most influential figures in Scotland. Far more than Red Clydeside or Keir Hardie, it was Chalmers who conditioned the thinking of Scots until well into the 20th century.

The high noon of Unionism was during and after the Second World War, when Scotland and England united first against Fascism and then against poverty and disease through the creation of the welfare state. But thereafter the Unionist universe began to disintegrate, as Scotland lost confidence in Empire, the Kirk and Great Britain, in that order. The precipitous decline of the church in the 1960s was a cultural revolution that wiped away many of the certainties of the old Scotland, and hastened the decline of the Scottish Unionist Party as new forms of middle-class radicalism emerged in what is now called Scottish "civil society". Out of this maelstrom emerged the SNP which ran Labour close in the 1974 General Election only to fall back again into internal divisions and electoral irrelevance.

The attempt by Westminster to defuse Nationalism by offering devolution led to the abortive referendum of 1979 and a sense of national humiliation and introspection in Scotland. But the industrial clearances of the 1980s and Margaret Thatcher's poll tax provided the impetus for the creation of the first significant political home rule movement in Scotland since the 18th century. The 1997 referendum campaign united the political tribes of Scotland for the first time and led to the restoration of Scotland's Parliament in 1999. This provided an incubator for a fully fledged Scottish Nationalism which has come to dominate Scottish political life.

In the final chapters, I deal with the experience of the Scottish Parliament: Scotland's disillusion with devolution, and how the fall of the Scottish Labour Party, as much as the rise of the SNP, has brought us to where we are today. The SNP commanded the political agenda in Scotland after its first historic victory in 2007, and under Salmond won the 2011 landslide that changed Scotland forever.

All this has happened so fast that Scots have barely had time to catch up with themselves, and there is understandable confusion about what independence means. The Scottish National Party suggests that independence would involve a new "social union" with England and even a continuation of the UK, while Unionists promise more powers without specifying what they are. I then look at the Unionist campaign and its unfortunate tendency to suggest that Scotland is "too poor, too wee, too stupid" to be an independent country: propositions that are no longer true, if they ever were. Meanwhile, the SNP's pick-and-mix approach to independence under Salmond raises the question of whether they are still truly Nationalist.

I also invite the reader to spend an evening with "the most dangerous man in Britain", Alex Salmond. The "wily" and "devious"

SNP leader of Unionist demonology, whose "lying" and "cynicism" have, according to detractors, duped the Scots into the antechamber to independence. Salmond has certainly made the Scottish National Party what it is today by converting it into a broadly based home rule movement which can be supported by Nationalists and non-Nationalists alike. This has infuriated Unionists and Nationalist purists alike, and allowed Salmond to bring Scotland to the verge of independence without having to define what independence means. Now the cards are finally on the table, which side is he really on?

CHAPTER TWO
THE STRANGE CASE OF
SCOTTISH NATIONALISM

WHEN I WAS an infantile leftist at Edinburgh University in the 1970s I regarded the SNP with profound suspicion. Nationalism was one of the forces of darkness, an ethnic passion risen from the sump of history, the preserve of racists and chauvinists. What was Hitler, after all, but a *National* Socialist? We talked heroically of a world without borders, without ethnic divisions, united by a hypothetical Socialist Internationalism that held the key to history. I used to annoy my late mother, a prominent Scottish Nationalist who had joined the party principally because of its opposition to nuclear weapons, by comparing the SNP to the National Front in England, which in the 1970s, was a potent political force on the streets of London and other English cities. Well, what's the difference? Aren't all Nationalisms essentially about ethnic purity, chauvinism, division, narrow-minded selfishness? It's Scotland's oil indeed. The politics of greed more like.

It seemed to many on the Left as if the only purpose of the SNP was to divide the working class, hand Scotland to the US oil majors and undermine British social achievements, such as the National Health Service, by appealing to the worst instincts of the selfish Scot. The image presented by the SNP propagandists in the 1970s of Scots driving around in Rolls-Royces like Saudi Arabian sheiks was a dismal one. Indeed, many Nationalists now accept that the "It's Scotland's oil" campaign, with its grasping and materialist overtones, may have contributed to the SNP's failure in the late 1970s. This was the age of proletarian romanticism – the working-class hero who knew no nation and had nothing to lose but his chains.

Unfortunately, this stateless paragon of proletarian virtue came and went without creating the Socialist commonwealth, leaving only the rusting chains of historic Nationalisms, corroded by international alliances like the European Union. It is the Left it seems which has been swept into the dustbin of history while Nationalism, in Scotland at least, has reinvented itself as a new form of communitarianism that looks to the small Nordic countries as a model for the good society. Critics like me have had to recognise that all Nationalisms are not the same. The SNP has demonstrated that it is possible to have a form of Nationalism which is not defined by race or ethnicity, and which can be outward-looking, inclusive, organic and kind to animals.

Oil-fuelled Nationalism burned itself out after the SNP's electoral collapse in 1979 which led to the final split in the movement, when the left-wing '79 Group, led by Salmond among others, was expelled, only to return as inheritors of the SNP in the 1980s when Scots turned against Margaret Thatcher. No more talk of tartan sheiks. After New Labour adopted much of the Thatcherite economic programme in the 1990s, the SNP was left as one of the most radical forces in the largely depoliticised culture of modern Britain. The Scottish National Party is the only party committed to unilateral nuclear disarmament ever to have been elected to government in the UK. It is not only committed to redistribution of wealth and to free personal care for the elderly, but also to restoring council housing and ending the sale of social housing stock. It is enthusiastically promoting community right to buy in the Highlands. Despite hydrocarbon revenues still being centrally important to its economic prospectus, the SNP is one of the greenest parties in Europe, committed to generating the equivalent of 100% electricity through renewable sources by 2020. In place of "Scotland's oil", Salmond talks nowadays of Scotland's "second energy bonanza" – green energy.

Nor will you hear any overtly anti-English sentiments expressed by delegates at SNP conferences – except perhaps by old-timers in the bar late at night. If any prominent SNP member were to give "Anglophobia" as their hobby in their *Who's Who* entry, as the late Hugh MacDiarmid used to, they would be shown the door. The SNP has even tried to tame the notoriously offensive "cybernats" who roam newspaper comment postings attacking any Unionists who dare show their heads. Modern Nationalists largely avoid using Scottish history as an organising principle of their movement, something visitors to Scottish SNP conferences find almost as surprising as the absence of kilts. They come expecting to hear of

William Wallace and national liberation, but all they hear about is corporation tax, keeping the pound and remaining in Nato.

The SNP spends much of its time turning away fraternal delegations to its annual conferences from other less liberal European equivalents. The Scottish National Party, unlike so many Nationalist parties in Europe, such as Italy's Lombard League or the Finland's True Finns, has no anti-immigrant or xenophobic tendency, at least not since the short-lived "Seed of the Gael" militants were expelled in the 1970s. Nor has the SNP been overly keen on welcoming representatives from the new small nations of what used to be called Eastern Europe, like Hungary or the Baltic states, which have tended to be governed by parties of the Right. The only Continental Nationalists who find they are truly welcome at a Nationalist conference are the Catalonians, whom the SNP regard as a comparable civic Nationalist movement, though *The Scotsman* reported[3] that even they had been cold-shouldered recently.

Unlike Basque or Quebec Nationalism, which spawned military movements in the 1970s, Scotland has never had anything like an ETA or an FLQ. A handful of extremists who called themselves the Army of the Provisional Government of Scotland were jailed in the 1970s for blowing up radio masts and electricity pylons, but unlike the Provisional Irish Republican Army they sought to emulate, they had no popular support and the SNP condemned them unconditionally. If anything, the SNP in the 1960s and 1970s was a pacifist organisation, inspired more by Gandhi than Gerry Adams.

The Scottish National Party has shown that multicultural Nationalism is not an oxymoron. You can be Nationalist without being nasty, without being xenophobic or chauvinist, or having any concept of ethnic exclusivity. It defines as "Scottish" anyone who happens to live in Scotland and positively celebrates immigration. The SNP boasts that it had the first Muslim MSP, the late Bashir Ahmad. The SNP's Minister for External Affairs is Humza Yousaf, whose mother is Kenyan and whose father came from Pakistan. One of Salmond's advisers is Osama Saeed, the head of international affairs for al Jazeera and a Muslim activist who once argued in favour of the return of the caliphate. Noel Dolan, the special adviser to the SNP deputy Leader, Nicola Sturgeon, was born in Balham of Irish descent, and sounds about as Scottish as Bob Hoskins. Scottish Nationalism is a postmodern Nationalism in which being Internationalist and multicultural are as important, indeed arguably more important, than the celebration of Scottish national identity. Which is just as well – the SNP is unique among European Nationalist parties in having more votes from non-Nationalists than Nationalists.

Scots have voted SNP in recent years, not to celebrate their race or ethnicity or even to define themselves culturally against another nation, but to express their repugnance at another political creed: Conservatism. If pressed I would have to admit that this has often been referred to by Nationalist supporters as "English Conservatism", and was embodied in one figure, Margaret Thatcher, widely referred to as "that Bloody Woman" on the doorsteps by Scottish voters in 1980s elections. If the rise of Scottish Nationalism can be credited to any one person, it is the former Conservative Prime Minister, who not only imposed the hated poll tax on Scotland, but is also held responsible in Scottish folk memory for the 1980s recessions that destroyed the industrial working-class communities of west central Scotland. There may have been elements of Anglophobia and sexism in Scottish attitudes to Mrs Thatcher, but it was primarily political. Scots from all classes and backgrounds seemed to find her hectoring manner and petit-bourgeois nostrums unbearable. Those posters in the 1970s of Margaret Thatcher with vampire teeth dripping with plundered Scottish oil were not the SNP's greatest propaganda achievements, but they certainly captured the spirit of the times.

However, Alex Salmond – the revisionist leader of the Scottish Nationalists – has even tried to stamp out anti-Thatcher chauvinism by remarking, in an interview in 2008, that the Scots "didn't mind her economic policies so much. But we didn't like the social policies at all."

"Aha," said Labour, "the SNP are tartan Tories after all!" The First Minister subsequently qualified his remarks to emphasise that he did not mean to suggest that he supported Thatcherite economic policies, or that Scots did either.

DON'T BE NASTY TO THE ENGLISH

Nationalists choose their words carefully, for if they lapse into anything remotely resembling anti-English chauvinism the largely

Unionist Scottish press leaps upon them. The Scottish media is probably unique in that it takes umbrage, not at slights on the Scottish nation but any hint of intolerance towards its neighbour, England. In December 2012, a largely innocuous article by the Scottish novelist and artist Alasdair Gray, which referred to the distinction between English "colonists" and "settlers" in arts administration, was rounded upon as an outburst of anti-English racialism. Gray was "fanning the flames of bigotry", according to an article in *The Scotsman*.[4] Yet two months later, when *The Guardian's* Steve Bell penned an offensive cartoon suggesting that the question in the Independence Referendum should be "Do you agree that Scotland should go and F*** itself", there was no comparable outbreak of indignation.

When the current Health Minister, Alex Neil, in 1996 compared the then Labour Scottish Secretary, George Robertson, to the Nazi collaborator "Lord Haw Haw", he was forced to retract by the SNP leader, Alex Salmond. When the Finance Secretary, John Swinney, told a closed session at the 2005 SNP conference that it was time for "Brits to butt out", he was again accused of anti-English racialism. Even when the former deputy leader, Jim Sillars, accused Scots voters of being "90-minute patriots" after they failed to eliminate the Scottish Tories in the 1992 General Election, he was accused of trying to import anti-English sentiment from the football terraces into politics. In fact, he needn't have worried. The 90-minute patriots went on to make Scotland Tory-free in the 1997 General Election when the party that dominated post-war Scottish politics lost every single Scottish seat.

Anti-Englishness does exist in Scotland, but it is isolated and episodic according to researchers such as Murray Watson, of Dundee University, in his book *Being English in Scotland*[5,] and not comparable to any recognisable form of deep-seated racial antagonism. In 2011, the number of racist incidents against people categorised as "white English" fell by 17%, though this was widely misreported as an increase because there had been an increase in incidents involving other white minorities.[6] There were some fears expressed about the impact of devolution in 1999 on the English community in Scotland after a school pupil in Edinburgh died at the hands of assailants who had allegedly made anti-English remarks. However, according to research by Asifa Hussein and Bill Miller of Glasgow University, the majority of English people in Scotland feel more secure since the creation of the Scottish Parliament.

This is despite the presence of some 400,000 English-born people who have come to live in Scotland since the 1980s – the largest inward migration since the wave of Irish immigration to Scotland at the end of the 19th century. In some Highland villages, indigenous Scots are in a minority, and in many rural areas most businesses have been taken over by incomers. But there have never been any of the "cottage-burning" campaigns against holiday homes in Scotland that took place in Wales in the 1970s and 1980s. The Human Rights and Equality Commission says it cannot cite evidence of any increase in specifically anti-English racism. However, what remains a very serious problem is religious sectarianism – the enduring enmity between Catholics and Protestants particularly in west central Scotland.

The SNP has always been careful to argue its case without falling into racial or ethnic stereotypes, or Scottish exceptionalism, and it would be taken severely to task if it did. The Nationalists have few fans in the mainstream Scottish media. In the year the SNP won a landslide victory in the Scottish Election of 2011, there was not a single newspaper in Scotland that actually supported independence as a matter of editorial policy. The virulence of the anti-Nationalist press in Scotland often surprises visitors from Catalonia or Quebec, or even Ireland, who are used to greater editorial diversity on the national question. On polling day in the 2007 Scottish Parliament elections, *The Sun* ran a front page with the SNP's logo remodelled as a hangman's noose, and other tabloids depicted Salmond as "the most dangerous man in Scotland". The SNP won the election, as it happens, confirming that newspapers don't tell people how to vote.

The SNP, clearly, has been able to address the Scottish voters over the heads of the media. But to avoid accusations of "separatism" and "breaking up Britain", the party has had to make significant changes to its policy and rhetoric in recent years. Gone are the SNP's old republican leanings – it now insists it wants to keep the Queen as head of state. In place of "throwing off the English yoke", as Nationalists like MacDiarmid put it, the modern SNP is calling for a new "social union" with England in a reformed UK. An independent Scotland would not only do without border posts, it would retain sterling and keep the Bank of England in charge of Scottish interest rates. Nationalists such as the former radical firebrand Alex Neil even now say that Scots can "still call themselves British" after independence.

This revisionism is perhaps understandable, given the Scottish voters' reluctance to embrace independence – even as they vote in large numbers for the SNP in Holyrood. However, the danger is that Alex Salmond empties the word "Nationalism" of any meaning. To paraphrase Herbert Morrison's remark on Socialism, Nationalism is whatever the SNP says it is. Indeed, it is what Alex Salmond says it is. This has left a lot of Scots wondering what point there is in voting Yes in a referendum if the United Kingdom is going to stay largely as it is. Indeed, so many Nationalist icons have been revolving in their coffins recently that if they plugged into the national grid it could provide a new form of renewable energy. What would Communist MacDiarmid have made of Salmond's desire to cut business taxes? What would pacifist Billy Wolfe have made of the party's support for Nato, a nuclear alliance? But Salmond seems to relish these apparent contradictions. One of the virtues of leading a party that has no fixed ideology and very little history, is that there is little risk of offending party purists. So long as he keeps winning, the SNP seems happy to let Alex make it up as he goes along.

INDEPENDENCE IN EUROPE

Since the SNP adopted its policy of Independence in Europe in 1989, which Alex Salmond supported, even though it was the brainchild of his great rival, the former Deputy Leader, Jim Sillars, the SNP has abandoned the "flags and armies" Nationalism of the past in favour of something much looser and federal. Like the 19th-century Italian Nationalist, Giuseppe Mazzini, Alex Salmond sees no contradiction between supporting independence and calling for a federal Europe. Independence in Europe has helped the SNP throw off the charge that it is a party of "narrow Nationalists" who want to split Scotland off into an isolated and introverted statelet on the fringes of European civilisation. It has allowed Nationalists to claim they are joining the community of nations rather than breaking up Britain or abandoning the UK.

Gradualists like Salmond had hoped – at least in the 1990s – that a drift of power from Westminster to the institutions of the European Union would help weaken the ties of sentiment and purpose that bind them to the UK as Scots increasingly came to see themselves as European. The Nationalists believed the EU President, Jacques Delors, when he said in 1992 that in future 80% of economic legislation would come from Brussels. They assumed that the Maastricht Treaty, ratified by the Conservatives under John Major in 1992, would lead to "ever closer union" and that Britain would join the European single currency in due course. What no one foresaw was the sovereign debt crisis in the eurozone which has shaken the EU to its foundations and raised serious questions about Britain's, and therefore Scotland's, continued membership of it. The SNP has been left with a commitment to a Europe that has declining support in England and Scotland.

EuroNationalism served its original purpose of making the prospect of independence less threatening to Scottish voters. But there is a further contradiction at the heart of SNP's policy of independence in Europe which is becoming increasingly problematic, though it has nothing to do with the synthetic row over Scottish membership of the EU after independence. The Nationalists want Scotland to have a seat at "the top table" in Europe by seeking independent representation on the Council of Ministers. They want to be full members of Europe, complete with voting rights in the European Parliament. However, in the UK – despite insisting there will be a new social union with England after independence – the SNP says unequivocally that it wants to relinquish political representation at the heart of this new confederal UK. It wants to pull all Scottish MPs out of Westminster for good and all. There is an obvious problem in arguing that being independent in Europe involves being represented at the centre in Brussels or Strasbourg, whereas being independent in the UK does not require representation at the centre of decision-making in Westminster.

This incoherence extends to the party's concern to remain in the sterling zone after independence – which arose as a pragmatic solution to the problem of monetary discontinuity, but has become a millstone for the Nationalists. The SNP's old policy of joining the euro, on the assumption that Britain would join, meant that currency need no longer be regarded as an independence issue. However, now that there is little prospect of Britain joining Europe's Economic and Monetary Union for the foreseeable future, the SNP is left with a policy of joining a currency zone – sterling – without having any representation at the centre of decision-making. The possibility of a seat on the Monetary Policy Committee – if the Bank of England grants one, is not the same as having a stake in the democratic oversight of the UK national economy. The UK Treasury, in April 2013, cast doubt on the viability of the SNP's proposed sterling union: "Would a newly independent Scottish state be prepared to accept significant limits on its economic sovereignty? To submit its economic plans to Westminster before Holyrood?"[7] In other words: would Scotland be content to be treated like Greece?

The UK Treasury is hardly an impartial source here, and the SNP was understandably annoyed that the Treasury was indulging in political attacks on independence. It argues that a currency union would be the most sensible and efficient arrangement, not least for English banks and firms with commercial operations in Scotland. But the Treasury has a point. There is a problem, as in the eurozone, of having a monetary union without a political union. The logical solution, for two countries in such an economic union, would be federalism – a division of powers, which would allow Scotland to have a say on UK issues such as monetary policy, foreign affairs and defence, while having substantial economic and tax powers retained by Holyrood. However, this is not an option on the table for the Scottish Independence Referendum. Nationalists continue to argue that only full political disengagement from the United Kingdom will allow the frustrated energies of the Scottish people to flourish.

SNP AS SCOTTISH LABOUR

The Unionist parties will continue to mock the SNP as a Nationalist party which doesn't want to be particularly Nationalist; and which is prepared to say whatever is necessary to win votes. Yet there is nothing wrong with gradualism and the SNP is perfectly entitled to reject separatism and narrow Nationalism. Most Nationalist parties celebrate and promote racial or cultural identity and seek self-government to protect it. But ethnicity and culture are not the organising principles of the Scottish National Party. The SNP has sought to present itself in recent times less as a vehicle for national liberation than as a replacement for Labour in Scotland – a reliable champion of social democracy against the neoliberal values of metropolitan political culture. The SNP's enemy, in this modern form, is not the English people or even the English state as such, but the political organisations that have sought to impose market fundamentalism on British society – through privatisation, deregulation, military adventurism, and latterly through the UK Coalition's austerity programme.

The SNP achieved its greatest success in the 2000s against a background of Tony Blair's New Labour governments. It was the marketisation of the NHS in England, the curbing of the welfare state, the introduction of university tuition fees and above all, the Iraq War that boosted SNP support in Scotland. Iraq became a defining moral issue after the invasion of Baghdad in March 2003. Teachers, university lecturers, trade unionists, liberal clerics and public sector workers in Scotland – the ones who embraced socialism in the 1970s – turned to the SNP as the only party that seemed to offer any resistance to the "illegal war" and the relentless commercialisation of public life. Scottish newspapers that were essentially Labour supporters, such as the *Sunday Herald*, began to give limited support to the SNP in Holyrood elections, on the grounds it seemed to represent what Labour had abandoned.

If the SNP has been a vehicle, not for national aspirations as such, but for a collection of social democratic political objectives then this leaves the obvious question: to what extent is it still truly a Nationalist movement? In fact, what is this strange Nationalism that seems to have come from nowhere, historically speaking, wants to remain in a union with England and whose programme appears to contradict its own mission statement? Until the 1980s, small 'n' Scottish Nationalism, like wearing the kilt, tended to be associated with the political right in Scotland. It was Scottish landowners and army majors who celebrated Scottish history and enjoyed Scottish country dancing. When I was growing up in Edinburgh in the 1960s, I wouldn't have been seen dead in a kilt, which I associated with what we called "Hooray Henrys" – upper-class twits who came in from the Borders for rugby internationals. All this has changed as the SNP has outflanked Labour as the champion of Scottish social democracy.

Over the years, the SNP has benefited from the rise of middle-class radical movements like the anti-nuclear movement in the 1960s and 1970s, and the environmental movement in the 1980s and 1990s. It has capitalised on the disintegration of the British Empire and the radical secularisation of politics that followed the collapse of religious observance in Scotland. It has exploited the divisions within the UK Labour Party and cherry-picked its social democratic policies and themes. But is this all it is? Has the Scottish National Party simply turned ideological opportunism into a programme for government? It is undoubtedly sincere about the collection of policies it has assembled. But where is the Nationalism?

Great political movements normally have antecedents. They come from somewhere, they have a basis. Labour emerged from the trade union movement and the industrial working class at the beginning of the 20th century; Tories were originally political representatives of the corn law landowners and monarchists; the Liberal Party emerged from the Whigs in the 19th century and articulated, broadly speaking, the political aspirations of the industrial bourgeoisie. The Scottish Unionist Party, which dominated Scottish politics in the first half of the 20th century arose from the split in the Liberal Party over Irish Home Rule in the 1880s, and expressed the views of the Presbyterian middle class and Orange or Loyalist working class. But where did the Scottish National Party come from?

Scotland's modern history is overwhelmingly Unionist. Attempts have been made to suggest that Scotland's very ultra-patriotic commitment to the Union in the age of the British Empire was itself an expression of Nationalism. The Unionist Party MP and author of *The 39 Steps*, John Buchan, famously said in the 1920s that "all Scotsmen should be Scottish Nationalists". But this romantic patriotism of the political right is very different to the political Nationalism of the modern SNP. Buchan wasn't talking about leaving the UK and setting up a Scottish state – quite the reverse, he was a true-blue British imperialist. The author of *John Macnab* was referring merely to the culture and identity of the Scots as it had been dressed in Highland garb by Sir Walter Scott in the 1800s and which had become part of the British Imperial myth.

If we are to believe that Scotland is now serious about independence and capable of voting Yes in September 2014 – and despite the opinion polls this cannot be ruled out – from where has this latent drive to independence come from? Given that Scotland has not shown any signs until the day before yesterday, historically speaking, of wanting to be independent, can there be the remotest possibility that Scottish voters will vote for independence? The very novelty of political Nationalism to the Scottish voters is one reason why they keep saying they lack sufficient information about independence to make a considered judgement. They made this clear to the Scottish Electoral Reform Commissioner, John Mc-Cormick, in the consultation over the wording of the Independence Referendum question in 2012.[8] Not having had a long history of Nationalist agitation, and given the ideological promiscuity of the SNP, they are understandably confused. If they vote Yes, will they end up with much the same arrangement as now but under a different name, as the modern SNP leaders suggest? Or would it involve borders and even a separate currency as the UK Treasury suggests? Would Scots continue as members of the European Union as the SNP insist, or would they be forced to reapply as a "third country" as the President of the European Commission, José Manuel Barroso, has proposed.[9]

ALL FEDERALISTS NOW

These are perplexing questions for an electorate that does not feel in any conventional way politically oppressed by England. The Scots realise they are on a journey – but the destination is opaque. The Scots are clearly not passionate Nationalists who feel their identity is being crushed and they don't go in for emotional, million-strong street demonstrations, such as those staged recently by Catalonian Nationalists in Barcelona. Scots are constitutional conservatives. They have had a very long and very bloody history and do not go in for radical change if they can possibly avoid it. Which suggests that Scots will only vote Yes in 2014 if they can be persuaded that not much will alter as a result.

Many Scots are unhappy with their present relationship to the UK and clearly do not feel in tune with the politics of the southeast of England. They continually express their desire for further constitutional reform, short of independence, to give the Scottish Parliament greater economic power. Opinion polls for the past 30 years have consistently registered this desire for further autonomy within the UK. Most recently, in 2013, the Scottish Social Attitudes Survey, an annual survey of 1,300 Scots, indicated that 67% support a form of federalism. If they have to vote Yes to independence to achieve this, they may well do so. History may judge that a tremendous opportunity to reform and revive the United Kingdom by consensus has been missed in the past few years. All the political leaders of the Unionist parties have made promises, at one time or another, about delivering a greater degree of fiscal devolution – provided that Scots vote No in the referendum. But none of them have been prepared to spell out exactly what they mean. Given the history of broken promises of "better devolution" after the abortive 1979 Devolution Referendum, the political parties would have to deliver a concrete plan which gives the Scottish Parliament effective control of the domestic economy.

Anyone with a sense of history looking dispassionately at the current constitutional impasse in the UK would argue that there is a rather obvious solution here. Since the House of Lords is going to be reformed anyway, why not turn this into a senate elected on a regional basis and make it the centrepiece of a modern, reformed, multinational United Kingdom? This has even been suggested by Labour Unionists, such as Lord George Foulkes. It's not as if anyone has any better ideas about what to do with the House of Lords, now that the hereditary principle has become unsustainable. The multinational character of British democracy will need to be recognised in some form anyway if only to answer the West Lothian Question; there will have to be changes to end the undemocratic anomaly of Scottish MPs voting, for example, on tuition fees for English universities, when fees have been abolished for their own constituents. The financial arrangement known as the Barnett Formula, which calculates Scottish public spending, has clearly outlived its usefulness. There is now a widespread consensus across all the parties in Scotland and England that, as the Labour-inspired cross-party Calman Commission argued in 2009, to be truly accountable a parliament should raise in taxation at least a large proportion of the revenue it spends on social policies.

What we have been left with is an unstable unilateral federalism in which Scotland has achieved a large measure of self-government without any corresponding adaptations to the unwritten British Constitution. There appears to be a lack of will to reconcile the conflicting interests of the nations and regions that make up the United Kingdom or to address the implications of the existence of the Scottish Parliament since 1999. But the "English Question" has been left to backbench Conservative MPs, some academic constitutionalists and people who post comments on newspaper websites. The inequity of the present arrangement has not led to English voters supporting the Campaign for an English Parliament in significant numbers. UK political leaders don't seem really to care enough about the constitutional anomalies involved in the West Lothian Question to want to have to set up an English Parliament and create the apparatus of a federal state to answer it. There is much to commend the British tradition of constitutional improvisation, of "muddling through", and we shouldn't rush to place our country in the hands of constitutional lawyers. Nevertheless, it is irresponsible of the UK political classes to ignore this and it is to the credit of the Scottish National Party that it at least has a solution to the problem – which is for Scotland to leave the UK in order to recreate the Union in a different form, as a partnership of independent countries.

It is one of the ironies of the current political debate that the SNP seems to be prepared to think more constructively about the United Kingdom than the UK parties. At least it has a road map out of the present predicament. Alex Salmond said he would welcome a second question in the referendum, specifically offering Devolution Max, a form of federalism whereby the Scottish Parliament would raise the majority of the money it spends while still contributing to common UK services such as defence and foreign affairs. But this was vetoed by David Cameron who feared the SNP leader might be trying to have it both ways, placing an each-way bet on a two-horse race. Perhaps he was. But this was an opportunity missed by the Unionist parties, a curious one, because had a second question been on the ballot paper, independence would almost certainly have been defeated by a very large margin.

Just as the status quo is not an option in the referendum, no change is not an option for the UK as a whole. Perhaps Scotland will just continue acquiring powers until it becomes a state within a state – what you might call independence in the United Kingdom as opposed to independence in Europe. That is what some gradualists in the Scottish National Party appear to believe. However, there is no guarantee Scotland will become an independent country by accretion. History doesn't move in straight lines; it moves by discontinuities and ruptures. There clearly have been powerful forces at work in the United Kingdom over the past three decades that have led us to something of a crossroads in the history of Great Britain and a fundamental renegotiation of Scotland's place in it. Which is why it is necessary to look at the origins of Scotland's place in the UK.

The Strange Case of Scottish Nationalism

Karl Marx said that history "weighs like a nightmare on the brain of the living". Seven hundred years of Scottish history will be weighed in the balance as Scots prepare to vote in the independence referendum. Even some Nationalists groan inwardly when they hear the names William Wallace, Robert the Bruce, Bannockburn. This is where Gothic fantasy meets populist Nationalism, emitting a whiff of ethnic chauvinism – Scots wha hae wi' Wallace bled. But these are potent myths which have endured through the centuries and still speak to many Scots today. Nations, for better or worse, are the arena in which civilisation developed, and modern concepts like democracy and human rights emerged from the process of struggle against political domination and tyranny. Scotland's myths have a peculiarly communitarian quality, arising as they did out of the struggle of a small country suffering oppression by a very powerful and overbearing neighbour. There is much debate about whether Scotland's Nationalist revolutions could be called in any sense democratic – the concept had no meaning to feudal society in the Middle Ages. However, in a sense it is irrelevant because the rebellion united the Scottish people in a struggle for freedom. As soon as people start to ask who they are, they look to the past and start to find a reflection of themselves, and it is in that self-discovery that they create new political forms.

Karl Marx also dismissed the ancient Nationalisms of Europe, like Scottish Nationalism, as "historical refuse" – which shows how wrong historians can be.

CHAPTER THREE
ORIGINS

✕

NOTHING INFURIATES Scottish historians more than the claim that most Scots under the age of 40 only know about the medieval Scottish patriot Sir William Wallace from Mel Gibson's 1995 biopic *Braveheart*. Some Unionists say the rise of modern Scottish Nationalism dates from the intervention of the diminutive Australian, who produced his epic account of the Scottish Wars of Independence just at the moment when the restoration of Scotland's parliament after 300 years was beginning to look like a real possibility. The film won five Academy Awards, including Best Picture and is actually rather enjoyable as long as you don't take it too seriously. It did exactly what it set out to do, which was to recreate, for a new age, the spirit of the old Hollywood epics like *Spartacus* and *El Cid*.

Braveheart is one of Alex Salmond's favourite films, which is perhaps why it generated a furious reaction among non-Nationalist Scots. The Scottish comedian Billy Connolly described it as "pure Australian shite". Many Scots, Nationalists and Unionists, claim to be offended by this antipodean intrusion into their copyright on the Scottish legends. A statue depicting Mel Gibson as Wallace, placed in the car park at the Wallace Monument, had to be removed in 2004 because it was continually vandalised. Others claimed to see in *Braveheart* a far-right agenda. The Nationalist commentator and musician Pat Kane called it a "neo-fascist tartan epic". And the film was also condemned in the gay press for homophobia, presumably because it portrayed Edward II of England as an effete homosexual who preferred hanging out with his lover, Piers Gaveston, to fighting the Scots. His father, King Edward, brilliantly played by Patrick McGoohan, is depicted throwing Gaveston out of a castle window, which never happened. Gaveston was assassinated by English nobles.

Hatred of the English is the racism that dares to speak its name, at least in Hollywood. When they are not murderers, the English are portrayed as privileged fops, while the Scots are naturally the heroic underdogs. But if you can endure the casual prejudice *Braveheart* did at least place a largely forgotten period of Scottish history back on the popular agenda in the 1990s. Scotland's leading historian, Professor Tom Devine, reflecting on *Braveheart* in 2010, said that the movie "dramatically raised Scotland's international profile and place on the world map, for good or for ill".[10] It sparked a revival of the Wallace cult not only in Scotland, where it has inspired a succession of Wallace-related festivals and conventions, but also across Europe, especially in Germany and Russia.

It certainly helped the tourist trade, and visitor numbers quadrupled at Stirling Castle in much the same way as they did at Rosslyn Chapel after *The Da Vinci Code* was published. VisitScotland has never looked back and there are numerous *Braveheart* tours of Scotland, even though the film was mostly shot on location in Ireland. The effect of the film on Scottish politics is less clear. There was no obvious increase in support for independence in the opinion polls. However, it coincided with the growing support for home rule and may well have contributed, if marginally, to the overwhelming vote for a Scottish Parliament in the 1997 Devolution Referendum. It may have also contributed to the rout of the Conservatives – who were seen very much as the English Party in the 1990s. In the 1997 General Election, they lost all of their Scottish seats – a wipe-out that was widely celebrated across Scotland.

WHO WAS WALLACE?

Braveheart is scorned by historians as a ludicrous Hollywood farrago that bears little relationship to the actual history of the man who led Scotland into the Wars of Independence and became Guardian of Scotland. But then, Wallace actually bears very little relationship to himself because very little is known about him. Most of what we think we know about Wallace comes from an epic poem composed 170 years after his death by the travelling minstrel Blind Harry. The modern myths about Wallace largely date from the Victorian era and the writings of Sir Walter Scott and Jane Porter. The Wallace Monument that stands over the scene of his greatest victory at Stirling Bridge was erected in 1869. Wallace is an archetypical popular hero, a people's champion, who is reinvented for different epochs. And as such, *Braveheart* – given that it is a popular film – as good a reinvention as any. It's certainly a great deal more historically accurate than Shakespeare's *Macbeth*, or Christopher Marlowe's *Edward II*.

We don't even know for certain when or where William Wallace was born, nor what he did before he became a guerilla leader harassing English garrisons and murdering the Sheriff of Lanark in 1296, allegedly for murdering his wife. Wallace was a tall man with a short temper and a long memory. He was born into a landowning family, was a brilliant tactician and must have had some advanced military training and experience on the field of battle, which has led to speculation he might been a mercenary – a profession that many Scots turned to in the Middle Ages. Contemporary accounts, like the *Lanercost Chronicle,* describe Wallace as a poacher and brigand and not surprisingly Edward I regarded him as a terrorist and murderer. What we do know is that Wallace was adopted by the bishops of Scotland as the only man who could stand up to the English invaders after King Edward I's bloody annexation of Scotland in 1296. He managed to defeat a vastly superior English army at Stirling Bridge on 11th September 1297 and changed the course of history.

English historians have long argued that Wallace's victory at Stirling Bridge was pure military opportunism. The English knights under John de Warenne, Earl of Surrey, and Hugh de Cressingham, the hated English Treasurer of Scotland, allowed themselves to be trapped crossing a narrow bridge as they were preparing to enter into battle formation. Under the chivalric rules of medieval military engagement, both sides were supposed to line up and face each other, formally, before charging into battle, but Wallace didn't play to anyone's rules except his own. He was a guerilla fighter, one of the earliest exponents of low intensity warfare. Taking advantage of the disarray in the enemy ranks, Wallace's men cut the English down as they crossed Stirling Bridge in twos and threes. There was chaos. The heavy English warhorses got caught in the bogs as they tried to escape. The sheer size of the English Army, three times larger than the Scottish force, became its major weakness as it tumbled over and into itself in a horrific maelstrom of armour, horse meat and human corpses. These were brutal times.

The slaughter of some 5000 English soldiers transformed Scottish and English politics overnight. Wallace had shamed the

Scottish nobility by showing that it was possible for a commoner, supported by a largely peasant army, to take on the English and defeat them. Had it not been for Wallace, the Scottish nobility would very likely have capitulated to Edward entirely and allowed their nation to be extinguished, as Wales had been in 1287.

Stirling Bridge also sent Robert the Bruce homeward to think again. The future King of Scotland had, at the time of Wallace's rebellion, been fighting on the side of the English, having signed with his father the hated Ragman Rolls of 1296, which recognised Edward I as Scotland's feudal overlord. Robert the Bruce was even a favoured member of Edward's court, before he briefly switched sides to back Wallace's rebellion.

As for Edward I, the military disaster at Stirling Bridge had a silver lining in that it united the fractious English barons behind him, and forced them to open their treasuries to finance the destruction of this new Caledonian menace. Edward Longshanks returned in force in 1298 to defeat Wallace at Falkirk, largely through the strength of English and Welsh longbowmen, who could fire armour-piercing arrows from a distance of several hundred yards. These were the machine guns of medieval warfare and the Scots in their schiltrons – fortified formations of spearmen not unlike hedgehogs – were slaughtered in their thousands. Falkirk was a personal humiliation for William Wallace, as well as a national tragedy, and he resigned his guardianship of Scotland and went into hiding. He continued the fight as best he could against the English for another seven years, but the magic had gone and his ability to raise an army was much reduced. Wallace was later betrayed, inevitably, by a Scottish noble, Sir John de Menteith, captured and sent to London. There he was tried for treason and terrorism and executed in Smithfield Market in 1305 in a gruesome spectacle, during which his innards were removed and burned before him while still alive.

This was another miscalculation by Edward I, who for all his skill as a war leader and "law giver", had little understanding of the power of martyrdom. Wallace dead, through this grotesque crucifixion, was far more dangerous than Wallace alive. He had been a discredited fugitive, largely disowned by the war-weary Scottish nobility who had wanted to come to terms with Edward to rebuild their finances. Now Wallace became one of the most potent martyrs of the last thousand years, a heroic fighter against tyranny who has been claimed as an inspiration by revolutionaries as diverse as George Washington, Giuseppe Garibaldi and Che Guevara. So enamoured was the 19th-century Italian Nationalist Giuseppe Mazzini with the Wallace myth that he even helped finance the building of the colossal 200-foot Wallace Monument that dominates the Stirling skyline to this day.

The image of Wallace as the outlaw man of the people, a Robin Hood who takes on the might of the state is of course a modern reinvention. There wasn't a lot of stealing from the rich to give to the poor. Wallace's main tactic was scorched earth – the destruction of farms, livestock and villages to deprive invading English armies of food. The Scottish peasantry could have been forgiven for feeling liberated to death. Even allowing for English propaganda, Wallace is thought to have behaved with brutality, even hanging farmers who refused to join his enlisted armies. In their forays into northern England, the Scots emulated the Vikings in their enthusiasm for looting and pillaging. The cost of Scottish independence was mostly paid for by the misery of the ordinary people on both sides of the border.

The feudal economy was largely built on warfare and the enrichment of a warrior aristocracy of Anglo-Norman or Scotto-Norman nobles like Robert the Bruce. Wallace was not a noble but he was a member of the landowning classes, and his revolution did not involve challenging the feudal hierarchy in the cause of some primitive Communism. Wallace as the tribune of the people is largely a projection back through the history of the political mindset of the 19th and 20th centuries. But these medieval warriors did clearly have some conception of the national community which went beyond the mere enrichment of their own dynastic houses. What is beyond doubt is that Wallace won the hearts and minds of a large swathe of the Scottish people, from a wide range of backgrounds, who showed almost suicidal bravery in their willingness to fight against one of the greatest military powers of the medieval world: England. Wallace arguably led one of the first people's armies in history and came near to ending the nobility's monopoly of the means of violence.

Yet there's a plausible case for arguing that the Scottish Wars of Independence were a historic mistake. There was nothing inevitable about the conflict between Scotland and England that erupted at the end of the 13th century and continued on and off for the next 300 years. The two countries had been at peace for more than a century. Scotland was a relatively prosperous independent country and culturally advanced, as evidenced by the great medieval cathedrals in Glasgow and St Andrews. Had it not been for a series of accidents, war with England might never have taken place.

It was unfortunate that Scottish King Alexander III – Edward I's brother-in-law – died in 1286, falling off his horse on his way, according to the *Lanercost Chronicle*, for a late-night conjugal call on his new wife, Yolande of Dreux. It was equally tragic that his successor Margaret, the infant Maid of Norway, died in Orkney on her way to Scotland, apparently after eating rotten food. Had she survived, the wars between Scotland and England might never have taken place. Indeed, since the Maid, though only seven years old, was being lined up to marry King Edward's son, the Union of the Crowns of Scotland and England might have happened 300 years earlier than it did. There was arguably a far greater community of interest between Scotland and England in feudal 1290 than there was in 1603, still less 1707.

Who was to blame for starting the war? We're not supposed to pass contemporary moral judgements on the actions of historical figures who lived to different codes in distant times. But it's hard not to see Edward Longshanks as the principal villain of the piece, though his actions probably arose as much from politics in England as malevolence toward the Scots. Edward I had grand ambitions to unify Britain under his rule and had successfully conquered and Anglicised Wales, which was now administered by English sheriffs. He was anxious to end wars on the British mainland, the better to deal with his main foreign enemy, King Philip IV of France, who was trying to take away English lands in Gascony. Edward also had trouble from his own barons who did not particularly like having to fight his foreign wars and who, since this was the era of Magna Carta, were no longer afraid to rein in the ambitions of headstrong monarchs. Edward was not above using the Scottish threat as a means of pulling his fractious English nobility into line.

But there was really no moral or military justification for brutally subjugating the Scots in 1296 because they presented no obvious danger to England at the close of the 13th century. In fact, the Scottish nobility and clergy had actually invited Edward, as a friend not an overlord, to arbitrate in the matter of the succession to Alexander III – the Great Cause as it became known. There were at least fourteen claimants to the Scottish crown including Robert the Bruce (the elder), his rival John Comyn of Buchan and the main contender, John Balliol, whose claim Edward upheld as the true heir to the Scottish Crown. But he only recognised Balliol on the condition he in turn recognised Edward as Scotland's feudal overlord. This proposal to turn Scotland into a vassal colony caused outrage in Scotland, as did the taxes imposed by Edward and his demands that Scottish knights should fight for England in France. It became clear that far from being a benevolent neighbour helping Scotland out of its regal difficulties, Edward had decided to use the uncertainty over the succession as an opportunity to extinguish the Scottish nation.

The hapless John Balliol came to be known as "Toom Tabard", which roughly translates today as "empty suit" and was regarded with contempt by his countrymen – the start of a long tradition of Scottish disregard for and suspicion of their national leaders. But even the compliant Balliol eventually rebelled against Edward, and negotiated a treaty with Philip IV of France in 1295, founding what became known as the "Auld Alliance" between Scotland and France. Edward regarded this as treason and promptly invaded Scotland, sacking Berwick and destroying Balliol's army at Dunbar in 1296. Berwick was one of the largest towns outside London, a northern European entrepôt and its destruction by Edward and the massacre of the townspeople was one of the great atrocities of the medieval age. Some 7,500 inhabitants – men, women and children – were put to the sword, and it was said that the water-wheels were being turned by blood. It was the medieval equivalent of shock and awe, intended to destroy Scotland's will to resist. Naturally, it did the reverse.

Edward intended that a line should be drawn, and Scotland turned into a region of England. He removed the holy relics and symbols of Scottish nationhood – the Crown Jewels, the Black Rood of St Margaret, supposedly part of the True Cross, and, most importantly, the Stone of Scone, or the Stone of Destiny, the block of sandstone on which Jacob's head had supposedly rested in Biblical times, and which had been used to crown Scottish kings. Edward took the stone to Westminster Abbey where it remained for the next 700 years until it was eventually returned by the Conservative Scottish Secretary, Michael Forsyth, in 1996, inadvertently fulfilling the prophecy quoted by St Columba that when the stone returns to Scotland so would Scottish sovereignty.

The image of Scotland being sat upon by every English monarch was a potent one – the proud nation reduced to the role of a resting place for the English backside. But Edward's attempt to extinguish Scottish nationhood failed, and instead he created a grievance among Scots that helped destroy him and his son, and which endured for centuries, wasting formidable amounts of English blood and treasure. At the very least it was astonishingly inept statecraft. The Scots were in no position to fight in the 1290s. They hadn't had much cause to wage wars since the Battle of Largs against the Vikings, and they lacked military training, knights, equipment and modern military tactics. Edward's army, by contrast, was one of the best equipped and trained in Europe, and was battle-hardened from campaigns in Wales and France. But, as so many armies of occupation have discovered, it is very hard to subjugate a people who just don't realise when they are beaten. It was a measure of Edward's ineptitude that he so antagonised this tiny, impoverished northern country that its people found the courage and determination to defeat his splendid army at Stirling Bridge in 1297.

THE BRUS MAKES UP HIS MIND

Wallace's life and death inspired the great opportunist of Scottish history, Robert the Bruce, who had been merrily slaughtering his countrymen on King Edward's behalf before the Scottish uprising. *Braveheart* dramatises this by suggesting that Bruce and Wallace fought on opposite sides in the battle at Falkirk in 1298 when Wallace was defeated, and though this is not historically accurate it is true in an artistic sense. Robert the Bruce fought in several of Edward's pacification campaigns in Scotland even through the early 1300s. He was among a party of English-supporting nobles who searched for Wallace in his hideout deep in Selkirk Forest in 1305. There is even a legend that he tipped Wallace off that they were coming for him, though this was probably an embellishment for the comfort of Scots who couldn't imagine the father of the Scottish nation being a turncoat.

Robert the Bruce, or de Brus, was of Norman descent and had lands in England as well as in Scotland. When Wallace was betrayed, Bruce was still a lively presence in Edward's court in

London. He fought, trained and hunted with English nobles in and around London and was a medieval man about town. It is quite possible that right up to the moment when Robert finally decided in 1306 that he was serious about becoming king of Scotland, he had still been angling to become sole guardian of Scotland under Edward. It seems hard to believe that the future king of Scotland might have been a quisling, but in the Middle Ages it was not unusual for Anglo-Norman magnates like Bruce to switch sides several times in their military career.

After the defeat of Wallace at Falkirk, King Edward I had actually installed Robert the Bruce as one of Scotland's regents, along with his deadly rival, John Comyn, and the Bishop of Glasgow Robert Wishart. After the dismal John Balliol finally threw in the towel in 1302, Robert realised he had a chance of becoming king rather than merely an agent of a foreign occupation. It seems that Edward realised around this time he had a traitor in his court and was about to arrest Robert the Bruce. But according to the epic poem *The Brus*, written by John Barbour in 1375, Robert fled after being handed twelve pence for a pair of spurs by his brother-in-law Ralph de Monthermer. The message was "get out of town fast".

Robert then finally met his rival, the Red Comyn, Lord of Badenoch, in Greyfriars Church in Dumfries in the cold February of 1306. They were supposed to be coming to an agreement on how to unite against the English overlords. Robert was prepared to hand over his lands in Carrick in exchange for Comyn's support in his bid for the crown. But it didn't quite work out that way. A fight began and the Bruce killed his rival near the altar of the church. It seems curiously fitting that Scotland's greatest king gained the throne after chibbing his main ally – No Mean City meets the War of Independence. It is also typically Scottish for its leaders to fall out among themselves – though in this case it perhaps served the cause of Scottish national history that they did.

Bruce became a renegade criminal, guilty of one of the most appalling crimes known to the medieval world – murder in God's house. This led to Bruce's excommunication and eternal damnation in the eyes of the Mother Church. The option of becoming King Edward's top man in Scotland was clearly no longer available to him, and Robert faced the sobering choice of whether to become king or a fugitive. Burdened by the sin of his crime, Bruce sought help from Robert Wishart, the Bishop of Glasgow, who appears to have offered him absolution provided he agreed to seize the vacant throne of Scotland. Clerics in those days were deeply involved in affairs of state and the Scottish bishops were militant Nationalists, if only because the Scottish Church didn't want to become controlled by the Archdiocese of York. Wishart had helped inspire Wallace's rebellion and had stashed a number of items of Scottish regalia which Edward had failed to remove in 1296.

Bishop Wishart raced off to get the new King of Scotland crowned before he changed his mind. King Robert I was thus installed on 25th March 1306 in Scone, though without the benefit of the eponymous stone which of course was in London. If it sounds a little hasty and improvised, it was. Robert became the only king in Scottish history to be crowned twice. This was because Isabella MacDuff, the Countess of Buchan – who incredibly was married to the uncle of the very Red Comyn who Robert had just murdered – insisted on exercising her clan's king-making right to place the crown on Robert's head. She arrived a day late – so they repeated the ceremony. It was perhaps unfortunate for her that they did, because Isabella – one of the great unsung heroines of Scottish history and probably Robert's mistress – ended up being imprisoned in a cage in the open air for four years in Berwick when Edward finally caught up with her.

Her family didn't do too well either. Robert realised he had to destroy the power of the Comyns, who derived their claim to the Scottish throne through the Balliol dynasty, so he waged war on Isabella's relatives in Buchan on and off for the next two years until they were no longer a threat. Bruce had to fight a civil war in Scotland even as he was fighting a war of independence against England. It was a precarious military situation, and required great tenacity to see it through, since for much of the time Robert had no standing army.

The war with England raged for the next eight years, with English armies heading north almost on an annual basis. Clearly, Bruce wasn't going to give up, and the Scots refused to be defeated even as they were mauled, repeatedly, in skirmishes on the field of battle. The outcome was by no means assured and for much of the time the Bruce was a lonely fugitive. He spent long periods in hiding, in Ayrshire, the Western Isles, probably also in Norway and Northern Ireland. It was during one of these periods hiding in a dank cave that he was said to have been inspired by the tenacity of the spider trying to spin its web and fighting against the relentless power of gravity. Such at least is the story, as retold by Sir Walter Scott.

But while the Bruce was resolving to try, try and try again, his family and followers were paying the price for his regal ambitions. Two of his brothers, Thomas and Alexander, were captured and executed; his sister imprisoned in another cage for four years – a peculiarly unchivalric form of punishment that meant not only exposure to the elements but also the humiliation of having to eat, sleep and defecate while exposed to the common people. Robert's wife, Elizabeth de Burgh, was held in captivity in England – though not in a cage because before the war she had been a face at Edward's court and was recognised as a lady.

Bruce gradually consolidated his hold on Scotland, skirmish by skirmish, castle by castle. Following the unorthodox military doctrines of Wallace, Robert avoided meeting the English army on the field of battle until it could no longer be avoided. He also appears to have inherited Wallace's support among the common people of Scotland – or at any rate those wealthy enough to afford to bear arms because he had unique ability to attract followers to what looked like a hopeless cause. This probably owed less to his personal magnetism than to the widespread reluctance from Scots of all ranks to accept Edward I as overlord of Scotland. And of course there was also fear – Bruce was one of the most ruthless warriors Scotland had ever produced, a desperate man, an excommunicated murderer who was not averse to killing anyone who got in his way, even in a church. Robert wasn't the first revolutionary to spend much of his time hiding in caves, but it was an extraordinary feat to keep the idea of Scottish independence alive in those years.

In his final years, Edward became obsessed with his inability to defeat the Scots. The rigours of 20 years on campaign took its toll and the Hammer of the Scots (*Malleus Scottorum*) died in 1307 of dysentery aged 68 on his way north at Solway for one final attempt to settle the matter. He is said to have ordered that his body should not be buried until the Scots were defeated. But his son Edward II was not so committed to subjugating this annoying and really rather insignificant northern country, and so he pulled the English army south. This was not a good moment for a tactical withdrawal as it boosted Bruce's image just as he was reuniting the country. Bruce's guerilla campaign continued until the only significant

English stronghold left in Scotland was Stirling, a near impregnable fortification of immense strategic importance, to which Bruce laid siege in 1313. When Edward II tried to relieve the English garrison there in 1314, Bruce seized his opportunity. Despite being outnumbered three to one, and having few cavalry, he defeated the English in the battle that secured Scotland's independence.

Bannockburn is probably the most famous battle in British history, but surprisingly little is known about it and even the location of the battle is a matter of dispute. The battle is said to have been preceded by an encounter between the Bruce and an English knight, Henry de Bohun, who, riding his warhorse, charged at the Scottish king. The Bruce, riding a diminutive palfrey, dodged the lance and then, according to legend, split his opponent's head open with one swipe of his battleaxe. This was the medieval equivalent of scoring a goal in the opening minute of a home international. Bruce – learning from Wallace's defeat at Falkirk – used his schiltrons of spearmen offensively – driving them at the English lines instead of using them as static formations. This prevented Edward from fully deploying his deadly Welsh bowmen, who had destroyed Wallace's schiltrons six years previously. Once again, the sheer size of the English army became its greatest weakness. The battle lasted two days and there is still controversy over exactly what happened. But what is not in dispute is the result. It was an epic defeat; an extraordinary achievement for a popular army with only 500 cavalry and 6,000 men against the biggest English army ever to invade Scotland, with 2,000 cavalry and 25,000 men. Edward only narrowly escaped capture, fleeing for the border. The existential crisis of the Scottish nation was over.

Yet, the fighting continued because Edward II refused to recognise Robert the Bruce as the true King of Scotland. And since he had been excommunicated – damned to Hell – by the Pope himself, this did somewhat undermine Robert's credibility. However, he kept his fractious nation united, showing discipline and political skill, since of course many Scottish nobles, himself included, still had connections and lands in England and were always liable to switch sides, just as he had, repeatedly. Edward II was not a ruler with the determination or the military skill of his father, and could never quite understand the need to spend so much time fighting the damned Scots. But whenever he retreated, after the annual military campaign, Bruce and his armies would invade the north of England doing what invading armies did. Plus, the Scots were always considered liable to form another anti-English alliance with France.

The fighting dragged on and on. In 1320, the earls and barons of Scotland signed the famous Declaration of Arbroath in the form of a letter to Pope John XXII, pleading "with devout kisses of your blessed and happy feet", for Scotland to be recognised as an independent country. The declaration applauded King Robert for liberating Scotland from the English and urged the Pontiff to lift his excommunication for murdering John Comyn – something the Pope never quite got round to doing. After a rather fanciful potted history of Scotland since Biblical times and inviting a comparison between the Scots and the Israelites (a comparison that would later also be made by the Covenanters), the letter appeals to the Pope to allow "those who live in this poor little Scotland" to be left in peace without being violently attacked by its powerful neighbour. The declaration goes on to say that if Robert the Bruce proved incapable of maintaining Scotland's independence, the Scots would "drive him out" and reserved the right to choose someone else as their king. Given Bruce's capacity for playing both ends against the middle, this might have seemed a prudent caveat.

This passage led to claims that the Declaration of Arbroath was an early expression of the doctrine of popular national sovereignty since it appears to have challenged the Divine Right of Kings and placed the monarch under the purview of the "community of the realm". Some claim it even inspired the American Declaration of Independence – Thomas Jefferson claimed descent from Robert I. This is stretching the point somewhat since of course the Declaration of Arbroath did not assert the right of common people to choose their ruler, still less suggest that all men are created equal. It was the nobility – the medieval earls and barons – who were warning Robert that they reserved the right to choose someone else if he didn't continue to defend Scotland against the English. It was more Magna Carta than the Rights of Man. Still, it was remarkable in that it placed King Robert I – the man who had liberated Scotland from English rule – effectively under threat of recall. The declaration may have influenced theorists of natural law, like the 17th-century political philosopher Thomas Hobbes and it undoubtedly inspired the Scottish Covenanters when they stood against Charles I and ignited the English Civil War.

The Declaration of Arbroath is memorable mainly for its

inspirational language. These words, written on the walls, greet visitors to the Museum of Scotland in Edinburgh: "For, as long as but a hundred of us remain alive, never will we on any conditions be brought under English rule. It is in truth not for glory, nor riches, nor honours that we are fighting, but for freedom – for that alone, which no honest man gives up but with life itself." Winston Churchill could have written that. He nearly did, because he was fascinated by Scottish history and is thought to have studied the declaration when preparing for his "finest hour" address to the nation in the Second World War. After the war, Churchill appealed to the Scottish voters to remember their heroic national history and not allow it to be extinguished by Labour's centralised Socialist state, which is one of the many reasons why the post-war Labour Party has tended to be ambivalent about Wallace and Bruce. These historical myths are malleable and can serve many purposes.

The Declaration of Arbroath is simply one of the finest statements of defiance in the English language, even though it was written in Latin. The Pope eventually listened and so did England and in 1328, at the treaty of Northampton and Edinburgh, King Edward III renounced any claim to Scotland and recognised Robert as King of Scotland in perpetuity. He even promised to return the Stone of Destiny, though he never got around to it. The Bruce was still alive but very sick, possibly with leprosy, and he died in 1329, asking for his heart to be cut out and sent to the Holy Land to atone for, among other things, his murder of Red Comyn in Greyfriars. Unfortunately, it never got there. As so often in Scottish history, the ambition was let down by the execution.

For good or ill, Scotland was in charge of its own destiny, though no one said it was going to be easy, and it wasn't. England didn't forgive or forget that it had been defeated by this ragged little country, a land of bogs and mountains, with no reliable allies and practically no wealth to speak of. Scotland and England continued to fight each other on and off for the next 300 years, and the Scots generally came off worst – as you would expect for a small poor country up against a military superpower. Flodden in 1513 was a particularly bad away defeat, in which Scotland lost one of its most enlightened kings, James IV and 12,000 men – the "floors o' the forest". But the existence of the Scottish nation was never again in doubt, until of course the Scottish nobles decided voluntarily to relinquish statehood in 1707 after the Treaty of Union. But even then,

Scots could still say they had never actually been conquered by the English and that Scottish nationhood was never extinguished.

WALLACE THE MYTH

What relevance does all this have for Scotland today? The exploits of Wallace and Bruce are tremendous stories for a start – murder, treachery and conspiracy. Game of Thrones is tame compared with the Scottish Wars of Independence, and the tales are forgotten and rediscovered every century or so. The Wallace myth underwent a significant revival in the 19th century, when Scottish history became a popular passion, largely thanks to the writings of Sir Walter Scott and Robert Burns. Wallace societies sprang up all over the world, alongside the Robert Burns cult, and 80,000 people crowded into Stirling for a Wallace commemoration in 1861, many from south of the border. The doings of Wallace and Bruce captured the imagination, strangely, of the English upper classes, and the Prince Regent became a great enthusiast for Scottish lore. Bruce's tomb, which had been lost in the Reformation, was discovered during the excavation of Dunfermline Abbey in 1818 and his body exhumed and analysed with great interest and a cast taken of his skull. This gruesome object is still on display in the Department of Anatomy at the University of Edinburgh, along with the skeleton of the grave robber William Burke.

The Victorian revival of interest in the Scottish Wars of Independence was not seen in any way as a threat to the Union. In the 19th century, Scottish soldiers were fighting the wars that spread the British Empire across the world. Indeed, it was part of the glamour of the Scottish regiments that they were descended from great fighting men such as Wallace and Bruce, and statues of the Scottish patriots command the entrance to Edinburgh Castle. Scots revelled in their bloody history, and jeered in the bars that the English had never defeated them and that Scots were all bravehearts. But this Anglophobic banter wasn't to be confused with demands for Scottish nationhood in the 19th century – the Scots were fully sold into the imperial project by this stage. Indeed, being patriotic involved regarding Scotland as the best of the British Empire, putting the Brave into Britain. The Scots saw themselves as the efficient, rather than the dignified, elements in the imperial constitution, who did the business and fought the wars, while the rather effete English built their grand mansions and lived the life of the rentier.

The Wallace myth, and the fact Scotland had fought against the English domination, also somehow absolved Scots from the uglier aspects of British imperial conquest. To this day, in former African colonies such as Malawi, Scots are somehow not implicated in English imperialism even though they fought the wars. Scottish missionaries in Africa regarded themselves, not only on a mission from God, but as representatives of a country which had thrown off the domination of a foreign power and celebrated liberty. Hence the slightly bizarre image of David Livingstone singing Burns's hymn to the common man, *A Man's a Man for A' That*, to bemused tribes in Central Africa while urging Lord Palmerston to turn Nyasaland into a British protectorate.

Interest in Scottish medieval history died away somewhat in the 20th century, particularly after the Second World War, when it became unfashionable and slightly anti-British to celebrate the exploits of Scottish patriots – though Churchill didn't seem to have any problems with it. The collapse of the British Empire and the independence movements in Indian and Africa further diminished the appeal of Scottish independence because Scots didn't think of themselves as some backward colony in need of national liberation. We were beyond that. The winds of change also revealed the dark side of the Empire which the Scots had idealised and it became politically incorrect in an increasingly Labour Scotland to talk about war, Empire and military prowess. In Scotland, in the 1960s, the middle-class leaders of the Scottish National Party became uneasy about celebrating Wallace too brazenly, partly because they feared encouraging the creation of a militant wing, a Scottish IRA. SNP leaders continue to attend the annual Bannockburn commemorations, but they don't want their civic Nationalism to be tainted by the image of hairy Highlanders waving fake claymores and threatening to kill English people. Nationalists still sing Burns's anthem, "Scots wha hae wi' Wallace bled/welcome to your gory bed or to victory", but only in the way Labour politicians sing the *Red Flag*.

The mainly working-class voters who started supporting the Scottish Nationalists in the late 1960s weren't so squeamish about Scottish history and lapped it up. This is partly because they knew so little about it. Scottish history wasn't generally taught in Scottish schools until the 1990s, and it was largely through the Scottish regiments that the stories were passed down. When I was at school in the 1960s in Edinburgh, I learned nothing of Wallace or Robert the Bruce, and I'd never even heard the word "Braveheart" until I saw the film. Alex Salmond was the same, and only learned about his country's history from his grandfather. It wasn't until the Standard Grade syllabus in 1990 that the teaching of Scottish history became compulsory in Scottish schools. But perhaps it was a good thing Wallace and Co weren't part of the curriculum, because there's no better way to kill legends than to turn them into homework. The fact they were hidden from history made Wallace and Bruce all the more compelling in an age in which popular culture is in love with Gothic romance. Alex Salmond likes to quote Robert Burns on how the story of Wallace ignited a fire "which will boil in my veins till the floodgates of life shut in eternal rest". Yea, and the horn of Helm Hammerhand shall sound in the deep one last time …

Alex Salmond was not amused when he went to see the progress of Historic Scotland's new "state-of-the-art" Bannockburn Heritage Centre, due to open in 2014, which claims to be using "immersive technologies" to give a "Lord of the Rings" feel. The significance of Bannockburn on the 700th anniversary of the battle is becoming something of an historiographical battleground. The National Trust for Scotland apparently wanted to present Wars of Independence as a regional conflict between Plantagenet dynasties, a bit like the Wars of the Roses only a bit further north. Historians, such as Dr Michael Penman, author of *The Scottish Civil War*, who is on the advisory academic panel to the project, find the whole anti-English aspect of the Bruce story just a little too, well, Nationalistic. They've sought to play down the nation-building aspect of Bannockburn and suggest it was a civil war between the Bruce and the Balliol families – a kind of *Godfather* interpretation of Scottish history. "Robert I's coup of 1306," writes Penman, "is now increasingly viewed in terms of a civil war between rival Scottish factions rather than the more black and white Nationalistic view which characterised Bruce's party as 'patriotic'."[11] Not by the First Minister it isn't.

Alex Salmond gave the project directors a lecture on Scottish medieval history, which the First Minister had studied at St Andrews University under the Medievalist Professor Geoffrey WS Barrow, and on which he considers himself an expert. William Wallace was no Plantagenet. Bannockburn was the climax to a struggle for national independence which mobilised the "community of the realm" against annexation by a foreign power. Barrow's research into the use of the phrase "community of the realm" by Scotland's guardians in the 13th century led him to regard it as a socially inclusive proto-Nationalist concept which "included the peasantry as well as the gentry and baronage in the national family – a considerable advance on the feudal doctrine of Divine Right".[12] In this interpretation, Bruce crowned himself King of Scotland not as a blood rival to Comyn but as a national freedom fighter.

Arguably, the Church was a more important player in the First Scottish War of Independence than either Bruce or the Balliols. It was Bishop Robert Wishart who put lead in the pencil of both Wallace and Bruce, organising the resistance, rejecting English sovereignty, preserving the Scottish regalia, promoting Bruce as king after absolving him of murder and presiding over the coronation at Scone. Wishart had a direct interest in Scottish independence because he didn't want his powers of patronage usurped by church leaders in England. But this doesn't mean that Bannockburn was really an ecclesiastical dispute between different branches of the Roman Church – though no doubt someone is writing a book to that effect even now.

This debate will no doubt continue all the way to the referendum and demonstrates how history itself becomes political. Everyone will have to take a view. My own is that to try to distil the Nationalism out of Bannockburn is fatuous historical revisionism, like the attempts to argue the American Civil War had nothing to do with slavery or the Russian Revolution was really about rivalry between Germany and Russia. Of course, it was about many things and the Bruce did conduct a civil war against the Balliols/Comyns and many other families before Bannockburn as he consolidated his hold in Scotland. He waged a three-year campaign to end the Comyn domination of north-east Scotland. This was a brutal era of blood feuds, treachery and violence. But to relegate medieval Scotland's struggle for independence to a footnote in order to avoid sounding anti-English is taking multiculturalism too far.

Edward's annexation of Scotland was not merely a dispute among English feudal dynasties with no national dimension. Edward had tried to force Scotland's nobles to pay homage to him as their feudal overlord, as Scotland's Lord Paramount, which would have extinguished Scotland's national autonomy just as surely as it did to Wales in 1286. Bruce was ambivalent about Scotland before 1306, had lands in England, and was as much a product of the circumstances of the time as he was an agent of historical change. But his genius was to realise that Edward, for all his military might, could not govern Scotland without consent. In the end, Bruce crowned himself King of Scotland after what was a military coup, certainly, but a coup which asserted Scotland's claim of independence from England.

STILL BRAVE AFTER ALL THESE YEARS?

These myths retain their potency even after 700 years. Unlike legend, folklore and romantic literature, national history is always there, solid, incontrovertible, a presence of the past; however it is mangled and refashioned to suit the politics of the times. You can never stamp it out. In the 1970s, the myths of the Scottish Wars of Independence collided with Alex Salmond's own very contemporary brand of left-wing Nationalism. Wallace was reinvented all over again as a modern freedom fighter. The Scottish Left in the 1970s were very keen on the writings of the Italian Marxist, Antonio Gramsci, and the idea of the "community of the realm" seemed to chime with Gramsci's idea of "civil society" – a kind of popular national dimension to class struggle. Gramsci in turn drew on the traditions of the 19th-century Nationalist Giuseppe Mazzini who – of course – had idealised Wallace and invoked his example in the struggle for Italian unification. All of which shows that when it comes to national ideology, what goes around comes around.

When the collapse of Empire and the rise of European integration began to undermine the integrity of the British state after the 1970s, Scottish history was around to provide a focus for Scottish political identity – a ready-made narrative to help explain and contextualise Scotland's sense of national grievance. It wasn't hard to see echoes of Edward I in Margaret Thatcher. The Poll Tax was straight out of the Longshanks's playbook. Few Scots still feel the English people are in any sense their enemies, but whenever relations between the two countries come under strain, as they did in the 1980s, Scotland's ancient Claim of Right to national sovereignty is there to be revisited. As it was in 1988 when the Scottish Constitutional Convention, under the clerical guidance of Canon Kenyon Wright, persuaded Scotland's MPs, trade unionists and charities to sign a declaration of popular sovereignty – a modern community of the realm. Though ironically, Alex Salmond, blood-boiling patriot, didn't quite make it because the Scottish National Party had boycotted the Scottish Convention.

Some things don't change. Scotland is still a small country that punches above its weight, has a harsh climate, some difficult people, and is bolted onto a much larger country that – for most of the time – doesn't really care all that much what happens in this windswept corner of Britain. And why should it? It has been an unequal struggle for Scotland being in bed with an elephant, as the late Ludovic Kennedy put it. Perhaps it would have been easier for everyone if the Scots had given up this Nationalism nonsense, accepted defeat 700 years ago and had become merely a region of England. But the point is that it didn't. Perversely, annoyingly, quixotically, Scotland refused to relinquish sovereignty, and that has remained down the centuries as one of those "facts on the ground" that American generals used to talk about in the Iraq War.

It is dangerous to make sweeping generalisations about national character, but clearly the resolve that was demonstrated by the people of Scotland in fighting for their independence has been of great significance to them. Scots still like to think of themselves as dogged and resolute patriots who do not give up easily and who are very difficult to dominate. "Nemo me impune lacessit," as it says on the Order of the Thistle. "Wha daur meddle wi me." This idea of Scotland as the undefeated has cropped up repeatedly in Scottish history, most notably in the mottos of the Scottish regiments in the 19th and 20th centuries. Even supporters of political union in 1707 insisted that Scotland had not been defeated by England and need not fear the loss of the Scottish Parliament. Like the ruins of Hadrian's Wall, testament to another era of Scottish resistance, the legends of Bruce and Wallace and their struggle will always be lurking in the national consciousness.

William Wallace nearly had the last laugh. The voting for the Scottish Parliament took place on September 11th 1997, the 700th anniversary of the Battle of Stirling Bridge. Unfortunately a few years later, 9/11 became memorable for altogether different reasons. Yet again, Scotland's founding myth was buried under the weight of another country's history.

CHAPTER FOUR
UNIONS AND DISUNION

$$\times$$

"LAND HO!"

One can only imagine Colonel John Campbell's relief and elation as he heard he had at last arrived on Scotland's promised land – a country with clear water, friendly natives and rich, dark soil. Caledonia was calling him, and he was going to his new home. And not a moment too soon, as the passengers and crew of the sailing ship St Andrew had experienced four months of, quite literally, purgatory on the voyage. Permanently nauseous, he had, as one of the chief officers, been responsible for organising the care of those dying from dysentery, diarrhoea and dehydration. He was trying to maintain some kind of discipline and order among a crew who seemed to have been recruited from the worst of the Edinburgh underground. And all the while having to put up with the ceaseless ranting of the Presbyterian ministers who kept up a running commentary on how God was punishing them for vanity. But Colonel Campbell, captain of the troop, had a strong stomach and a good pair of earplugs. He had seen a lot worse on the field of battle in Flanders where disease was always a greater enemy than the enemy itself.

But at last it was over, and as the little ship approached the coast of the Darien Isthmus in Panama, they could give thanks to God ...

Or then again, perhaps not.

As every Scotsman knows, it was downhill all the way for Scotland's fledgeling colonists in the ill-fated Darien adventure in 1698 to 1700. The area chosen as "Caledonia" turned out to be a disease-ridden swamp backed by dense jungle and almost uninhabitable. Within six months, a third of the expedition were dead. The natives were friendly but the Spanish weren't. The English refused to trade, resupply or help the Darien colony in any way, despite being a few leagues away in the West Indies. King William, at war with France, didn't want to upset the Spanish – or so went the excuse. The boycott was largely the work of the East India Company which feared for its monopoly of trade between the Atlantic and the Pacific.

The Scots couldn't seriously blame the English for Darien. No one made them come to this godforsaken corner of central America, which the Spanish had avoided, knowing it was a malarial death trap. They didn't even have reliable maps. What had made them do it? Most of the accounts of the bounty of the Darien Isthmus had come from Scottish pirates, told to the brilliant fantasist William Paterson – the man who set up the Bank of England – who then persuaded Scots to empty their purses into the Company of Scotland, set up to mount the venture. The Scots investors were victims of a mania, like tulip mania, or an early version of the South Sea Bubble. It was a 17th-century version of irrational exuberance; that combination of speculation, greed and intoxication that afflicts capitalism today, as we saw in the recent financial crisis. It ended in sickness, heartache and death, far from home.

Colonel Campbell had had more than enough of the hooded crows of the Kirk during the voyage and was under no illusions about their worth, spiritual or temporal. Sat in the ships, away from the fever, their contribution seemed to amount to praying while the rest of the expedition tried to build huts, break the soil, hunt turtles. The ministers of the Kirk seemed to believe their main function was to evangelise the natives – a singularly futile project, since they couldn't speak the native language and had no interpreters. The Indians didn't have much time either for the trinkets – combs, beads, mirrors – that the expeditionaries had brought to trade. The local tribes felt sorry for the despairing colonists and brought them plantains to ease their discomfort as they died. They asked for nothing in return.

After eight months fighting with ministers and the Spanish, and with colonists dying at a rate of ten a day, Colonel Campbell had had enough. He packed up and left, and the rest followed as best they could. Of the four ships that made it out of "Caledonia", as Darien was called, one sank, two made it to New York, and one, the *St Andrew*, limped to the West Indies, where it was not exactly given a warm welcome by the British pirates and plantation owners. Another 100 men died at sea before Campbell finally found refuge in July 1700 in the Black River area of south-western Jamaica.

He had to live on his wits, since there was nothing else to fall back on, and it's assumed the Scots used what could be salvaged from the St Andrew to set up a trading station. Jamaica had been colonised by the English for a century, and some Scots were already there, having been transported for crimes of rebellion alternately by the Stuart kings and by Oliver Cromwell. It was a wild place at the end of the 17th century. It was the haunt of privateers – buccaneers – who were under semi-licence from England to raid Spanish vessels transferring gold and silver from the New World. Port Royal, the capital, was called the "Sodom of the New World" and reputedly had a drinking den for every ten inhabitants.

Somehow, Campbell managed to fit in rather well with the Jamaican demi-monde and became a bit of a celebrity among the expat community. He married and within four years had become the owner of a substantial sugar plantation in Black River. Colonel John was the first Campbell to set foot on Jamaica, but he was by no means the last. Jamaica was not a bad place to live – in the upland areas you could escape the worst of the malarial fever that killed so many white men in hot countries. Also, there were no Spanish and few ministers. Unlike Darien, the soil was good, especially for planting sugar, a commodity for which there was now an insatiable demand in the Old Country.

Colonel Campbell advised his relatives to follow him, and many did – their name still under a cloud from the Massacre of Glencoe. There was only one problem. No matter how many Campbells made the trip, there were never going to be enough workers to cut all that sugar cane. The market was booming; fortunes could be made. Luckily for the Campbell clan, there was a ready solution to the problem. It was called the slave trade.

Since the 1630s, British vessels had been cruising the West African coast and loading up with slaves, readily provided by the local tribal chiefs who exchanged them for copper, linen and what passed for luxury goods. The slaves were transported to Virginia to work on tobacco plantations and also to the West Indies. Soon, Campbells were up to their necks in the most lucrative business in history. They dealt in sugar, rum, tobacco and black ivory, as the slave trade became known. His cousin, George Campbell, became one of the leading slave traders in Liverpool.

Colonel John became man of substance and renown. The soldier who had only narrowly survived the great colonial disaster of Darien ended up one of the richest planters in Jamaica. When he died in 1740, his son inherited an income of more than £10,000 a year, a fabulous sum of money.[13] And as his largesse spread far and wide so did his seed. One way or another, Campbell appears to have sired half the population. It is said that to this day there are more Campbells per square acre in Jamaica than there are in Scotland.

The islands became what Darien was intended to be: a predominantly Scottish colonial outpost. By 1750, one-third of the population was Scots – slave drivers, doctors, ministers (you couldn't escape from Scottish Presbyterianism for long), administrators and accountants. And they weren't all just working for the English. One-third of the plantations on Jamaica by 1800 was owned by Scots.

Colonel Campbell's extraordinary career offers a remarkable insight into Scotland's relationship with England, the United Kingdom and the British Empire as it emerged from the late Middle Ages. Frozen out of the New World and colonial trade, in the 17th century Scotland played at colonial catch-up with Darien before realising that, well, perhaps it wasn't going to happen. So in the 18th century they did the next best thing: they colonised the British Empire and took charge from within. In this, they were often extremely successful as the mansions of the Glasgow Tobacco Barons were to demonstrate. Darien in effect became Jamaica – the next best thing to an empire.

Enterprising Scots just made the best of whatever opportunities were available to them after the 1707 Act of Union allowed them access to colonial markets. And they weren't too bothered about how they did it. If you had asked John Campbell how he, a product of the great communitarian clan tradition of the Scottish Highlands, could make a fortune out of the misery of the black man; how this son of William Wallace, the freedom fighter who defied English slavery, could morally contemplate living off African slavery, he would no doubt have replied: "Look son, it's just business."

John Campbell of Black River was wealthy enough to have returned to Scotland and lived the life of the Scottish laird. Many of his compatriots did return, often building hideous castles in remote parts of Scotland that were impossible to keep warm enough for human habitation. But he refused to return to Scotland, allegedly because he never forgave England for the Darien disaster, for refusing to come to the aid of the 1,200 benighted Scots dying in the fetid heat. He wasn't thought to be very keen on the Union with England either. Unfortunately, the Union got the last word. On his grave in Black River, Jamaica, the Colonel is described as having been born in "North Britain" rather than Scotland.

DARIEN – NOT SUCH A DAFT IDEA

Scotland felt a deep sense of humiliation over Darien. It has been a stick with which Scots have beaten themselves for the past three centuries; a moral lesson in the perils of that greatest of all Scottish sins: getting above your station. Scottish Calvinism is an unforgiving, judgemental religion, at least it was in the past. From every pulpit in Scotland, the name Darien was used to flagellate the Scottish Presbyterian conscience red raw. The wages of sin. The curse of vanity. The folly of greed. Amen.

Most countries celebrate their victories, their achievements, their noble ventures. Not the Scots; they celebrate their failures. Scotland may have been a cradle of the Industrial Revolution, a hub of the European Enlightenment, and the country that invented everything from paper currency to penicillin, but what gets remembered is the Darien disaster. It has been added to the list of Scottish humiliations: Flodden, Cromwell, Culloden. After the new Scottish Parliament got into difficulties after 1999, there was a revival of interest in Darien, the 300th anniversary of which happened to coincide with the restoration of Scotland's parliament. Newspaper headlines drew the comparison – a "Darien Parliament". When *The Economist* turned to examine independence in 2012, it referred to the Darien disaster as if it were still relevant to modern Scotland, or "Skintland" as it called it.[14] When the House of Lords Economic Affairs Committee looked into the implications of Scottish independence in 2013, it mentioned Darien on page two.[15] It was the subject of a rather chaotic production by the National Theatre of Scotland, *Caledonia*, in 2010, which presented Darien as a morality play on greed and Scotland's misguided effort to muscle in on the ruthless world of colonial exploitation. Darien has become, for some Unionists, a metaphor for the folly of Scottish independence – an economic version of the Tartan Army's disastrous outing at the 1978 World Cup.

For some reason we hear a lot less of Scottish colonial ventures that did succeed, such as in Canada, where Sir William Alexander was granted a charter in 1621 in Nova Scotia – a colder version of Caledonia. Simon McTavish's North West Company in Montreal rivalled the mighty Hudson Bay Company until they merged in 1821. By then tens of thousands of Scots had set up in Canada, which is why 15% of the Canadian population, nearly five million people, declared themselves in the 2006 Canadian census as being of Scottish origin. The Hudson Bay Company itself, which was once the largest landowner in the world, was largely run by Scots, many from Orkney. In the late Middle Ages, Scotland had been a very effective trading nation, with long-established links with the Baltic States and the Low Countries, which were disrupted by wars and by English sea power.

In fact, the Darien Scheme was a rather good idea – at least on paper. The USP was to link the Atlantic and the Pacific oceans, allowing trade from India to pass over the 40-mile isthmus instead of risking the waters of Cape Horn. Darien is what ultimately became the Panama Canal 200 years later. It was simply ahead of its time and could have worked if it had been better organised, if it had English resupply, and if the Spanish hadn't got there first. Big ifs, perhaps. The 1698 expedition was poorly led, badly researched, ill-equipped and lacked proper finance. However, it wasn't as daft as it has been presented.

Darien failed because Scotland was up against an emerging imperial power that was determined to protect its mercantile interest. The project threatened the monopoly of the powerful English East India Company, which put pressure on King William to curb this nominally Scottish operation which initially had a great deal of support from south of the border. The Dutch East India Company didn't like it much either. The King declared the enterprise illegal, which meant the departure of Dutch and of English investors, who were supposed to put up half the capital. To make matters worse, the Spanish claimed the territory of Darien for themselves and regarded the expedition to Darien as an act of war. So when the colonists got into difficulties and started to die in their hundreds, they were left on their own – *pour encourager les autres*.

It became clear that Scots could not benefit from a place in the sun as long as it was in the shade of England. Darien didn't lead to the Treaty of Union with England, though it is hard to believe it would have happened if the venture had been a great success. However, it was a painful, but relatively minor conclusion to a very distressing century. The Treaty of Union that extinguished the first Scottish Parliament came at the end of the bloodiest era Scotland had experienced since medieval times, in which religious armies clashed over apparently obscure doctrinal issues in shifting alliances on regional and monarchical lines. These religious passions have little reality to us today, which is why historians tend to view events through an economist prism, which filters out what people at the time thought they were doing.

Putting it all down to Darien and bribery saves a lot of intellectual effort, but at the cost of a lack of proportion. The Union of 1707 wasn't simply about economics. It had more to do with avoiding war, ensuring the protestant succession in England and entrenching the Presbyterian religion in Scotland. It came in the wake of an earlier union – the Union of the Crowns in 1603 – when the son of Mary, Queen of Scots, King James VI, succeeded to the English throne. This was supposed to have placed the two countries on a common path to peace and prosperity. It didn't.

CROMWELL AND THE COVENANTERS

Scots were dismayed at the speed with which "their" James VI disappeared to London to become King James I in 1603 and appeared to ignore Scotland altogether. He took the court with him, and since the King was head of state and head of the government, it deprived Scotland of much of the apparatus of the state and all of its foreign policy. His son, Charles wasn't much better and didn't visit Scotland for 30 years. He boasted of ruling Scotland with a pen when others could not rule it with the sword.

Both countries were nominally Protestant, but the Scots took the Reformation and Calvinism rather more seriously than the English. In Scotland, the old Catholic bishops were replaced by Presbyteries, conventions of elected parish representatives, who governed in God's name. This was the system devised by the leaders of the Scottish Reformation, John Knox and Andrew Melville, in the previous century for embedding Protestantism in the people by underpinning theocracy with an element of democracy.

When Charles I succeeded the throne in 1625, he decided that

Britain should be united spiritually and politically by harmonising religious observance north and south of the border. He also wanted to introduce episcopacy – installing bishops to act as instruments of royal power in church affairs. Charles not only restored much of the Catholic power structure in England, he also had a weakness for "papist" ceremonials like kneeling for holy communion. Worst of all, his wife, Henrietta Maria of France, was a Catholic and didn't try to hide it. Charles was also a firm believer in the Divine Right of Kings – the notion that kings were effectively gods and should be regarded as infallible no matter how licentious, egocentric, inept and tyrannical their behaviour.

In Scotland, the Reformation had taken power from the old Church and the King, and placed it largely in the hands of the Kirk – the equally infallible manifestation of God's true purpose for humanity. There wasn't going to be a meeting of minds here.

The trouble began with a book. A new *Booke of Common Prayer* was introduced by Charles I in 1637 without consultation with the Scottish Parliament or the General Assembly of the Church of Scotland. When the new Anglican liturgy was given its first Scottish outing in St Giles' Cathedral in Edinburgh in July 1637, complete with kneeling and communion, a market trader, Jennie Geddes ,was said to have hurled her stool at the minister crying: "Daur ye say Mass in my lug," or: "How dare you say mass in my ear." There is doubt about her existence; there is no doubt about the riots caused by Charles's neo-Catholicism.

The Scots Protestants set about drawing up the National Covenant, based on the Covenant of the Israelites in the Old Testament. This document signed, often in blood, by 300,000 mainly Lowland Scots (the Highlands weren't so enthusiastic) has been described by Allan Macinnes as "a Nationalist manifesto asserting the independence of a sovereign people under God."[16] But this wasn't an early version of the SNP manifesto, and nor was it an assertion of the democracy or national sovereignty as we understand it. It was primarily about religion. The Covenanters believed themselves to be predestined to establish God's commonwealth on Earth. This was an early version of what became known as "Scottish exceptionalism".

The Prayer Book and associated works were rejected and the bishops were expelled from the Scottish Church. Charles didn't take kindly to this and launched the Bishop's War of 1639 to encourage his puritanical countrymen to change their minds. Scottish Covenanters under the Earl of Argyll then assembled what some historians now regard as the precursor to Oliver Cromwell's New Model Army. Led by Alexander Leslie, the First Earl of Leven, a veteran of Dutch and Swedish wars, this force was well-trained and equipped and enlisted thousands of hardened Scottish mercenaries. It marched into battle singing psalms and prayed late into the night; its zealous discipline making it all the more lethal. The Scottish rebellion effectively dethroned Charles I and asserted the sovereignty of Parliament and the General Assembly of the Presbyteries against the divinely ordained monarch. They blazed a trail that the Westminster Parliament would follow a couple of years later.[17]

Scottish Calvinism was a revolutionary creed that defied absolutism, not in the name of the people, but in the people's religion: Presbyterianism. It was here, in Presbyterian Scotland in the 17th century, that the concept of constitutional monarchy arguably first emerged. Presbyterians accepted the right of the king to rule, but only with the "consent of the people", according to the Scottish Presbyterian theologian Samuel Rutherford in his book, *Lex Rex* or *The Law Is King*, in 1644. There was more than an echo here of Bruce's community of the realm, and also the Declaration of Arbroath, which also challenged the Divine Right of Kings– though no self-respecting Protestant was likely to quote from a letter to a Pope. It also placed the Kirk at the centre of Scottish civil society, a de facto government, especially during long periods when the state had been exported to London.

The English Civil War broke out in 1642, when the English Parliament united with the Scottish Covenanters and eventually defeated Charles at Newark in 1646. The Scots handed their king over to Oliver Cromwell's Puritans, who executed him in 1649 – an event that shook Europe in an age when monarchs were still believed by many to be in a direct line of descent from God. You might have thought this would have led Scotland and England joining in a republican union under a common Protestant faith. But it didn't. The Scottish Covenanters fell out with the English Parliament, essentially because they wanted to impose their Presbyterian religion on England. This wasn't acceptable to the English Puritan parliamentarians, led by Cromwell. After Charles was relieved of his head in 1649, the Scottish Covenanters, somewhat perversely, decided to support the restoration of Charles II, provided he signed the Solemn League and Covenant, as it had now become known, and promised to rule a Protestant Scotland free from English control. It was an act of stupefying naivety.

Infuriated at this apparent attempt to restore the Stuart dynasty and thus threaten the Puritan revolution, Oliver Cromwell invaded and occupied Scotland after the Battle of Dunbar in 1650. The Covenanters were comprehensively defeated at Worcester in September 1651, after which many of the losing Scots were sent as indentured slaves to the West Indies, where some of their descendants probably worked for Colonel Campbell. Scotland was "incorporated into the English Commonwealth" by an act of the English "Rump" parliament. The Scottish Parliament was abolished and Scotland fell under the military occupation of the English General George Monck, who continued to transport Scots to the plantations abroad. Cromwell had succeeded where Edward I had failed – incorporating Scotland into his "Godly Britannic Union". At home, Scots needed passes to move around their own country. However, in 1659, Monck himself switched sides and started supporting Charles II, after whose restoration in 1660, episcopacy was restored, complete with bishops, prayer books and kneeling. It was back to square one.

The cost of these incomprehensible holy wars was appalling. More than 100,000 Scots are believed to have died through battle, disease and pacification in the Wars of the Three Kingdoms – out of a population of little more than one million. The passions unleashed by reformed religion were proving to be as devastating and divisive as medieval Nationalism. It seemed as if Scotland and England simply couldn't find a way of coexisting on these islands, whether under a Protestant theocracy, under absolutist monarchy, or under Puritan dictatorship. A lot of blood had been shed, but for what?

The answer was another 20 years of repression, as the Restoration of the Stuart dynasty turned into another cycle of religious repression and rebellion. As soon as he gained the throne in May 1660, Charles II immediately renounced the Covenants, effectively outlawing the Covenanters. They took to the hills where they staged outdoor religious gatherings or "conventicles" after which many faced torture and execution. Charles's suppression of the Covenanters, who had restored him to power, was more brutal than anything seen in Scotland since the Middle Ages. The climax in the period called the Killing Time in the 1680s was marked by mass executions and torture of Covenanters and anyone who refused to accept the supremacy of the king.

Henry Buckle, the 19th-century historian, said that 1660-89 Scotland experienced "a tyranny so cruel and so exhausting that it would have broken the energy of almost any other nation". David Hume said that "nothing could equal the abject servility of the Scottish nation during the period but the arbitrary severity of the administration". Even allowing for Hanoverian hyperbole, this was a rough old time. And as if that wasn't enough, Scotland also experienced severe famines towards the end of the 17th century as a result of the "little Ice Age", which shortened the growing season and led to crop failures. This further depleted the energies of a country that had been wracked by conflict and hardship for longer than anyone could remember.

Seen in this context, the thousand or so who died in the Darien adventure were a drop in the ocean, to use an admittedly tasteless pun. Far more Scots died in the battles, or the epidemics of bubonic plague that followed the armies as they swept across the countryside, or in the Stuart repressions, or the famines. The loss of treasure in the cycle of rebellions, invasions and restorations was incalculable. Like the Massacre of Glencoe in 1692, the Darien adventure achieved iconic significance largely because of the political story it told about Scotland, and continues to tell. If it hadn't been for the Irish Jacobite journalist, Charles Leslie, who publicised King William's "cover-up" of the massacre of 78 MacDonalds in Glencoe, it would probably have just been another clan feud in the north. Only 38 were actually killed and far worse atrocities were perpetrated by the Highland clansmen billeted in the Covenanter communities in South Ayrshire during the Restoration. Similarly, Darien was useful both to the Jacobites, who used it to tell of the perfidy of the English, and to the Hanoverians who wanted to demonstrate Scotland's economic inadequacy the better to justify union with England.

The 1707 Union happened because Scotland was exhausted – not just financially, but spiritually and physically. Scots Calvinists wanted an end to spiritual uncertainty through a guarantee that their own Presbyterian religion would be safe from interference from the south or from episcopalian monarchs. The English for their part wanted Scots to guarantee the Hanoverian succession, end the threat to England from Stuart absolutism and, frankly, stop being so bloody difficult. The Union was primarily about security rather than bribery of the Scottish nobility – though that undoubtedly happened as well. It was very difficult to see any resolution to the cycle of violence unleashed by the Union of the Crowns, short of the two countries somehow becoming dedicated to a common economic purpose: a union, rather as the European Economic Community was seen as the solution to the inability of France and Germany to stop going to war with each other in the 20th century.

THE END OF AN AULD SANG

After the Glorious Revolution of 1688 drew a line under the Stuart dynasty, an articulate body of opinion in Lowland Scotland started to look, if not to formal Union with England, then at least to some kind of federal arrangement. Leading figures of the time, the Duke of Argyll and Dalrymple of Stair, had been in exile with William of Orange in Holland and they thought Scotland could be remade along Dutch lines as a small, enterprising trading country. Both were Presbyterians, but they were more interested in economics than in doctrinal purity and they had had enough of religious violence. This seemed a reasonable business plan, but it had one important flaw: England wasn't prepared to endorse it.

Scotland was effectively locked out of the growth areas in international trade because England's Navigation Act of 1660 outlawed Scottish ships from trade with the English colonies in the West Indies and America. There was no way Scotland could compete militarily with the world's pre-eminent naval power. Enterprising Scots merchants found ways of getting round their exclusion, sailing under flags of convenience and landing their sugar in ports that were similarly convenient. Smuggling was big business too, and some Scots became infamous as pirates, such as Alexander Selkirk, the model for *Robinson Crusoe*, and Captain Kidd, born in Dundee, and hanged for his crimes in Wapping in 1701. But ingenuity and piracy could not compensate for Scotland's exclusion from the New World.

It wasn't just exclusion from the colonial trade that bothered Scottish merchants. There were tariffs on the export to England of cattle and linen. The Alien Act of 1705 treated Scots in England as foreigners who couldn't secure inheritance rights and imposed embargoes on Scottish beef, linen, corn and coal. Scottish merchants were excluded from doing business with the fastest-growing market in the world, England, which didn't yet speak the language of free trade as it would be spoken by Adam Smith. The only way to get access to these markets was to seek a closer union with England.

Hanoverian England had its own reasons for looking again at political union with Scotland. Queen Anne, who succeeded William of Orange in 1702, had eighteen children, all of whom died leaving England with another succession crisis. Protestant England wanted to maintain the Hanoverian succession as a guarantee of the Glorious Revolution of 1688 which entrenched constitutional monarchy as well as the freedoms of the Bill of Rights. But the difficult Scots weren't prepared to accept any old monarch and the Scottish Parliament insisted on the right of Scotland to choose a king of its own. This raised the possibility of another Stuart restoration. Both countries feared another civil war, having experienced a century of it. But Scotland feared it more than England.

Queen Anne summoned commissioners from the Scottish Parliament to come to London in 1705 to discuss a political union. Though there wasn't a lot of discussion. It was an offer the Scots could not refuse. Nationalist historians, such as Paul Henderson Scott, believe that Scots were told that, if they didn't agree to the 1707 Union, they would be invaded by the Duke of Marlborough, who had just defeated the French at Blenheim, and that Scotland would fall under military occupation again, as it had under Cromwell. There were certainly troop movements in England which could have been interpreted as a prelude to invasion.

Scotland was in no condition to fight a war of national independence, having been punished by war and impoverished by peace. Much capital had been lost. The key lay with the Church, which had assumed a quasi-governmental role through the turbulence of the 17th century. The Kirk was prepared to accept Queen Anne's diktat, and political annexation, so long as it received a guarantee that Presbyterianism would remain in Scotland in perpetuity as the established Church. The Kirk wanted neither absolutist monarchy, nor English domination, a factor that is often overlooked in accounts of the period which tend to follow the money that changed hands.

And so followed the Treaty of Union of 1706, with its 25 articles, and the hated Acts: the Union with Scotland Act of 1706, passed by the English Parliament, and the Union with England Act, passed by the Scottish Parliament in 1707. This was an incorporating union, the objective of which was to create a new single kingdom named "Great Britain" – though neither side believed this was actually going to happen. "There's an end of an auld sang," said the Earl of Seafield, Chancellor of Scotland, as he signed the Treaty of Union on 1st May 1707.

WHATEVER HAPPENED TO SCOTLAND?

There has been a lot of constitutional debate in the past year about the significance of the Acts of Union, and whether Scotland was legally extinguished along with the Scottish Parliament. The constitutional expert Professor James Crawford, of Cambridge University, set feathers flying in February 2013 by suggesting that Scotland had ceased to exist after 1707. "Scotland certainly was extinguished as a matter of international law," he wrote in legal advice to the UK government on the constitutional implications of Scottish independence, "by merger into either an enlarged and renamed England or into an entirely new state."[18] Nationalists like Paul Henderson Scott were understandably outraged. Scotland never went away he insists – just look around you, man.

However, in a technical sense Crawford is correct. The Acts of Union were supposed to create "one united kingdom by the name of Great Britain", an entirely new state that would replace the pre-existing countries. However, this was a bit like the union of marriage, in which two are supposed to become one, until death they do part. It was an expression of hope rather than a statement of constitutional reality. England certainly didn't see the Act of Union as the extinction of the country of England. Scotland didn't think it was ceasing to exist just because its parliament was going south. It had seen its government move south before, in the Union of 1603 when James VI took it to London and didn't come back. The mistake is to take the treaty too literally – neither of the signatories was in the business of national liquidation, whatever the wording might have said. It was a marriage of convenience, and neither party wanted to look at the small print.

What arguably happened was that the Kirk became the principal vehicle through which Scotland's national identity was projected, a kind of shadow parliament.

The people of Scotland felt genuine anger at the loss of the Scottish Parliament – even though they didn't have a right to vote in it. Not a single petition in favour of Union was received by the Scottish Parliament. There were widespread riots and estimates at the time said nine out of ten Scots opposed the Union. This is remarkable given that the Parliament could in no sense be regarded as equivalent to a democratic legislature, or an expression of the people's will. It was the property of the nobility, the merchants and burgesses of the towns, and the representatives of the Kirk.

It was as much the manner of the Union as its political impact that turned the stomachs of Scots. So much money was sprayed around the Scottish nobility that it began to look more like a version of the Louisiana Purchase than a voluntary union of equals. Under Article 15, a sum of £398,085, known as the Equivalent, was given to Scotland to "offset future liability towards the English national debt", an obfuscation of which Chancellor Gordon Brown would've been proud. This compensated Darien investors by stealth. It wasn't paid by England because the debt became the liability of taxpayers in Scotland. Tens of thousands were also distributed in patronage and pensions to the nobles and burgesses. Even with hindsight this was a miserable start to a marriage. Daniel Defoe, novelist and English spy in Scotland, reported that he didn't believe the Union would last. Strangely, it did.

Scots merchants got what they wanted: access to the colonies and imperial markets. The Navigation Act was repealed allowing Scots to trade in sugar, tea and cotton, though it took around 30 years for this business to really take off. In the meantime there were riots in Scotland, and repeated demands for repeal of the Union after Scots discovered they were expected to meet the cost of buying off the Parcel o' Rogues through higher taxes. Some taxes, like the Malt Tax, which increased the price of beer and whisky, were supposed to have been specifically ruled out by the Acts of Union. Few things made a Scotsman in the 18th century angrier than an unreasonable hike in the price of drink, and in 1725 riots were so violent in Glasgow that General Wade had to be sent in with 400 troopers to put down what looked like a rebellion against the Union itself.

In the Act of Union, Scotland gave up its political independence in exchange for access to the common market of its day. But England didn't take over bankrupt Scotland in a spirit of neighbourly altruism. London needed reserves of troops for its growing Empire – Defoe called Scotland "an inexhaustible treasury of men" – and it needed taxes to help pay for its new national debt (another of William Paterson's clever ideas) which financed military expansion, especially at sea. Scots were expected to pay an array of taxes on windows, soap, alcohol and just about anything that moved. Nevertheless, Scotland eventually got a piece of the action, or the upper classes did. Glasgow's location on the Atlantic seaboard allowed it to become an entrepôt for tobacco, sugar, cotton and other "slave goods" in the second half of the 18th century. Glasgow's rise was founded on the wealth of the Tobacco Lords, who artfully combined the exploitation of slave labour with the promotion of a highly addictive drug – nicotine. This was when Scotland's moral principles collided with commercial reality.

SCOTLAND AND SLAVERY

Which brings us back to Colonel Campbell's priapic activities in Jamaica. It was the fourth of the 25 Articles of Union passed in 1707 that allowed Scotland access to the lucrative slave trade. Scottish merchants tended not to deal directly in negroes, but they benefited from the "triangular trade", which transported slaves from West Africa, to pick tobacco, cotton and sugar in the plantations of the West Indies, which was then shipped back to the warehouses of Port Glasgow and Greenock for sale in Britain and Europe. The names of the Tobacco Lords are written on the very streets of the city: Buchanan Street, Ingram Street, Glassford Street. Also immortalised are the plantation colonies: Jamaica Street; Tobago Street; Kingston Bridge.

Scotland's involvement in the slave trade tended to be ignored by historians until comparatively recently. The publication in 2006 of Iain Whyte's *Scotland and the Abolition of Black Slavery* was a wake-up call. There was an outpouring of national guilt in 2007, when the 200th anniversary of the abolition of the slave trade clashed with the 300th anniversary of the Act of Union. In the febrile atmosphere of that Holyrood election year, slavery became a live issue. Unionists found it hard to conceal their glee at this secret history, which they claimed undermined the SNP's tendency to assume that Scots, since Wallace, have somehow been morally superior to the English. People were shocked to learn that Scotland's national poet, Robert Burns, the author of *A Man's A Man for A' That* had accepted a plantation post – though he didn't take it up and later became an articulate opponent of the slave trade. There were calls for an apology to the descendants of those who had worked for Scottish slave plantations.[19]

Scots participation in the slave business also jarred somewhat with Scotland's reputation as hub of the European Enlightenment. There has been a lively debate about whether or not David Hume, Scotland's greatest philosopher, was a racist[20], largely based on a footnote he wrote to an essay "Of National Characters" in 1748. "I am apt to suspect the Negroes to be naturally inferior to the whites," he declared. "No ingenious manufacture among them, not arts, no sciences." Hume based this assessment, as with all of his speculations, on empirical evidence. He had never come across negroes who appeared more civilised or more intelligent than white people so he assumed there weren't any. The only black people he had any direct experience of were the blackamoors who served at table in fashionable Scottish dinner parties. Slavery was legal in Scotland until the 1770s. This perhaps shows the limitations of Hume's empiricism, but should not be taken necessarily as evidence he actively supported slavery or was inherently racist. Like his Enlightenment colleague, the Scottish economist Adam Smith, he viewed slavery as a "barbarous practice". Though even Smith was equivocal. He thought slavery was bad economics, as well as being morally repugnant, but even he had to concede that running a West Indian plantation was simply the fastest possible way for a young man to get rich.[21] A bit like being a derivatives trader in the City of London in the early years of this century, it was good money for bad business.

At the time of the Union in 1707, apologists for slavery still argued that it was sanctioned by the Bible – which it is, at least on some interpretations of the Old Testament. The Kirk accepted slavery as part of the natural order of things until the 1770s, when the growing evangelical movement helped persuade the Kirk it was wrong to enslave souls who could instead be brought to God. Ministers like James Ramsay became highly vocal critics of the trade, both in Scotland and England, and large abolitionist meetings were held in Scotland in the early 19th century. Scottish missionaries such as John Campbell (no relation) opposed the slave trade because it undermined their attempts to convert Africa to Christianity.

The Kirk never quite got round to petitioning Parliament to abolish the slave trade, possibly because so many of its members were actively involved in it. The Lord Advocate, Henry Dundas, who effectively ruled Scotland at the end of the 18th century, accepted the case for abolition, but did everything in his power to delay it. There was simply a very great deal of money to be made out of the sweat of the black man, mostly by the English upper classes, and Scots just carved themselves a lucrative slice of a business from which they had previously been excluded. Thereafter, fortunes made in tobacco and sugar were partly invested in the development of manufacturing in and around Glasgow, providing clothing and wares for export to the New World.

The Carron Iron Works were established near Falkirk in 1759, a spark of the Industrial Revolution, producing parts for James Watt's steam engine and becoming one of Europe's biggest iron producers. Scotland had prodigious quantities of coal and ironstone, and deep water in the Firth of Clyde. The abundance of cheap Scottish labour, displaced from agriculture, made Scotland an attractive place to do business. Iron allowed the manufacturing of tools and equipment for export – including, it is said, the shackles in which the slaves were transported. Scotland's Industrial Revolution was based largely on the textile industry, much of which was devoted to the production of coarse cloth for the slaves in the colonies.

However, when it comes to questions of collective guilt for slavery, it should be noted that Iain Whyte's book, while exposing Scottish involvement in the evil trade, is entitled *Scotland and the Abolition of BLACK Slavery*. There was no shortage of what could, and was, called white slavery happening closer to home, in the satanic mills of the Scottish Industrial Revolution. In the early 19th century, the condition of the Scottish industrial worker was little better than that of the slave. The only difference was that in Scotland the slaves were hired by the hour. The life expectancy of a factory worker in the 1820s was probably less than that of a Virginian plantation slave, as William Cobbett pointed out to the abolitionist William Wilberforce. Arguably, the lives of Scottish child labourers were held even more cheaply than the offspring of slaves, because on the American plantations, after 1807 at least, the children of slaves had a financial value. This was because of the restriction on the import of "fresh-water" slaves from Africa by the abolition of transportation from Africa. Children in Scotland were almost literally ten a penny, from orphanages or destitute families who'd been cleared off agricultural land in the Highlands and Lowlands. The exploitation of children continued well into the Victorian era. Until the Mines Act of 1842, boys and girls of eight worked underground hauling tubs of coal for 14 hours a day. Very young children were working in clothing factories for 12 hours a day until the Factory Act of 1863. This is not in any way to condone black slavery or exonerate Scots for their involvement in it.

The Tobacco Lords may have built some large baronial piles, but it would be wrong to suggest ordinary Scots of the period benefited from the slave trade. During the early years of the Industrial Revolution, the majority of the population's lives were brutal and short, few of them seeing their mid-40s. Much of the wealth that arrived from the plantations was recycled in Highland estates and in the purchase of flocks of Cheviot sheep. These hardy animals could cope with the Scottish climate and produced vast quantities of high-quality wool and meat, which was more profitable than the produce yielded by the Highland peasantry. Moreover, the Cheviot didn't become a burden to the laird when crops failed. Throughout the 19th century, many Scottish peasants were forced or priced out of their own ancestral lands, often by the descendants of their own clan chiefs. And if they didn't gravitate to the cities, the Highlanders were often made to endure immense hardship, migrating to the New World on vessels that were little better than slave hulks. Though they had the consolation they were nominally free men and women if they arrived there alive.

The Lowlands of Scotland were also cleared of farming communities. At the close of the 18th century, 90% of Scots still lived on the land. By 1911 only 11% did so. Agricultural workers who had been used to seasonal working of perhaps 220 days a year were thrown into factories working 14-hour days all year long. Scotland suddenly became the second most urbanised country in Europe and the populations of cities like Dundee and Glasgow tripled and quadrupled resulting in intolerable living conditions. In the 1860s, in Glasgow, two-thirds of all families lived in one-or-two room houses. As late as 1911, Scottish cities were five times as over-crowded as English cities, with the majority of families living in one or two-room slums. One child in five died before the age of one. Tens of thousands were wiped out in cholera and typhus epidemics that swept the urban areas before the Glasgow middle classes – in fear of their own lives – finally invested in sewage works and fresh water from Loch Katrine in the Trossachs in the 1855 Glasgow Waterworks Act.

The Industrial Revolution was arguably a disaster for most Scots, at least in the first half of the 19th century.[22] The relatively nutritious rural diet of oatmeal, salted herring and potatoes gave way to white bread, tea and sugar for the urban masses. Rickets, a city disease, restricted the physical mobility of generations of Scots, and tuberculosis, which incubated in the slums, was translated back to the county areas and became endemic in the villages. By 1900, infant mortality in Scotland was higher than at the dawn of the century, despite all the medical advances, water works and the rise in industrial wages. Some 40% of Glaswegians lived on less than £1 a week – the bare minimum for survival at the end of the 19th century. And for Glaswegians even the fresh water supply brought an insidious new contamination: lead from pipes dissolved into the supposed saviour that was Loch Katrine water.

So, while it is important not to bowdlerise Scotland's history by ignoring the slave trade, it would be wrong to claim that Scotland's Industrial Revolution was simply built on black African slavery, as is sometimes suggested.[23] The sweat and blood that made Scotland a manufacturing power were shed by Scottish wage slaves in the mills of west central Scotland not just by the negroes of the plantations. Why did they put up with it? Scottish workers in the 19th century earned less than their English counterparts and their living conditions were invariably worse. Women and children made up a third of the manufacturing workforce until the middle of the 19th century. Employers took no responsibility for their workers when they were injured, as they frequently were, or when they became too old to work. And they had no automatic right to poor relief as workers had in England – the Scottish Kirk opposed welfare. Perhaps if they had any energy left they might have rebelled against their exploitation, but there was very little of the revolutionary anger that swept Europe in the years up to 1848. It may have been the "Springtime of Nations" in the rest of Europe, but it was still winter in Scotland.

There was, however, great fear of revolution among the Scottish middle classes at the supposed threat from the urban poor but there were no popular revolts of any significance. The so-called "Radical War" of 1820, led by weavers Andrew Hardie and John Baird, was little more than a series of skirmishes, and seems to have been encouraged by agent provocateurs. The uprising has been described, by the historian TC Smout as a "pathetic rising".[24] Others dispute its insignificance, but it bore no comparison to what was happening in Europe or even in England. There were some Chartist meetings in Scotland in the 1840s, but on the whole, the Scottish workers were too impoverished for politics, Nationalist or Socialist, and many still lived in fear of religion, even if many of the urban masses had stopped being regular church-goers. The Scots working classes spent much time on the streets because their homes were so crowded, but instead of political organisation they sought consolation in alcohol, fought among themselves and vented their frustrations on Irish immigrants.

This was not a revolutionary country. Political Nationalism, of the kind that was on the march in Italy, Hungary, Poland and Denmark, was non-existent in Scotland in 1848. Karl Marx published the Communist Manifesto in London in that year, but it had very little resonance among Scottish workers. The only social class that had any political visibility in 19th century Scotland were the lairds, the urban middle classes and the skilled workers in the industrial centres, and they saw their future, economic and social, as inextricably bound up with the Union. Nor did the Kirk have any interest in political reform. Scotland was locked down, tight, for most of the Victorian era.

CHAPTER FIVE
IT'S SCOTLAND'S EMPIRE

$\times$

BLANTYRE COTTON MILL, eight miles south of Glasgow was founded by a group of entrepreneurs at the end of the 18th century to process cotton largely from the slave plantations of America. Considered one of the more enlightened factories in Scotland in the early 1800s, it still employed large numbers of children in circumstances unimaginable today. They were generally malnourished and were expected to perform tasks that were beyond their strength in an extremely dangerous occupation where serious injuries were a daily occurrence, not least because the children often fell asleep on the job. One of them was a young boy called David Livingstone.

Livingstone went on to become a missionary and explorer and one of the greatest celebrities of the Victorian era before disappearing into the heart of Africa looking for the source of the Nile – and being rediscovered by the American journalist, Henry Morton Stanley. The original "lad o' pairts", Livingstone was a religious self-improver, who combined Scottish exceptionalism with a love of progress, science and Presbyterian egalitarianism. He has also been branded a racial supremacist, a domineering husband, an incompetent geographer and self-publicist who chose adventure over missionary work. As a leader, he was a nightmare. But to get into the mind of the Victorian Scot, and to understand the ideological universe inhabited by many Scots almost until the Second World War, David Livingstone is a good place to start.

The 200th anniversary of his birth passed on 13th March 2013 without much public interest, yet when he died of dysentery in 1874, kneeling in prayer in a hut in what is now Zambia, he was probably the most famous Scotsman in the world. A national hero in Scotland and England, and the subject of endless adulatory books and articles, he was the first white man to cross the African continent on foot and the first white man to discover the Victoria Falls (Mosi-oa-Tunya, "the smoke that thunders" as it was known locally). He was also a fierce, lifelong enemy of slavery.

David was born in Blantyre in March 1813, but the Livingstone family had moved from Ulva, "the isle of wolves", a tiny island off Mull, where his grandfather had been a tenant farmer until the "improvements" led to him being removed from his ancestral lands. From the age of ten, David worked 14-hour days in the Blantyre mill, from 6am till 8pm, to support his family. However, the mill owner, Henry Monteith, did offer two hours of rudimentary school education after 8pm, for those children with any energy left. Livingstone had extraordinary energy and taught himself Latin in his spare time. He was to discover that the renowned Scottish education system, established by John Knox in the Reformation, did allow the occasional mill slave to escape poverty, provided they had the determination. When he was 16, he began training to be a physician in Anderson's College in Glasgow, a technical institute that became the University of Strathclyde. He emerged a product of what Scots educationalists today call "the democratic intellect" – Scotland's meritocratic system of low-cost higher education.

Profoundly religious, as many Scots were, Livingstone was motivated by evangelical Protestantism rather than politics, which hardly seem to have figured in his life. Religion was a popular passion in Scotland, as it had been since the Reformation. Figures like John Knox were idolised, though not of course in a devotional sense, and the blue-bonneted Covenanters were popular historical figures. Religion was recreation as well as moral instruction. Livingstone and his father – an impoverished tea salesman – often spent evenings attending religious meetings to hear fashionable evangelical preachers. Presbyterianism, though morally austere and intensely sectarian, was not an entirely dogmatic religion and was becoming open to ideas of progress and science, which fascinated Livingstone. This impoverished mill urchin spent much of his free time arguing with his father about the meaning of predestination, while amusing himself by making technical drawings of steam engines.

Livingstone wasn't a Scottish Nationalist, but he was a patriot, proud of Wallace and Bruce and given to quoting Robert Burns, often to bemused natives in Africa. He believed passionately in the virtues of Scottish culture, but like most Scottish meritocrats, he left for London as soon as he qualified as a physician. After training in the London Missionary School, aged 26, he went abroad –

again like so many of his Scottish contemporaries. When he arrived as a medical missionary in southern Africa in 1840, it was still "the White Man's Grave" where missionaries suffered casualty rates almost as high as foreign postings in the British Army – the real enemy was disease. But Livingstone believed he could stave off the worst effects of malaria with quinine, making a bout of the fever, as he called it "no worse than the common cold". This proved just a little over-optimistic. Many of the friends and missionaries he lured to his Malawi mission posts died almost as soon as they arrived, lacking his natural immunity. One of the casualties was his wife, Mary.

After his "discovery" of the Victoria Falls, named after the British Queen, Livingstone was lionised by London society and revered in Scotland. His books were bestsellers and his speaking tours made him a lot of money, most of which went to finance his expeditions and agricultural experiments in Africa. As revisionist biographers such as Tim Jeal[25] have noted, David Livingstone was a pretty useless missionary, having only converted one tribal leader to the faith. He doesn't appear to have been a very good geographer, having – as Jeal points out – mistaken the source of the River Congo for the source of the Nile. Livingstone was probably what we would call a manic depressive today, though during his mania he was capable of extraordinary feats of endurance, such as his trek across the continent. Members of his later Zambezi expeditions, like the artist Thomas Baines whom Livingstone accused of theft, were severely critical of his leadership skills. In 2006, the Scottish writer, Julie Davidson, wrote a biography of his wife, in which Livingstone is cast as a domineering, sexist self-publicist with little regard for the safety of those around him. This seems a little unfair. Born in Africa and the daughter of a Scottish missionary, Mary Livingstone was a formidable woman who crossed the Kalahari Desert twice while pregnant and wasn't anyone's idea of a victim. We have to be careful judging people who were born two centuries ago by the standards of modern gender politics.

I'm sure Livingstone was an extremely difficult and driven individual and he talked of being part of "a superior race". But he was a product of his times. He didn't regard "savages" as innately inferior, as did many in Victorian Britain, but simply lacking in Christian education. The tribal societies he came across in Central Africa were involved in bitter blood feuds – often with guns supplied by the West – and practised slavery themselves, aided and abetted by Old World entrepreneurs in "Black Ivory". His hatred of slavery was utterly sincere and he used his celebrity status largely to campaign against it. Accounts in his journals, many of which are now available online, of navigating rivers filled with corpses of those massacred by the Arab and Portuguese slave traders, are horrifying. We may scoff at his ethnocentrism – after all, his superior "English races" had been responsible for enslaving millions of Africans in the plantations of the West Indies and America. Even as Livingstone was leaving the spread of the gospel in Africa, Britain was conducting a war in China over our right to peddle addictive drugs in the Opium Wars. Nevertheless, to understand how Scots viewed the Empire, you have to see it through Livingstone's eyes. It was above all a moral project as well as an economic one. Commerce was seen as an engine of progress, not as a means of exploitation, and technology was its fuel.

Today, we look on colonialism as the ruthless oppression of subject races by the British state, but to Livingstone it was the only way to prevent ethnic cleansing, and he lobbied a reluctant Lord Palmerston to make the country now called Malawi into a protectorate, Nyasaland. He was an early exponent of what Tony Blair would have called liberal interventionism. Livingstone thought that colonialism was the only way slavery could be extinguished, but he wanted it to be Scottish colonialism because he believed in the innate moral superiority of Presbyterian Scotland, the Scotland of Burns and the Covenanters. And there has never been a better statement of Scottish exceptionalism than the speech he gave to members of his expeditions:

We come among them as members of a superior race, and servants of a Government that desires to elevate the more degraded portions of the human family. We are adherents of a benign, holy religion, and may, by consistent conduct, and wise, patient efforts, become the harbingers of peace to a hitherto distracted and trodden-down race.

People who think of Livingstone only as an explorer or a missionary miss the point of what he was doing in Central Africa. He discovered Lake Nyasa (now Lake Malawi) and mapped the Zambezi while exploring areas which could be developed for cash crops. Most of his journals are not about the tally of souls saved, but the quality of the soil, rainfall, drainage. A bit like William Cobbett's Rural Rides, only in some of the most inhospitable areas of the planet. His greatest discovery was not the Victoria Falls but the fact that Central Africa was not a desert and had a relatively benign climate, which meant it could rival the New World as a source of commercial agricultural produce. And he saw this as the solution to both the Highland Clearances and the slave trade:

At present we in England are the mainstay of slavery in America and elsewhere by buying slave-grown produce. Here there are hundreds of miles of land lying waste, and so rich that the grass towers far over one's head in walking. You cannot see where the narrow paths end, the grass is so tall and overhangs them so. If our countrymen were here they would soon render slave-buying unprofitable.

Livingstone advocated emigration from over-populated Scotland to Nyasaland, where industrious Scottish farmers would render slavery uneconomic by producing cotton, sugar and other marketable produce in Africa, rather than in Jamaica or Virginia. The idea was that there would be no point in exporting black slaves to America because they would produce the plantation goods there, in Africa, under the moral guidance of Protestant Scots. It was perhaps naive; it was probably racist, and may have been impractical because of the vulnerability of Scots to fever. But it has to be said that it was, like Darien, a brilliant idea. The only reason it failed was because he couldn't persuade the British government that the interior of Africa wasn't like the Sahara, which was what everyone in London believed at the time.

Livingstone believed that slavery could be abolished by Commerce, Christianity and Civilisation. This was humanitarian capitalism, wedded to a muscular form of Christianity that was all about getting stuck in and changing things here on Earth, rather than waiting for compensation in the afterlife. His self-belief, which was unshakeable, arose from his Presbyterian conviction that his actions were guided by the hand of his maker. This gave evangelical Christians a formidable drive and a tendency to project their faith by example rather than indoctrination. His missions weren't about inducing the fear of God into the native savages; in fact he envisioned a fairly benign and humanist version of Calvinism, but in the complex process of economic development:

Colonization from a country such as ours ought to be one of hope, and not of despair. It ought not to be looked upon as the last and worst shift that a family can come to, but the performance of an imperative duty to our blood, our country, our religion, and to humankind.

Livingstone's exploits in what was called "darkest Africa" were related by the popular press to an enthusiastic Scottish readership. He nearly lost an arm in a fight with a lion and had some narrow escapes from Portuguese slave traders. Livingstone was the original Scottish popular hero. A follower of Adam Smith who recited Burns in the jungle and could cope with immense physical hardship, partly because of his experience in the mills. He was probably intensely vain as well, certainly driven, and was overprotective of his achievements, against his many detractors. Traits, it has to be said, that are not unknown among Scots even today. He ended his life lost in the heart of Africa, so crippled by disease that he had to rely on the Arab slavers to stay alive. A fate which, for him, must have been almost worse than death itself.

Unfortunately, Livingstone was followed by genuine hard-nosed British imperialists, during the "scramble for Africa", who were rather less high-minded and primarily concerned with the extraction of raw materials. The image left by the British Empire in Central Africa is of true white supremacists like Cecil Rhodes, whose private armies, flying a British flag, secured military domination for personal financial gain. Livingstone's Nyasaland became an adjunct to racist Rhodesia. The colonisation of Africa by the West led to exploitation and a new form of economic slavery in many parts of the continent.

However, it would be wrong to blame Livingstone for this, and he is not regarded in Africa today as just another British colonial adventurer. In fact, the continent has been rather kinder to his memory than hostile biographers in Britain. Most colonial towns changed their names after de-colonisation, but not Malawi, where you can still visit the town of Blantyre he founded, named after the place of his birth. Kenneth Kaunda famously described David Livingstone as Africa's "first freedom fighter". It might seem odd to suggest the first opponent of colonial rule was a white man. What Kaunda was referring to was the resistance offered to rapacious colonialists by missionaries such as David Livingstone and to the fact that, historically, it was in the Africanised churches that agitation for self government began.

MR MCCONNELL, I PRESUME

In 2004, the Scottish First Minister, Jack McConnell, sought to reconnect with this legacy of benign Scottish imperialism when he launched the Malawi Partnership with Scotland as a means of improving Scotland's image abroad and helping the Central African country deal with its chronic health problems. He was criticised by some in the UK Labour Party for this attempt at a Scottish "foreign policy". It was also thought to be faintly politically incorrect to honour Livingstone because of his identification with racial supremacism and even sexism. But Malawi, which has suffered terribly from AIDS, didn't seem too worried and eagerly adopted McConnell's initiative. The Scottish National Party has been eager to follow this up, partly because it wants to promote the idea that Scotland was in some way more ethical in its participation in colonialism – a proposition that is almost impossible to defend. In March 2013, Alex Salmond welcomed the first woman President of Malawi, Joyce Banda, to Scotland on Livingstone's 200th anniversary and promised a further £5 million from Scotland's International Development Fund. Not exactly a king's ransom, but still welcome in one of the poorest countries in the world. Ms Banda reciprocated by announcing she was going to auction her private jet and 60 limousines, which rather put the First Minister's contribution in the shade.

Scots like David Livingstone believed that, as products of the most literate nation on the planet, they had been chosen to educate the world. Sceptics tend to refer to this as the "myth of Scottish education". Scotland certainly had a head start in public literacy, since there had been, mostly, free parish education in Scotland since the Reformation. This was organised by the Kirk Session so that the ordinary people could read the Bible and understand the word of God; though questioning it was not part of the deal, and science was rather frowned upon until the 18th century. Education was a cherished part of Scottish self-image in the 18th and 19th centuries, even though the use of child labour in manufacturing led to a decline in educational standards in the first half of the 19th century. It was hard to study arithmetic when you were working 14-hour days in the mines or mills. But the idea of "the lad o' pairts" is embedded in the Scots folk memory, which is one important reason why the abolition of university tuition fees was such a touchstone issue for Scots in the 2011 Scottish election. Scotland's budget universities in the 19th century turned out legions of generalist graduates who sought posts in the colonial administration, the Church, the army and the trading houses of East India. It was said that, whereas Oxford and Cambridge taught a young man how to spend £1,000 a year, the Scottish universities taught him how to earn £1,000 a year. That rather summed up the practical approach Scots had to the business of learning.

Scots were prepared to go where the Empire took them, largely because of the limited opportunities for advancement in Scotland, especially for the sons of Scottish landowners and minor nobility. As child mortality fell sharply at the end of the 18th century, there was a lot more minor nobility around. Between 1751 and 1800, 85% of medical graduates in Britain were trained in the Scottish universities.[26] This academic overproduction was impressive, but the doctors, lawyers and clergymen couldn't expect to be employed in small backward Scotland, and it wasn't always very easy to break into the professions in London. Many looked to the colonies to get on, just as Scots had always looked abroad for work, the difference being that there was now fabulous wealth to be made in certain of Britain's territories overseas, especially after the opening up of India. That's if they survived, since most of the foreign destinations in the West Indies or India were death traps: a Scots emigrant working for the East India Company in the 18th century had a 50% chance of not coming back to tell the tale.[27] Scots were useful to the expanding Empire because they were prepared to go where many in the English middle class feared to tread.

Two intrepid Scots, James Matheson, an Edinburgh University graduate, and William Jardine, a Scottish doctor, set up a nice little trading operation in Canton in the 1830s, called Jardine Matheson and Company. This did a healthy business in tea, cotton and opium, which when mixed with tobacco delivered a formidable hit and was sold in great quantities to the Chinese. Once again, Scottish merchants were making a good living out of promoting addictive drugs. Tobacco barons had become the opium lords. When the Chinese Emperor tried to ban the stuff, on the not unreasonable grounds that too many of his people were addicted, the British

Government sent gunboats from India to make him see reason.

If nothing else, the Opium Wars revealed the breathtaking hypocrisy of many of the Scottish mercantile classes, who used a debased free-market morality to justify human enslavement – on plantations or in opium dens – so long as they were allowed to make a great deal of money out of it. This wasn't what Adam Smith meant by the wealth of nations. When Sir James Matheson came home in 1844, he bought the Isle of Lewis where he built an incongruous mock-Tudor castle, Castle Lews, and turned himself into a caricature of a Scottish laird. Jardine Matheson, the inspiration for the novel *Tai-Pan* by James Clavell, went from strength to strength, and the company is one of the largest conglomerates in the world. Only now it is based in Bermuda. And it has given up the drug trade.

The urban middle-classes, who dominated Scottish society in the 19th century, were falling in love with Great Britain and the Empire, not least because of its money-making potential. This was the basis of the popular "canny Scot" image, one who combines toe-curling piety with a grasping attitude to money. Scots saw working hard in their vocation to be an expression of grace, even if it involved the ruthless exploitation of economic opportunity. Max Weber called it the "Protestant Ethic", a legacy of Calvinism. We might call it having it both ways. Whatever, Scots were certainly imbued with the spirit of capitalism and, though they voted Liberal, rather than Tory, the Scots middle-classes bought heavily into the imperial project. And they followed the money wherever it took them. Scotland's biggest export has always been its people. Since the Middle Ages, Scots have been wanderers – merchants and mercenaries. But in the era of the British Empire the Scottish middle-classes flooded the colonial marketplace as officers, administrators, clerics, plantation managers. One-third of colonial governors between 1859 and 1939 were Scots.[28]

This embedded the Scots middle-classes so firmly in the expanding Empire that the thought of independence seemed outrageous and even faintly anti-Scottish, almost unpatriotic. Instead, they flattered themselves that they were the moral spearhead of the modern imperial project. They were all David Livingstones, bringing civilisation to the world. The Empire fitted rather well with the spiritual doctrines of Calvinism, especially predestination – the idea that humanity was divided into God's elect and the rest. No prizes for guessing who the elect were in this enterprise: it was the Scots, with their "perfect" Presbyterian religion which could be projected across the world using the vehicle of the British Empire. Missionaries like Mary Slessor, the "White Queen of Okoyong", followed in Livingstone's footsteps, her exploits recorded in magazines such the *People's Journal* and *The Scots Magazine*.

The Empire was itself a kind of religion for many of the more humble Scots who didn't get fancy jobs, but were prepared to sacrifice their lives for Great Britain without question by dying in hot places for "King and Country". Many of even the most impoverished Scots, especially those with military connections, felt a strong sentimental attachment to the Union and to the civilising project of Great Britain's Empire. We treat such attitudes today with incomprehension and derision – what did the British Raj mean to a struggling family in a "single end" in a Glasgow tenement? While Scottish soldiers were doing their stuff in the Crimean War, back in Dundee, a city of nearly 100,000 people, there were only five WCs, and three of them were in hotels. In Edinburgh, things were no better where the teeming closes of the High Street were incubators of disease. According to one contemporary account, "sanitary arrangements [are] of the most defective description ... as a consequence, the atmosphere is foully tainted, and rendered almost unendurable by its loathsomeness at those periods when offal and nuisance require to be deposited on the streets".[29] While the Scottish soldiers were fighting rebels in Calcutta on behalf of the East India Company, the real Black Holes were back home in Scotland.

This emotional attachment to the British Empire was itself a political constraint on Scottish radicalism. Socialist leaders later in the century failed to understand the tenacity with which working people clung to the bitter consolations of Protestant religion and the racial idealism of the British Empire. The Scottish founder of the British Labour Party, James Keir Hardie, despaired when the workers he had been lecturing on Socialist Internationalism marched off to fight the British Empire's wars in 1914, ending up in tens of thousands of anonymous graves in France. Fighting for King and Country really meant something to these people and to their bereaved relatives. But the truth is that the Scots had been dying in other people's wars for a very long time.

"SCOTLAND FOREVER!"

Like many impoverished countries, Scotland had for centuries been sending many of its young people abroad as mercenaries. As far back as the 13th century, the axe-wielding gallowglass, who fought in Ireland and across northern Europe, were valued for their aggression and their loyalty to their paymasters. The Auld Alliance led to many Scots soldiers of fortune making their way to France, often to fight the English during the Hundred Years' War. In the 15th century it was said that France had "too many of three things: rats, mice and Scots". Scottish mercenaries fought for the Poles against Sweden and vice versa at the close of the 16th century. In fact, there seem to have been very few wars of significance in which Scots didn't fight. By the early 17th century, during the Thirty Years War, up to one-fifth of adult males were involved in fighting abroad.[30] One reason that Alexander Leslie's Covenanter Army was so effective was that it included thousands of seasoned Scottish mercenaries attracted back to Scotland to fight the good fight.

And, of course, Scots had been fighting on their home turf, mostly against the English, but often among themselves, since the Wars of Independence. The trick of the Empire was to turn this militant tradition to the service of Great Britain after the 1707 Union when the standing armies of Scotland and England were merged. How could Highlanders, who had been pursued by the Butcher Cumberland and whose very tartan had been outlawed by the 1746 Dress Act, turn around and don the English redcoat? Well, since the Scots were used to fighting for whoever was around to pay them, this integration into the British Army was not as improbable as it might sound. Scots were professional fighters – it was what they did.

Pitt the Elder boasted that he had harnessed the aggression of the Highland clans after the 1745 Rebellion by enlisting them into the wars against France. "I sought for merit wherever it was to be found," he told Parliament. "And I found it in the mountains of the north." British generals favoured Highlanders for more practical reasons. "They are hardy, intrepid, accustomed to a rough country, and no great mischief if they fall," as General James Wolfe described Highland troops, before he was killed leading them in the capture of Quebec City in 1759. And he should have known, since he fought against the clans at Culloden. Bringing together Highland rebels and Lowland Hanoverians in the same British Army was an ex-traordinary achievement so soon after the Jacobite wars. It was here that "North Britain" was born.

The military contribution of the Scottish regiments, such as the Black Watch, was the most important factor in the propa-gation of a distinctive Scottish input into British imperial activity. During the Seven Years War, one in four male Scots was in military service. The historian Linda Colley, in *Britons: Forging the Nation 1707-1837*, claims that it was through fighting against the Catholic French – the "other" – that Protestant Scots discovered their British-ness. However, it is a historical fact that Catholic Scots did their share of the fighting, too. Many former Jacobite clansmen fought on the British side in the American Wars of Independence in the 18th century, and quite a few hung on there, making their way across the border to Canada, contributing to the long tradition of Scots emigration to that part of the New World. Others went south to the plantations of Virginia, where they united with earlier Jacobite refu-gees from Culloden. Their descendants and Ulster Scots became in-volved in the secessionist politics of the southern states of America in the years up to the American Civil War. It's not for nothing that the Confederate flag is based on the St Andrew's Cross.

Paradoxically, the growing Scottish identification with Great Britain coincided with a liberation – or reinvention – of the symbols of Scottish national identity, in particular the kilt and sporran. The British Army saw the value of the mystique of the Highland clans-man, and in the 19th century, the tartan and bagpipes were adopted by Lowland military forces, who had hitherto dressed in the same redcoats as the English regiments. The kilt worn by the new Scot-tish regiments bore very little relationship to the belted plaid worn in the Highlands before the Union. Indeed, some say that the small kilt, or philabeg, was invented by an Englishman, Thomas Rawlin-son, in the 1720s. But it became the most distinctive military dress code in the world – allegedly causing the Germans in the trenches of the First World War to run in fear from the "Ladies from Hell". The kilt was also a rather great way of provoking fights in bars, because non-Scots couldn't resist testing the manliness of the wearer of the tartan skirt.

Scots were flattered by this new image of Highland heroism, even though it was fashioned for them, like their national dress, by English military propagandists. For the wearing of tartan, like the new patriotism, was not an assertion of national autonomy, still less a protest at Scotland's unequal relationship to England, but a celebration of Scotland's role at the sharp end of British imperialism. However, the military reputation of the Scottish soldier was hard won. The roll-call of British battle honours shows how the Scots regiments were generally used in the front line, as assault troops, stormtroopers even. Scottish Nationalists have tended to blame British generals for the high casualty rates among Scottish soldiers in wars up to and including the First World War. However, there is ample evidence that the Scots soldiers genuinely favoured being in the front line.[31] After Waterloo, in the Crimean War and the Indian Mutiny, Scottish soldiers went out of their way to show they were even better at fighting against Indians, Russians and later against the tribes in Southern Africa and the white tribes of the Boers. The Scots were physically smaller and weaker than soldiers from England largely because of their poor nutritional intake and their crowded living conditions, but they made up for it by their aggression on the field of battle. Though their dress bore little relationship to the plaid of the Jacobite Highlanders, there was nothing synthetic about their aggression. However, there was always a suspicion that the Scottish soldiers enhanced their reputation because they were able to write home about it – twice as many Scots as English could read and write in the middle of the 19th century. Scotland was becoming the biggest newspaper-reading country in the world, and the press was filled, just like today, with accounts of wars – and the exploits of Scottish soldiers were always the top line.

"Scotland forever!" is supposedly what the Royal Scots Greys cried as they charged the French lines at Waterloo, at least in Lady Butler's epic 1881 painting of the same name, one of the many Victorian depictions of the Scots at war. If this is what they did actually shout, it didn't alter the fact that they were fighting for Great Britain. Some 50,000 Scottish volunteers were mobilised during the Napoleonic Wars. The leading role played by Scots soldiers in the great British "national project" of these wars began the Victorian love affair with the Scottish soldier. Artists made a good living reproducing images of fierce warriors in tartan fighting in exotic corners of the Empire. Possibly the most famous is *The Thin Red Line* – the stand made by 500 soldiers of the 93rd Highlanders at Balaclava during the Crimean War in 1854. This was depicted in numerous works, of which the most notable, by Robert Gibb, is on display at the Royal Scottish Academy in Edinburgh. These paintings were the war movies of their day, and combined with the journalistic accounts (the "thin red line" phrase came from *The Times* war correspondent William Russell) had mass appeal.

Why would Scots wish to lay down their lives in such great numbers for an enterprise, the British Empire, which was first of all the project of the English upper classes? In what way did they or their families benefit? Some British workers – especially skilled workers in the emerging Scottish engineering industries of the 19th century – perhaps benefited from the British Empire when Glasgow became the Second City of the Empire. But whether this had any material value for the Scottish working masses, in their overcrowded slums, is debatable. The martial tradition has to be at least part of the answer. It was the stories the Scots told themselves, in the pubs and publications about their collective valour that made them so susceptible to imperial propaganda. Through organisations like the volunteers, territorials and what became the biggest youth movement in Scotland, the Boys Brigade, founded in Glasgow in 1883, Scottish male culture became inextricably linked with organised violence. The Kirk was heavily sold up to the regimental culture, too, and had no truck with pacifists and Socialists. It said that to fight for King and Country was the highest duty of the Christian. This was a militant religion. Dr Wallace Williamson, a Scottish minister who addressed soldiers in the trenches put it this way in 1915: "Remember there is only one way to peace in this dread hour of history, through the bloodstained path of war."[32] In the streets of Glasgow, in times of peace, young men fought boredom by organising themselves into semi-military gangs, like the Penny Mob, and later the San Toi and Bridgeton Billy Boys.

This was a potent imperial brew. You had Scottish exceptionalism, the Scottish Presbyterian tradition, mixed up with a presumption of white racial superiority and laced with the Scottish martial culture which was then expressed through symbols of Scottish national identity. False consciousness it may have been, but it was a powerful moral force. The emerging industrial working classes were developing a political identity in the late 19th century, but it had little impact on this psychology of popular imperialism. The heroism of Scottish soldiers, measured in the anonymous graves in France, was at the disposal of the British ruling class for fully two centuries after 1745. More than half a million Scots signed up to fight in the Great War and 26% of them were killed – against only 11% for the rest of the British forces.[33] It wasn't just a case of Scots lions being sent to their graves by English donkeys. Scots were sent into battle by Scots because of the preponderance of Scots in the army high command, from Field Marshall Douglas Haig down.

Scottish casualties were very much higher in Scottish than in English regiments because the Scottish battalions also fought as the front line in the Western Front and Gallipoli. This debt will no doubt be recalled in the run-up to the 2014 Scottish Independence Referendum, which coincides with the 100th anniversary of the outbreak of the Great War. There will be lamentations at the flower of Scottish youth hurled pointlessly at German machine-guns by dumb British generals. However, the inconvenient truth for Nationalists is that Scots soldiers did generally lead from the front out of choice, and seemed willing, since the days of the Seven Years War, to risk their lives to demonstrate their bravery. Even in the Second World War, the Scottish regiments at Arnhem were marching into unequal combat to the tune of the bagpipes. The evaporation of all this after the war, principally in the 1960s, is one of the great moral transformations which cleared the way for the rise of modern Scottish Nationalism.

SIR WALTER SCOTT

In the early 19th century, Scottish national identity was used to cement the Union, with sometimes surreal results. Sir Walter Scott rummaged through the chaos of the previous two centuries to salvage an idealised Scottishness to promote the visit of King George IV to Scotland in August 1822, the first visit from a reigning monarch since Charles II. Fictitious clansmen clad in improbable tartans dreamed up by the Highland Society of London were lined up for inspection by the corpulent king, in pink tights, dressed in a fantasy costume that cost the equivalent of £110,000 today and featured a tartan called "Royal Stuart". This was pantomime Nationalism. A Hanoverian king in a phoney tartan named after the Jacobite dynasty.

Scott was an Edinburgh lawyer who became fascinated by the folk music and popular culture of Scotland. In his popular Waverley novels – about a Hanoverian soldier who switches sides to Bonnie Prince Charlie, and then back again – he created a synthetic image of a heroic Scotland based on the warrior clan system which had, of course, been destroyed after the 1745 Rebellion. Scott was a Unionist Hanoverian who wanted to play the patriot game and didn't see why the Jacobites should be allowed to monopolise the myth of the Highlander. He was also worried about the possibility of political radicalism spreading to Scotland following the Peterloo Massacre in Manchester in 1819. What better way to unite the nation than to offer a heroic image of Scottish identity to assuage the anger of the dispossessed?

In fact, Scottish national identity had been almost, literally, buried after the Union. The Honours of Scotland – Scotland's Crown Jewels – had been lost to history until Scott and his friends unearthed them in 1818 stuffed in a trunk in Edinburgh Castle where they had been locked away after 1707. The last king who had used them was Charles II, whose coronation in 1660, the Restoration, is not an event Unionists like Scott would have been expected to celebrate. But his genre was the historical novel, the reinvention of the past, and Scott believed it was possible to mash up Scottish history to erase the distinctions between Highlander and Lowlander, Jacobite and Hanoverian, Catholic and Protestant by creating a convenient fantasy in which they are both aspects of the same archetypal Scottish personality. Scott was not entirely cynical about this: he was genuinely concerned that Scotland's history and culture was being effaced in "North Britain". But there was a level of artifice involved which made the whole enterprise thoroughly bogus.

Scott was an influential figure, the first internationally renowned novelist, whose books had phenomenal reach. He almost single-handedly created the image of Scotland that has filled a million tourist buses and adorns an even greater number of shortbread tins. His heroes, like Waverley, are generally figures caught between conflicting loyalties, but his books celebrate the Jacobites who had fought against the Union. It is a mark of just how integrated Scotland had become with England that all this glorification of Highland rebellion was seen as no danger to the Union. Queen Victoria herself became a great enthusiast for the new romantic Highland and helped turn kilts and tartan into essential fashion accessories. Following her construction of Balmoral Castle in the 1850s, Scotland's national architecture lapsed into what became known as the "Baronial style". Suddenly, turrets and crow-stepped gables appeared on every middle-class mansion in Edinburgh or the south side of Glasgow.

The Victorians became infatuated with Scottishness, and after the railways were built it became fashionable for every middle-class English family to visit Scotland to chase the deer and watch the Highland Games, which were also largely a Victorian invention. Scotland became a Celtic theme park, a tartanised construct. Soon, wealthy English "lairds" were buying large tracts of Scotland to turn into sporting estates devoted to the hunting of deer, pheasant and anything else that looked good on a wall. In the Edwardian era, half the Cabinet of the UK departed to the Highlands for the Glorious 12th and the parliamentary year was built around the shooting season. The annual slaughter of stags and game birds added a new dimension to the Highland Clearances. It also led to even more of the crofting population being priced out of their home lands.

The empty and desolate Highlands we see today are the result of centuries of depopulation and de-forestation. Originally cut down for charcoal burning, the trees that once covered Scotland were unable to recover because of grazing by sheep and latterly deer. The lack of roads, other than those built by General Wade, in the Highlands of Scotland testifies to the paucity of human habitations. Scotland is now much prized as a European tourist destination because of its supposedly "wild" and "natural" landscape. There is nothing wild or natural about it. It is only because of the pattern of Highland land use over the past 200 years that the Scottish hills look so barren and bleak.

Scott and Livingstone represent two sides of the Victorian Scottish consciousness. They were British imperialists who insisted they were Scottish patriots. Scott, the Tory Unionist, reinventing Scotland for the delectation of the English middle-classes, as well as the Scots, and projecting the myth of the Highland soldier across the English-speaking world. Livingstone, the humble lad o' pairts working his way up through the meritocratic Scottish education system and exporting Scottish Presbyterianism to Africa. Both were capable of feats of hard work – Scott's literary output was prodigious, especially after he was effectively bankrupted by the collapse of a publishing company in which he had invested. Livingstone walked across a continent, alone except for a couple of native porters. Both became international celebrities because of the spread of the mass media – newspapers, books and magazines. Neither was living entirely in the real world.

CHAPTER SIX
HOME RULE IS ROME RULE

$\times$

I T I S often assumed, by people who aren't familiar with British history, that Scottish Nationalism has followed a broadly similar course to the struggle for political independence in Ireland. That, to quote an essay in the *New Orleans Historical Review*, devolution in the 1990s was "a response to hundreds of years of Scottish Nationalist sentiment" – Scots must been trying to assert their political autonomy in the way Irish home rulers and republicans did in the 19th and 20th centuries. The American sociologist Michael Hechter argued in the 1970s in an influential book, *Internal Colonialism: The Celtic Fringe in British National Development*, that Scotland was, like Ireland, an internal colony of England – a last outpost of empire. He suggested there had been a pan-Gaelic movement against English domination, which Scotland just happened to join a bit late in the day. Even the Irish Republican Army subscribed to this notion of Celtic solidarity, at least in that it reputedly exempted Scotland from its mainland bombing campaign in the 1970s.

In fact, nothing could be further from the truth. The Scots and Irish saw Great Britain very differently in the 19th century. Not only did Scotland's Lowland middle-classes appear quite happy with the union with England, they vigorously opposed Home Rule for Ireland and ended up voting in large numbers after 1912 for a party, the Scottish Unionist Party, that defined itself by its opposition to Irish Home Rule. Many working-class Scots, in the west in particular, were militantly Orange and Unionist in their outlook until comparatively recently. It's understandable that Scottish historians, some of whom who are sympathetic to the Labour movement and Red Clydeside, should have been reluctant to suggest there were a lot more Protestant bigots in the shipyards than militant Socialists, but that's how it was.

The two weren't always mutually exclusive. My grandfather worked as a foreman in Weirs after the First World War and believed himself to be a Socialist. He was a teetotaller, too; he knew his Burns. But he didn't have any Catholics in his yard. Even after 1931, during the Great Depression years, Scottish workers voted in large numbers for what was, in effect, the sister party to Ian Paisley's Ulster Unionists/UDC.

Even in the Highlands, where "improving" landlords before 1850 had cleared tens of thousands of Scots off their land, there was no significant Nationalist response. Scotland's peasants were dispossessed by one of the most mercenary landlord classes anywhere in the world. But there was very little resistance until the end of the century. The Highland Land Wars of the 1880s and 1890s may have contributed to the founding of the Scottish Home Rule Association, but they were primarily about securing tenancies for subsistence farmers, the Highland crofters. It was not a home rule movement. There was no Scottish Nationalist Party in 19th century Scotland – Scotland's party of choice remained the Liberals, who were staunchly in favour of the union until the end of the 19th century, even after Gladstone promised home rule for Ireland.

Nationalism of the kind promoted in Ireland by Daniel O'Connell, Charles Stewart Parnell and James Connolly, who had different ideological outlooks but all sought repeal of the Act of Union, simply did not exist in Scotland in the 19th century, at least not at levels that were politically significant. Ireland was never reconciled to the union with Great Britain after 1801 in the way the Scots were with England after 1707. The only similarity was the partiality of members of both the Scottish and Irish Parliaments to English gold. But what happened after the pay-off was very different. Daniel O'Connell's Irish Repeal Association in 1840 launched nearly a century of political struggle against the Union and the British state, which became increasingly violent in the 20th century and ultimately led to the Easter Rising and Irish War of Independence in 1919. Pretty much the reverse happened in Scotland. Riots spread across Scotland in the decades immediately after the 1707 Union, culminating in the Jacobite Rebellion in 1745. But thereafter, the union with England enjoyed wide support across all classes in Scottish society, even among the radical movements after the Napoleonic Wars, who wanted to improve the condition of the Scottish working-class, but did not see political Nationalism as relevant to this objective. This identification with Great Britain intensified throughout the 19th century as the Empire spread, aided by the popularity of Sir Walter Scott's romanticised image of the Jacobite Highlander. Victorian Scots' celebration of patriotic heroes like William Wallace did not mean they wanted their country back; they didn't think then that they had lost it.

There was a Scottish Home Rule Association in the late 19th century, partly in the wake of Gladstone's attempt to placate Irish Nationalism with a form of devolution. But in Scotland this had limited appeal and was not an attempt to end the union with England – quite the reverse, in fact. Most Scottish home rulers hoped to cement the union further by improving the quality of governance in Scotland, initially through measures like the creation of the Secretary of State for Scotland in 1885. Several Scottish home rule bills were presented to Westminster by the Liberal governments but none was passed. There was little enthusiasm for Scottish home rule after the Liberals Unionists went off to form the Scottish Unionist Party with the Tories in 1912. There were, however, some unlikely individuals who supported Scottish devolution one of them was Winston Churchill, who delivered a speech in Dundee in 1913 calling for a federal reconstruction of the United Kingdom, with "home rule all round". But even his enthusiasm for devolution died away rapidly after the First World War, as the politics of home rule gave way to Socialism and the rise of the Unionist Labour Party. Unionism of the Left and Unionism of the Right were the two poles between which Scottish politics oscillated throughout the 20th century. Nationalism was nowhere.

Many Scottish voters had switched from Liberal to the Scottish Unionist Party to register their opposition to mass immigration from Ireland. Half a million Irish had settled in Scotland by the end of the 19th century. The sectarianism that mars contemporary life in Scotland's housing estates to this day dates largely from this period. The Protestant working-classes in west central Scotland feared this invasion of cheap labour from Ireland might spread to the shipyards and engineering works on the Clyde. Catholics were barred from many yards, leaving the immigrants to seek second-rate occupations like dock work and warehousing, street cleaning and labouring.

The Church of Scotland, and especially its Orange fundamentalist wing, feared also that the Catholic immigrants would carry with them the contagion of Popery. Ministers in their Protestant pulpits delivered furious tirades against the Irish incomers. It is hard to believe that the politically correct and ecumenical Church and Nation committee of the Church of Scotland we know today could have published, as late as 1923, a pamphlet called *The Menace of the Irish Race to our Scottish Nationality*. But it did. Catholic Irish were regarded, not just as second-class citizens, but as an inferior race who brought diseases like typhus and whose moral pestilence infected the pure stream of Scottish Presbyterianism.

And this wasn't some ancient enmity, dredged up from pre-Enlightenment ignorance and fear among the Scottish lower classes. Sectarianism was really rather respectable. One of the most influential figures in the Church of Scotland in the first half of the 20th century, the Moderator of the General Assembly, John White, was a virulent anti-Catholic who called for the ending of Irish immigration and wanted a "racially pure" Scotland. Though what he meant by that is not at all clear given that Scotland has absorbed waves of immigrants from Europe, like the Poles and Lithuanians, who have become a part of the fabric of Scottish society. Some on the other side of the Irish Sea might have pointed out that many Scots had compromised their own racial purity by emigrating to Northern Ireland in the 17th century, seizing land from Gaelic tribes to form the Plantation. But the Ulster Protestants were seen as part of the Orange "race" and welcomed into the lodges and flute bands of Glasgow.

This manufactured fear of the Irish made Protestant Scots feel even more attached to the Union. "Home Rule was Rome Rule", went the mantra of the Orange Unionists, who believed that Catholic Irish immigrants wanted to reverse the Reformation. This passionate loathing of the Irish led to some glaring moral contradictions. West of Scotland working-class culture could accommodate both Socialist Internationalism and religious sectarianism. Rent strikes and John MacLean alongside Orange marches and racial intolerance. So intense was the antagonism that Catholics were granted the right to have their own religious schools under the 1918 Education Act, a defensive action that was understandable given the intensity of discrimination, but it unfortunately wrote the sectarian divide into the very educational system. In Glasgow, it is still common for people who have been introduced to each other for the first time to ask what school they went to. And they don't mean grammar or comprehensive.

Immigrants are often victimised and scapegoated in the

host country, as the Irish were in Scotland, and as Afro-Caribbeans were in England. But why did Scots feel quite so strongly opposed to political home rule for Ireland itself? What difference did it make to Scots whether Ireland was in or out of the Union? Again, it was the Empire. Scots feared Irish independence because they feared that secession would undermine the integrity of Great Britain, and that might damage the British Empire which, before the First World War, covered one-quarter of the planet and 500 million people. The Unionists, like the Liberals before them, regarded Scotland as the dynamic, intellectual and even moral spearhead of the British Empire. In the 18th and 19th centuries, Scots colonised the British Empire, fighting its battles, keeping its books, organising its trade, managing its plantations, and looking after its soul.

Internal colonialism probably did accurately describe the condition of Ireland during its century as part of the United Kingdom. Certainly, southern Ireland remained an essentially agrarian and underdeveloped economy throughout the 19th century, when Scotland was a site of the Industrial Revolution. The crisis over the Irish Potato Famine exposed the double standards applied by the British. There was very little sympathy in Britain and the relief effort was grudging and sporadic even as the Great Famine claimed one million lives and caused one million more to emigrate. It looked, to Irish Nationalists, like passive genocide inflicted by a Protestant Britain on Catholic Ireland. The realisation that the wealthiest Empire in history would stand idly by while a part of Great Britain starved convinced the Irish people that their future did not lie in ever closer union. Similar potato blights in Scotland led to famine, hardship and death, but on nothing like the same scale as in Ireland. Ireland's union with Britain in 1801 preserved the country in neocolonial underdevelopment; while Scotland's union after 1707 did the opposite by allowing Scots to colonise the world, so long as they accepted they were the junior partners.

TROUBLE IN GOD'S COMMONWEALTH

Puzzled by the absence of Nationalist politics in 19th century Scotland, some historians have sought to infer a kind of unconscious Nationalism from the behaviour of essentially non-political institutions such as the Presbyterian Kirk.[34] The Church of Scotland certainly occupied much of the space left by the lack of Scottish state-hood after 1707. In the absence of a Scottish Parliament, the General Assembly of the Church of Scotland in the 18th and 19th centuries debated matters of national importance and was a form of clerical self-government. But this analogy cannot be stretched too far. The General Assembly was not a democratically elected national parliament and it had no formal legislative powers. It was the governing body of the Church of Scotland, an institution that dominated the consciousness of Scots and regulated their moral lives, but did not exercise political power on their behalf. The Kirk was responsible for poor relief until the middle of the 19th century – discriminating the "deserving" from the undeserving poor by awarding the former a lead tag – and organised the parish schools. But its primary objective was to bring sinners to the true faith, and keep them there.

Scots weren't Presbyterian because they were National-ists; Scots were Presbyterian because they were intensely religious and still militantly Protestant in a way we can hardly comprehend today. God was a living presence in the lives of many ordinary people, and the Kirk was regarded as God's eyes and ears in the community, especially in rural areas. The primary unit of ecclesiastical government was the parish, overseen by the elected Elders of the Kirk Session, who imposed strict moral discipline on the congregation. Those who transgressed the Kirk's laws could be punished in various ways, through fines and public acts of repentance and abasement before the congregation – traditionally with the sinner dressed in sackcloth. The Session did adjudicate on some civil matters, like debt repayments and minor land disputes, but it was primarily interested in moral crimes like fornication, blasphemy, illegitimacy and working on the Sabbath. Scotland in the 18th and much of the 19th century must have been rather like the Muslim theocracies of the Middle East – Iran for example. With one important difference: secular affairs were governed by a parliament in another country.

So, although the organs of the Church may have occupied some of the space of national politics, that doesn't mean this was a political system in religious guise. Some historians have suggested[35] that the landmark event of 19th-century Scotland, the Disruption of the Church of Scotland in 1843, was a kind of displaced independence movement, even that it was an explicitly Nationalist revolt. There may have been echoes of the National Covenant in the evangelical movement in the Kirk at the start of the 19th century. The only problem with this analogy is that, unlike the Covenanters, the Free Kirk that left on 18th May 1843, was not seeking the restoration of a parliament nor was it defying the authority of a king. The Disruption was essentially a theological or spiritual dispute in a country which was profoundly religious, almost to the exclusion of secular politics. In 1843, when the Free Kirk ministers walked out of the General Assembly, they were followed through the streets of Edinburgh by tens of thousands of cheering Scots. It looked like a revolution; it was a revolution, but only within the confines of established religion. Edinburgh bankers did not fear for their assets and no Chartists made declarations of aims when the Reverend Thomas Chalmers declared spiritual independence.

There was arguably a class dimension to this schism. The Disruption was an essentially middle-class revolt against aristocratic privilege embodied in the 17th-century Patronage Act, which allowed wealthy landowners to nominate ministers. Evangelicalism turned into a popular mass movement ranged against the London Government because of Robert Peel's support for the moderate status quo. This did not mean that it was class conflict as such, or a challenge to the established political structures, and it certainly wasn't an assertion of Scottish national identity against the Union. Reverend Chalmers, who led the Free Kirk after Disruption, was opposed to Socialism and Nationalism or indeed anything that interfered with his Presbyterian theocracy, which he called "God's Commonwealth". He also fulminated against trade unions, welfare, immigration and anything remotely resembling Catholicism. His fear that he might have unleashed a popular revolt – this was the era of radicalism and Chartism – made him even more politically reactionary, and he went to great lengths to prevent any radical ideas infiltrating the Free Kirk he led. Chalmers loathed popular democracy –"the lawless spirit of insubordination" – and saw political agitation for civil rights and the extension of the franchise as a threat to the Church.

Nothing could have been less like the Irish Nationalism that emerged after the Great Famine, which took place around the same time as the Disruption in the 1840s. That constituted a direct political challenge to the Union and to the British Empire, which had left the Irish Catholic population to starve. By contrast, the Scottish evangelicals who revolted against the powers of patronage of the

Anglicised landowners in the 1830s and 1840s did so primarily for religious purposes, to promote their fundamentalist and almost charismatic version of Reformed Christianity. Confusingly, the Moderates who defended patronage, were actually more willing to come to terms with Enlightenment rationality than were the evangelicals, many of whom were still suspicious of science. It is hard for us to understand these disputes with our modern secular outlook, and there is an understandable tendency to try to recast the Protestant evangelicals as a movement for popular democracy – as a kind of religious Chartism.

But the evangelicals were fighting essentially to resist the intrusion of the secular state into ecclesiastical affairs. This brought them into conflict with the political establishment in England, if only because the Patronage Act was defended by the Tory Government of Robert Peel in Westminster. But the Disruption wasn't an unilateral declaration of political independence, or a call for an extension of the franchise, or a challenge to the ruling classes. It wasn't through some clerical false consciousness that Scots generally did not support political Nationalism in the 19th century; it was because they didn't regard home rule as important. Religion was what motivated most Scots, and the preservation of their Protestant faith dominated public life.

Religious observance may not have extended throughout all layers of Scottish society in the Victorian age, and there were many who were indifferent to the Church's message, especially among the slum populations of the Scottish cities that were exploding in size in the mid-19th century. Chalmers despaired of the faithlessness of the urban masses, and wanted a return to a pre-industrial, agrarian golden age of the parish village, where church attendance had been almost universal. But few escaped the authority of the Church even in the cities because the Kirk defined the limits of social policy and still dominated the intellectual life of the entire country. There was very little organised challenge to this essentially theocratic approach to public affairs. Even the Chartists in Scotland, who organised large demonstrations in the 1840s in favour of voting reform and trade unionism, marched behind banners depicting the Covenanters and singing psalms.[36]

The Church was opposed to state intervention to ameliorate poverty essentially because the Rev Thomas Chalmers believed that only religion could help people help themselves, and that handouts would lead to dependency. Mrs Thatcher would have found a lot to like in his sermons.

"The remedy against the extension of pauperism does not lie in the liberalities of the rich; it lies in the hearts and habits of the poor," said Chalmers in *On Political Economy*. "There is no possible help for them if they will not help themselves. It is to a rise and reformation in the habits of our peasantry that we look for deliverance, not to the impotent crudities of a speculative legislation." Chalmers was opposed to state poor relief and thought that the solution to social problems like poverty lay within the soul of the individual. Only once people were brought to God could they begin to improve their social and material circumstances, and stop drinking. Chalmers was a clerical radical and a social conservative and worried that the passions of evangelicalism should not spill into politics. "Nothing will ever be taught in our theological halls," he said at the opening of New College Edinburgh, "which shall have the remotest tendency to disturb the existing order of things, or to confound the ranks and distinctions which now obtain in society."

This was a profoundly reactionary philosophy and betrayed a wilful ignorance of the social consequences of industrialisation. How could people live decent lives when they were living in the degrading squalor of Edinburgh's notorious slums? Chalmers spent much of his time working in poor areas of Edinburgh, but faith blinded him to the reality of the lives led by the people he tried to evangelise.

Chalmers is referred to by most of his biographers without irony as a "social reformer". This is partly because he urged wealthy people to donate to charity and believed that the accumulation of wealth for its own sake, if not contrary to the teaching of the Bible, was spiritually valueless. Right at the end of his life, he was finally persuaded to accept that the ten-hour working day might give workers more time and energy to devote to church attendance. But throughout, he advocated the most extreme form of laissez-faire economics and was a resolute opponent of state regulation and welfare. However, Chalmers was a towering figure in Victorian Scotland and his attitudes were deeply ingrained in Scottish public life. This is very much how middle-class Scots thought in the 19th, and most of the 20th century – and they were the only group that counted politically. The Scottish Unionist party drew its social philosophy largely from Chalmers.

The presumption that Scotland was essentially a Labour country – a land of egalitarian values like those attributed to Robert Burns – falls down when you look at the Kirk-dominated Scotland of the Victorian age. Burns was hugely popular in Scotland, and his work was celebrated in annual festivals – the T in the Park of their day. But the attendees did not see any contradiction between their miserly approach to poor relief and his celebration of the virtues of the common man in *A Man's a Man for `A That*. Most Scots who had the vote in Victorian Scotland supported the Liberal Party, rather than the Tory Party which was never a political organisation with much electoral support north of the border. But this was old-style, laissez-faire liberalism of the kind Chalmers advocated in his extensive writing on political economy. The Liberals begat the Scottish Unionist Party after the division over Irish Home Rule, and that was the movement that projected Scots into the 20th century. It was patriotic, both in a British and Scottish sense, socially conservative and, naturally, Unionist.

KEIR HARDIE AND THE SCOTTISH LABOUR PARTY

When Socialism did come along in Scotland, with James Keir Hardie, the founder of the British Labour Party, at the end of the century, it was not an overnight success. Hardie, like David Livingstone, grew up in poverty and started work in the Lanarkshire coal mines in 1866 when he was ten years old. He was almost completely self-educated. The supposedly democratic Scottish education system didn't reach child labourers like him. Hardie was a Christian long before he was a Socialist, and worshipped in the same evangelical Congregational church as David Livingstone, whom he emulated in many ways, not least in his passion for social reform. But his first stop was the temperance movement, the war against the demon drink, which was a kind of surrogate social movement in the Scotland of Thomas Chalmers.

Cheap alcohol had made Scotland one of the most sozzled states in the world. The urban poor, living in slums and having little else to do in the few hours left to them after work, drank heavily and publicly. Chalmers saw this as the Devil's work, not the brewers'. If only the Scots could be prevented from drinking they would turn more readily to God. Perversely, however, as an advocate of laissez-faire, he opposed any increase in the price of drink. *Plus ça change*. Scotland has recently had an similar debate about minimum pricing of alcohol, which was proposed by the SNP Government in 2010 and opposed by Labour. When drink prices were finally raised toward the end of the 19th century, alcohol consumption fell rapidly from 1.6 gallons per year in 1861 to 0.4 in 1931, according to the Scottish census.[37]

It was Christian preaching and temperance rallies that revealed Keir Hardie's formidable abilities as a public speaker, and he would go on to address meetings of more than 100,000 people using his lungs alone. He also became a miners' union organiser, after which the mine owners blacklisted him from working in the pits. Hardie was compelled to become a full-time union organiser and journalist, making his name during the strikes that hit the Lanarkshire coal mines after the owners tried to cut wages in the 1880s. Curiously, he also persuaded Lanarkshire miners to start playing cricket, a game that was thought in many parts of Scotland to be a quintessentially English pastime.

Hardie at this stage was still a member of Gladstone's Liberal Party, which had developed a radical reforming wing after the Reform Act of 1867 granted some male workers the vote and inaugurated the era of industrial politics. He realised that organised labour would soon outgrow the Liberals and needed a party of its own. Seeking to attract these new worker votes, Hardie stood in 1888 as an independent labour candidate in Mid Lanark. He finished last. The Socialist dawn had not arrived in Scotland. However, that year he formed an alliance with the extraordinary Scottish Liberal MP and adventurer Robert Bontine Cunninghame Graham. Nicknamed "Don Roberto" because he had spent much of his youth as an unsuccessful rancher in Argentina, Cunninghame Graham became the first president of the Scottish Labour Party and went on to help found the National Party of Scotland in 1928, which became the SNP. They don't make politicians like that any more.

Keir Hardie was a supporter of home rule for Scotland, but he didn't find much support for it north of the border, or for Socialism, and in 1892, he left Scotland to stand in West Ham South, a working-class seat in Essex. He won, thanks largely to Liberal votes, and entered parliament as the first representative of the working man. His tweed suit and deerstalker were considered a sartorial affront to Parliament at a time when politicians wore top hats and frock coats. The society magazine *Vanity Fair*, declared: "Hardie's headgear has endangered the foundations of parliamentary propriety." However, he didn't shake the foundations of the British establishment, at least not yet.

His attacks on the monarchy caused even more outrage than his dress sense or his Socialism, and he lost his Essex seat in 1895. Hardie didn't return to Scotland, even though his wife and family still lived there, and became a notable figure on the London Left, forming a close relationship with Sylvia Pankhurst, the suffragette with whom it is assumed he had an affair. Hardie wasn't a Marxist, though he took an interest in the *Socialist International* and he had many conversations with Marx's daughter Eleanor. He remained very much a Christian Socialist, campaigning for specific reforms such as votes for women, free schooling and pensions. In 1900, he formed what became the modern British Labour Party, and went on to become Labour's first chairman, winning its first seat – not in Scotland but in Wales – in Merthyr Tydfil. Hardie had become another member of the Scottish diaspora.

Modern Scottish Nationalists like to claim Keir Hardie as the father of Scottish home rule, but the truth is that he wasn't particularly interested in Scottish politics and devoted more energy to the campaign for home rule for India than for Scotland. The Labour Party insists that its founder had nothing to do with Nationalism and resent the SNP's attempt to enlist him into its cause. The Keir Hardie Society, accused the SNP of "body snatching" their icon. Keir Hardie, they insist, was "an Internationalist" and regarded Nationalism as a means by which the capitalist class divided the workers against each other. He remained a pacifist and was appalled when the country, and the Church, were gripped by war fever in 1914. Like many on the emerging 20th-century Left, he underestimated the enduring appeal of the Empire and Great Britain for many working people. His attempt to organise a general strike against the war led to his being frozen out of the very British Labour Party he had created. Hardie died in September 1915 after a series of strokes.

The rise of Labour politics was of course important in Scotland as in the rest of the UK, and the Labour Party effectively replaced the Liberal Party in Scotland in the general elections of the 1920s. But Scots' imperial conservatism was never far from the surface. Throughout the Great Depression after 1931, Scots voted overwhelmingly for the right-wing Unionists. The middle class in

Scotland was too small to have delivered these votes on its own. The history of Scotland before the 1960s was not just about the rise of the working class, but about the enduring support shown by all classes for the Union, Empire and Church.

Scotland was by all accounts a relatively docile country in the 19th century, led by a pushy and self-confident middle class and a reactionary Kirk that used spiritual power to stifle any progressive political movements. Large parts of the Highlands had become little more than sporting playgrounds for the English aristocracy. The poor in the slums dominated Scotland's population, but were almost entirely invisible to politics during the course of the Industrial Revolution, even after the Reform Acts. Scotland has acquired a reputation for being a Labour country, but that doesn't accurately describe the political culture of Scotland in the 19th century or in most of the 20th century.

DR JEKYLL, I PRESUME

Of course, there were corners of social radicalism, like the municipal socialism pioneered in Glasgow after the First World War by the Independent Labour Party. And church missionaries like David Livingstone had a social conscience and a belief in progress, though of a very Scottish kind. But the Kirk kept it all firmly under control. Its brooding presence cast a shadow over Scotland and gloominess came to be associated with the Scottish character. This "dark" quality to Scottish Presbyterian life emerged in the literature of the times. In 1824, James Hogg published *The Private Memoirs and Confessions of a Justified Sinner*, which tells us a lot about the psychological universe of the Scots. Sometimes described as the first Gothic novel, Confessions is a kind of satire on the Calvinist notion of predestination – the doctrine that all humans are either members of the Elect or of the damned, and that their destiny is fixed by God even before they are born. Hogg's anti-hero decides, not unreasonably, that if he is already guaranteed eternal salvation in the afterlife, then there's no reason to behave well in this life. Hence the "justified" sinner takes to murder.

Unsurprisingly, few Calvinists agree with this interpretation of their doctrine and insist that if a person is of the Elect, he or she, will by definition behave like one. Therefore, it is inconceivable that a murderer could be predestined to grace. The message here, of course, is that Scots have to work damn hard to persuade themselves, and others, that they are indeed members of the chosen. This, it is said, is why Scots became so obsessed with outward appearances – with good conduct. Hogg's novel of split personality is said to have influenced another literary dissection of the Scottish psyche: Robert Louis Stevenson's *The Strange Case of Dr Jekyll and Mr Hyde*, published in 1886. This novel, set in London, has a strong air of Presbyterian Edinburgh, where Stevenson grew up with a very troubled relationship to religion and a distaste for the hypocrisy of Victorian morality. It is another case of the upright and respectable appearance concealing violent tendencies within, and many see this as an allegory of strait-laced Scotland struggling with its inner demons. Jekyll and Hyde was written as a Christmas horror tale and Stevenson never intended much significance to be read into his "penny dreadful". But it has generated an industry of morbid self-examination by literary Scots who rather like the idea of the beast within.

Scottish writers of the 20th century have been fascinated by the idea of the Scottish hard man – from *No Mean City* by Alexander McArthur about the Glasgow razor gangs in 1935, to William McIlvanney's *The Big Man* in 1985 and the current top seller in the Tartan Noir genre, Ian Rankin's Inspector Rebus series. These novels have done a lot to shape how England sees Scotland, and how Scots see themselves in the 21st century. Typically, the story involves a working-class autodidact with a troubled relationship with the bottle and the opposite sex, who defies authority and generally ends up in a fight he didn't start. As a Scot myself, I would have to say that it is not unknown for my countrymen to correspond to this psychological profile. But there are many more who don't. Popular Scottish literature has a tendency to recycle the same, stereotypical images of brooding Calvinists, drunken wife beaters, mean-minded bankers, honest street fighters, puritanical hypocrites, tortured sexual repressives. Or perhaps it's just that London publishers like to commission works that feature one or other of them, or all at the same time.

Which brings us, inevitably and unpronounceably, to the Caledonian Antisyzygy, a term applied to Scottish literature by George Gregory Smith in 1919. The strict definition of the term is the presence of duelling polarities in one entity. The concept was used in a 1932 essay by the modernist poet Hugh MacDiarmid. *The Caledonian Antisyzygy and the Gaelic Idea* has been used as a conversation-stopper by literary show-offs ever since. If it means anything at all, and I am not entirely sure it does, the antisyzygy means the divisions in Scottish psychology, history and politics as reflected in literature – such as the divisions between Highland and Lowland, Jacobite and Hanoverian, Protestant and Catholic, Glasgow and Edinburgh. Sir Walter Scott's *Waverley* involved an antisyzygy, because Edward keeps wavering between polar opposites of Jacobite romanticism and his own Hanoverian origins. *The Justified Sinner* is an antisyzygy as is *Jekyll and Hyde*, since they both involve an unstable psychological dualism. Calvinism is an antisyzygy between the Elect and the Reprobate.

It seems rather facile to describe James Keir Hardie and the Rev Thomas Chalmers as a Caledonian Antisyzygy, but if the term does mean anything, then it must presumably relate also to the contradictory nature of Scottish political culture in the 19th century. There was a distinct egalitarian strand running through Scottish society from Robert Burns to Hardie, which never really emerged as mass politics in Scotland. Meanwhile, there was a genuinely revolutionary impulse generated by the evangelical movement in the Scottish Kirk, led by Chalmers, which was radical but wasn't proletarian. Somehow, these contradictory forces prevented the social and political Nationalism that swept Europe in the middle of the 19th century from disturbing the pond of Victorian Scotland.

The Church was very disturbed, of course, and provided a kind of surrogate radicalism in the passions released by the Disruption. The Kirk was becoming less oppressive in the era before 1843 and there was less emphasis on the doctrine of Predestination. A more liberal and humanist form of Presbyterianism was certainly around in the 19th century, though it got lost in the proliferation of "Wee Free" churches that followed the Disruption, like the fragments of Marxism after Trotsky left the church of Soviet Communism. The problem that contemporary Scots – most of us raised through 1960s secularisation – have in making sense of their intellectual origins in the Victorian era is that forces such as religious evangelicalism are distant and hard to understand.

What emerged from Victorian Scotland was a Scottish Unionism which had widespread popular appeal and which, along with the mystique of Empire, helped suppress or diminish political radicalism of the kind seen elsewhere in Europe. Keir Hardie was a product of the Scottish Kirk, and translated Presbyterian values into politics, even though founder of the British Labour Party couldn't get himself elected in the country of his birth. He followed the well-trodden path of Scots, taking the high road to London. The Scotland he left behind was a conservative country, with an increasingly class-conscious working population which still saw Great Britain as a cause worth fighting for. And dying for.

CHAPTER SEVEN
THE HIGH NOON OF UNIONISM

$\times$

T H E R E I S nothing quite like aerial bombardment to bring people together. On the nights of 13th and 14th March 1941, Clydebank, the heart of Scottish shipbuilding, was largely destroyed by the Luftwaffe. Actually, the main target, John Brown's shipyard, avoided serious damage, but more than 500 people were killed and as many seriously injured, while 35,000 people were made homeless. The nearby city of Glasgow and surrounding areas were left traumatised. The panic that spread through one of the most densely populated urban concentrations in Europe can only be imagined. In that incendiary moment, Scotland and England became one in the war against Fascism.

Scotland had never experienced anything like this before. London at least had memories of the Zeppelin raids in the First World War. Scots had been vaguely aware of the dangers of bombing from the raids on Guernica, during the Spanish Civil War, in which a number of Scots had fought in the International Brigades. But Scotland had not been invaded and occupied for three hundred years. The last battle on Scottish soil was Culloden in 1746. The fear that Hitler's invading armies would try to land in Scotland led to the construction of a chain of bunkers and tank barriers along the beaches of East Lothian which remain to this day. The German bombing was never repeated in Scotland, at least on the same scale, and Scottish cities suffered nothing comparable to the destruction of London or Coventry. But the Clydebank Blitz, coming as it did relatively early in the war, cemented Scots in their commitment to the British war effort.

The bombing did something else: it helped create the National Health Service. Pre-war planners, expecting widespread bombing, had built and staffed seven new emergency hospitals to deal with the Scottish casualties. But as the bombing never took place, at least in Scotland, these were largely surplus to requirements, until the imaginative wartime Labour Secretary of State for Scotland, Tom Johnston, turned them into an engine for improving the health of the working people of Scotland. The tens of thousands of Scots who had been languishing on waiting lists for the charity and voluntary hospitals were finally given the treatment they needed. Even the luxury Gleneagles Hotel was pressed into service as a convalescent home for injured miners. It is no surprise that Tom Johnston was regarded as a secular saint in Scotland. He cured the sick and enabled the lame to walk.

In fact, the Second World War did more for the health of the working population of Scotland than had been achieved in the century since the Factory Acts. The rate of infant mortality fell by 27% between 1939 and 1945. Indeed, by VJ Day it was one-fifth of the level recorded at the turn of the century when Glasgow had supposedly been the Second City of the Empire.[38] What a hollow boast that now sounded. During six years of war, the average height of 12-year-old Scottish children increased by nearly two inches. Preventable diseases like diphtheria and rickets were finally tackled. By June 1941, 440,000 children in Scotland had been immunised, according to the Scottish census, 40% of the age group. By 1942, the figure had risen to 792,000 or 69% of the group. There could be no greater indictment of the failure of the policies of successive governments of Liberal, Labour or Tory than that it took another world war to generate the political will to combat this needless suffering and early death.

Politicians and civil servants had been fully aware before the war that most of Scotland's health problems were preventable. In 1935, the Nobel Prize-winning Scottish nutritionist Sir John Boyd Orr, in his *Food Health and Income* report, had stated the blindingly obvious in terms that even the dullest bureaucrat could understand: you could not expect a nation to be healthy when half of the population had an inadequate diet because they couldn't afford to buy food. Only when the workers were required to fight and manufacture munitions did the means become available to deal with Scotland's health and social problems. Rationing showed that people could be properly fed, even during times of wartime scarcity, at relatively little cost. Programmes like the provision of free milk and orange juice, as well as elementary health education for mothers, had an almost miraculous impact on the health of children.

But the most dramatic improvements in the health of Scots

owed nothing to rationing. It was the doubling of average wages and full employment during the war years that did most to make Scotland better. People were healthier because they could afford to eat, wash and clothe their families. The claim of Kirk ministers since Thomas Chalmers that want and disease arose from moral deficiencies in the individual character was finally exposed for the nonsense it always had been. Never again would governments be able to wring their hands, as they did in the Great Depression, when half of Scotland was unemployed, and say they could do nothing in the face of implacable market forces. For politicians of all parties, it came to be seen as self-evident that if the state could create full employment, higher wages, better health and a dynamic economy during wartime, then it could do it in peacetime, too. The doctrines of laissez-faire capitalism were discredited.

The Beveridge Report in 1942 was therefore largely a recognition of a wartime reality. Its promise of social security "from the cradle to the grave" was the foundation of the post-war consensus and represented a political acceptance that governments could no longer allow living standards to fall below levels needed to sustain civilised life. Nor could the state allow human and productive capital to lie idle. Rearmament had released the industrial capacity that had been rusting away in the 1930s. During the war, the state became the dominant economic force in Scotland, as Tom Johnston acquired unprecedented powers to redirect industry and labour through the Scottish Council of Industry.

MUNICIPAL SOCIALISM IN ONE COUNTRY

Tom Johnston was Labour's greatest-ever Scottish Secretary of State. A former Red Clydeside left-winger and journalist – the founding editor of the radical news sheet *Forward* – Johnston had been part of Glasgow's "municipal socialism" movement, before and after the First World War, and which had used local government to clear slums and provide utilities like gas and water at public expense. Johnston saw the opportunity presented by the wartime command economy to apply "gas and water socialism" more widely. He introduced rent controls, promoted council housing and even launched a primordial version of the NHS. It was the policy of the wartime coalition government to decentralise the administration of Britain to make it more resilient to enemy bombing. Johnston simply exploited this new machinery to the full. Unusually for a Socialist, Johnston was an expert on life insurance, having been involved with the working mens' Friendly Societies in Glasgow, and he largely devised the social insurance scheme proposed in the 1942 Beveridge Report.

Johnston was a Unionist and he used the threat of Nationalism to bully the UK Cabinet into directing jobs to Scotland. This threat was almost totally fictitious. The SNP had only been in existence since 1934 and was in no condition to threaten anyone, since it had largely fallen apart shortly after the war began. Nationalism of all kinds had been tainted by the rise of Fascism in Germany, and the alleged flirtation of some Nationalist intellectuals, such as Hugh MacDiarmid, with national defeatism – as in his remark that the English bourgeoise was "a far greater enemy" than the Germans.[39] Moreover, the Republic of Ireland's neutrality in the Second World War was considered a betrayal of Britain and a demonstration that Nationalists were prepared to acquiesce in the defeat of democracy. The SNP had also passed a motion in 1937 calling for Scotland to remain neutral in the event of war with Germany.

MI5 had been all over the tiny Scottish Nationalist movement because the SNP had also opposed conscription, but this was because they were mostly pacifists rather than Nazi sympathisers. The Nationalists claimed that the disproportionate Scottish casualties in the First World War showed that England's war leaders could not be trusted not to use the flower of Scottish manhood as cannon fodder. The SNP leader from 1942 to 1945, Professor Douglas Young (he taught Greek at Aberdeen University), was imprisoned for encouraging young men to refuse the call-up. It was further claimed he had discussed whether and how Scots could negotiate with the Nazis if Britain fell in the invasion that many expected was imminent in 1940.

The police appeared to be convinced that there were SNP fifth columnists who wanted to use the war to set up an independent Scottish republic. *The Sunday Times* in 2005 revealed documents from the National Archives[40] allegedly showing that Arthur Donaldson, a future leader of the SNP, had praised Germany and had said that the Nationalists should make a deal with the Nazis to run Scotland after England had fallen, in the manner of Vidkun Quisling in Norway. Donaldson was arrested and interned for six weeks in Barlinnie in 1941 for "subversive activities". The allegations were vehemently denied by his family and friends and was probably born of paranoia in the Security Service. In reality, most Scottish Nationalists were part of the Allied war effort, including Ian Hamilton, one of the Stone of Destiny thieves, who volunteered for service. He believed the SNP was out of tune with Scottish opinion during the war. "The programme was Scotland, free and neutral, and even as a school boy I could see that wasn't exactly the kind of programme that was gonna win a lot of votes, particularly in places like Clydebank which had been just bombed to Hell."[41]

Labour took full advantage of the SNP's equivocation on the eve of the war against Fascism. The Scottish Secretary of the Labour Party during the war, John Taylor, said it should be called the "Scottish Nazi Party". Tom Johnston wasn't above exploiting the SNP threat also, and while he didn't exactly call them traitors, he warned that they might soon threaten the integrity of the UK. He told Lord Reith in 1943 that the SNP could become the Sinn Fein of Scotland.[42] Scotland's economic future had to be secure if the Union was to be secure. This was the first outing for an argument that was used in Cabinet by every Scottish Secretary of State, Tory and Labour, for the next half century – deliver jobs to Scotland or face the consequences. By "playing the Scottish card", Johnston claimed to have attracted nearly 100,000 jobs to Scotland. Rolls-Royce at Hillington, producing Spitfire engines, alone employed 25,000 workers at its height. He certainly had a dramatic impact on the economic life of the country. Johnston devised a plan to electrify the Highlands with hydroelectric power, using the National Grid to unite Britain in a union of common voltage.

During the war, some Conservatives suggested that Johnston was himself a proto-Nationalist because he created a quasi-state in Scotland to promote public health, clear slums and promote industry. In his earlier days in the ILP, he had certainly been a supporter of home rule. Winston Churchill famously called him the "King of Scotland" and the Scottish Office did increase in size during his reign, though most of the administrative devolution to the Scottish Office had actually been introduced before the war under the Tory Scottish Secretary, Walter Elliot, who was largely responsible for the remarkable "moderne"-style St Andrew's House building on Edinburgh's Calton Hill. Johnston was also accused by the Conservatives of building, like Joseph Stalin, Socialism in one

country. However, this wasn't independence, but municipal socialism on a grand scale. Scotland became one big county council. But
Johnston's determination to create a Nationalist threat where none
existed may inadvertently have contributed to its emergence at
the end of the war. Politics abhors a vacuum, and having created
a political space for Nationalism something had to fill it. This duly
appeared in 1945, when the Nationalist Dr Robert McIntyre gained
Motherwell in a by-election, becoming the first-ever SNP member
of Parliament.

Labour said McIntyre only won this seat because he received
the tacit support of the Conservatives who, like the other parties in
the wartime coalition government, had agreed not to stand against
each other while conflict continued. This momentary victory did
not represent the emergence of a Nationalist movement as such,
and McIntyre lost the seat three months later in the 1945 General
Election when the SNP returned only 1% of the entire Scottish vote.
Nevertheless, Scottish Nationalism had achieved political representation, however briefly. The national question was on the political
table.

The administrative autonomy won by Johnston during the
war raised the question of Scotland's lack of political autonomy. If
all this good work could be achieved by the Scottish Office with its
army of civil servants, was there not a case for democratic oversight
of this devolved machinery of government? After all, every local
council is elected. Why should there not be a democratically elected
body to oversee the work of Johnston's super-council? It was almost
as if the state that had been removed from Scotland in 1707 had
partially been restored, albeit in a pre-democratic form. There was
a perceived democratic deficit here that demanded to be filled. This
is what led to one of the most intriguing episodes in the history
of Scottish Nationalism – the emergence of the National Covenant,
a demand for Scottish home rule that was signed by nearly two
million Scots by 1951.

This National Covenant was loosely based on the document
signed by the Covenanters in 1638 demanding religious autonomy
from Charles I. It was the brainchild in 1942 of an unsuccessful SNP
election candidate, and one of the founders of the National Party of
Scotland, John MacCormick – "King John" as he was called after a
heckler had suggested during a Glasgow University debate that he
wanted to rule an independent Scotland. The history was perhaps

questionable, since the Covenanters had not been seeking independence as such, but expressing their opposition to episcopacy in Scotland. But then, John MacCormick, though one of the founders of the SNP, wasn't really a Nationalist. He was an advocate of devolution, of home rule, who left the SNP in 1942, called himself a radical and ended up joining the Liberal Party. On his departure from the SNP, he set up a non-party body, the Scottish Convention, to promote broad-based home rule within the UK. This split in 1942 created a division in the Nationalist movement between gradualists and fundamentalists which lasted until Alex Salmond became leader in 1990.

The National Covenant called for a federal Scottish Parliament with power over domestic affairs only. MacCormick's initiative was a brilliant one – to take the home rule debate out of the hands of the Scottish political parties and hand it to the people, to what today is called "civic Scotland". And it worked. The Covenant was signed by two-thirds of the Scottish electorate, which was a considerable achievement, even if some of the names appeared more than once. When the Yes Scotland campaign tried to emulate the Covenant with its Yes Declaration in 2012, it sought only one million signatures, but in its first year had attracted just 200,000.

The National Covenant achieved nothing – at least not directly, because it was disowned by all the political parties and there was no mechanism for its proposed parliament to be put into effect. But it anticipated by half a century the decisive result of the 1997 Scottish Devolution Referendum, which set up a parliament similar to the one envisaged by MacCormick. His Scottish Convention was the template for the Scottish Constitutional Convention set up in 1988. The present leader of the SNP, Alex Salmond, is in some respects a political descendant of John MacCormick in that he aligned the Scottish National Party with this broad home rule movement in the 1990s and achieved unprecedented electoral success as a result.

Yet, when the National Covenant was being signed, the United Kingdom had never been more united, and support for the Union in Scotland had never been stronger. Scottish Nationalism, after the war, was politically insignificant and intellectually discredited. The very idea of creating a separate Scottish country based on ethnic identity seemed petty-minded if not positively reactionary. During the war, Scots had fought with English soldiers across North Africa and Europe in a great project to save Western civilisation.

They had been fighting, not in the interest of a British Empire or a ruling class, but for the people of a country, Great Britain, which had stood alone against tyranny and had led the world in a just war against fascism. Like the citizens of Clydebank during the blitz, they felt part of something that transcended domestic politics and national boundaries. This was a new popular Unionism, not based on tartan romanticism or imperial chauvinism. It was a Labour rather than a Tory Unionism.

THE WELFARE UNION

The Beveridge Report had been widely circulated and discussed before the end of the war. When soldiers were demobilised and saw the unprecedented improvements in public health achieved by wartime planning, they resolved that there should be no return to the 1930s, to economic depression, want and disease. The returning warriors voted Labour by a landslide, to the shock and surprise of Winston Churchill, who expected an electoral reward for his wartime leadership. This really was going to be a land fit for heroes, and the land in question was Great Britain. The Scottish Unionist Party, which had dominated Scottish general elections throughout the 1930s, found it was also left behind by the flight to Labour in 1945.

What remained of the British ruling class in 1945 understood as well as the demobilised soldiers that a return to the depression economics of the hungry 1930s would probably lead to the extinction of the capitalist system itself. Indeed, in Scotland under Johnston it arguably already had been. Scots had fought on the same side as the Russians in the Red Army, and the Soviet Union appeared to represent an alternative to the capitalist model. That the social achievements of the war years were largely retained after the war represented a triumph of political will over economic circumstances. Britain may have been bankrupt, and government debt levels were far higher than they are even today, but that didn't stop the Labour Government of 1945 setting up the National Health Service and implementing the Beveridge plan for social welfare.

The armoury of controls over industry acquired by the Scottish Office, mostly retained after the war, would have been inconceivable before it. Orthodox economists, which included former Labour Chancellors like Philip Snowden, believed that state intervention on any scale was incompatible with property rights and a violation of the laws of the market. But after the war, state interventionism advocated by the economist John Maynard Keynes dominated economic thinking. It took 40 years for neoliberal economics to be rehabilitated in the UK by Margaret Thatcher. Keynes wasn't a Socialist; he was a Liberal, but he realised that if capitalism was to survive it would have to be saved from itself and the state would have to undertake responsibility for ensuring that economic depressions didn't happen. Full employment became an explicit objective of national policy, and remained so, essentially, until the 1980s.

Above all, the post-war settlement was about social security for the whole of Great Britain. The National Health Service, the landmark achievement of the 1945 Labour government, was welcomed in Scotland with national rejoicing. In a country where half the population still lived in overcrowded conditions, and had suffered in relative silence for 200 years, this was nothing short of miraculous. Jim Sillars, the future SNP deputy leader, recalls that "my father and a miner's wife who stayed beside us were dancing up and down the path" when the Attlee government was elected in 1945. "It was a wonderful thing," he said in *Road to Referendum*. "We really believed that Socialism would cover Britain from John O'Groats to Land's End."

Because Scotland's health and economic problems had been much worse than England's, Scotland could expect to benefit disproportionately from the resources of the entire UK being devoted to the eradication of "want and idleness". Nationalisation of coal, the railways, and iron and steel industries by the Labour government of Clement Attlee also seemed to mark the dawn of a new age in which the means of production would at last be under democratic control. The Red Clydesiders had scarcely dared to dream in the 1920s that anything like this could happen. The Distribution of Industry Act of 1945 promised development areas to which manufacturing would be located by public finance or by government direction. It was hoped this would rectify the North/South imbalances in the UK economy.

In the 1930s, while Scottish heavy industry slumped, a new economic cycle had begun in the south of England based on the new consumer industries. They manufactured cars, radios, vacuum cleaners and washing machines – the artefacts of the new world of leisure. Scotland had missed out on all this because most capital investment had been attracted to London. There had been no real market for consumer goods in Scotland because of the small size of the Scottish middle-class and the low wages of industrial workers. What the Distribution of Industry Act promised was nothing less than a reversal of this relentless concentration of economic activity in the south-east of England. It also aroused hopes among the relatively impoverished Scottish lower middle-classes that Scotland could become part of the future and afford labour-saving devices and even motor cars. The growing state bureaucracies in health, education and central government also provided white-collar jobs for middle-class Scots, like Alex Salmond's civil servant parents. For the first time in 200 years, it began to look as if young professionals would not have to leave Scotland to seek careers.

At first, it was the middle-classes, too, who benefited from council housing because they were able to afford the relatively high rents and had secure incomes. But as housebuilding turned into something of a national obsession in the early 1950s, the working classes started migrating en masse from the slums of the city centres to peripheral schemes and new towns. In the 20 years after 1945, more than half a million houses were built in Scotland, three times as many as in the two decades before the Second World War. In the peak year of 1953 alone, 40,000 new houses were completed in Scotland, enough to house a small city of 100,000 people.[43]

The vast majority of these new homes were council houses, which left Scotland, in the late 1960s, with a rate of home-ownership that the future Scottish Secretary Malcolm Rifkind observed was "lower than in Communist Hungary or Czechoslovakia".[44] Unfortunately, some of the council housing estates had a distinctly Stalinist quality to them, too. A dull uniformity of design, grey harling, no pubs and very little recreation space turned them rapidly into what the comedian Billy Connolly called "deserts with windaes". But compared with what had gone before, the stinking inner-city slums riddled with disease and despair, even these uniform homes were an immense social achievement. Before the war, 40% of Scots lived in houses with fewer than two rooms and with communal privies. The families who moved into these bright new homes with bathrooms and kitchens could hardly believe their good fortune. It was only when system-building and multi-storey blocks marched over the landscape in the 1960s that council housing became discredited.

Housebuilding was an economic strategy as well as a social one, driving the consumer economy of the 1950s, creating jobs and spending power among the working classes of Scotland. It is often assumed that when Harold Macmillan said that most people had "never had it so good" he was only referring to England, but Scotland boomed in the 1950s as well. Average working-class incomes in 1959 were nearly three times what they were in 1939. Scots began to acquire televisions and washing machines. Unemployment remained below 3% until well into the 1960s. Even the supposedly declining Clyde shipyards were working near capacity through the 1950s. Shipbuilding was still the biggest industry in Scotland at the end of that decade. Lithgow's was the largest ship and marine engine-building firm in the world.

Many people had expected that, after 1945, Scottish industry would collapse in a post-war depression as it had after the Great War demobilisation. But the expansion of the European economies thanks to the cash pumped in by the US Marshall Plan meant that history did not repeat itself. Moreover, there was no competition in the 1950s from Germany, whose industry had been devastated by Allied bombing. The Luftwaffe's blitz of Clydeside, by contrast, had been almost entirely counterproductive – it had united the people of Scotland and England in their determination to fight Germany, while failing to inflict any lasting damage to the Scottish shipbuilding industry which simply picked up from where it left off.

Scots believed that the social transformation had been achieved through being part of Great Britain, and they were right. The welfare state had been introduced UK-wide, and the economic planning was being mounted on a British-wide basis. Income levels between Scotland and England converged through the 1950s. The government in Westminster, elected in part on Scottish votes, produced a truly national NHS and provided security for all citizens of Britain on an equal basis. This was a legacy of the collective spirit generated across Britain by the war effort. It was widely believed that public ownership of industry – rail, steel, mines – could only make sense on a UK-wide basis, too. Certainly, the compensation to the previous private owners needed the clout of the UK Exchequer.

Working-class Unionism was no longer based on fear of Roman Catholicism, but it remained a powerful force against Nationalism and home rule. The Scottish trade unions saw solidarity as the means of promoting the interests of workers across Britain. Unity, after all, was strength, and the combined forces of the British working class were considered necessary to combat the political power of capital. Collective bargaining in industry worked when workers stood together, irrespective of geography. Communism did not appeal to many British workers but there was considerable support for Socialist Internationalism on the intellectual Left in the 1950s and 1960s. Scottish Nationalism had very little to offer in response to the UK welfare state. What could independence possibly achieve that was better?

SUEZ AND THE END OF EMPIRE

But while the Union between Scotland and England had never been stronger at home, the ties that bound the British Empire together were loosening, rapidly. The South-East Asian colonies were lost during the war. India, "the Jewel in the Crown", achieved independence in 1947. The British Empire appeared to be crumbling as between 1945 and 1967 no fewer than 26 former British colonies declared independence. The Suez crisis in 1957, when a misconceived British invasion of Egypt was effectively vetoed by America, confirmed that Britain was no longer a military power of significance in the world. As the writer William McIlvanney put it, "Suez was for me, a full stop on the fantasy that the British still had a kind of clout."[45] Harold Macmillan's wind of change blew then away the rest of the African colonies, culminating in the Rhodesia crisis in 1965. David Livingstone's Malawi went its own way in 1964.

The Empire was no longer either a source of national pride in Scotland or a field for material advancement. Scots could no longer go abroad to manage colonial administrations or run companies that depended on imperial preference, still less sell opium to the masses in China. Missionaries still worked in Africa, but the scramble was over. Scottish soldiers still fought in Aden and Malaya, but the glory days were past and the regiments were fading into history. One of the biggest single issues in Scotland in the late 1960s was the campaign led by Lt Colonel Colin "Mad Mitch" Mitchell to "Save the Argylls" – the Argyll and Sutherland Highlanders Regiment. The Commonwealth, which succeeded the Empire in the 1950s, was essentially a device for managing the decline of Empire rather than perpetuating it. Scots continued to emigrate to former British colonies like Canada and Australia in the 1950s and 1960s. But as the British flag was rolled up in dominion, territory and protectorate, there were fewer and fewer foreign lands in which Scottish soldiers could fight and die for the British flag as they had been doing for 200 years.

Historians such as Richard J Finlay insist that "Scots were more imperially minded than other parts of the United Kingdom".[46] That may seem hard to believe today when, for most Scots, the Empire is ancient history. It is not easy to understand quite why people in this relatively impoverished part of the UK should have felt any great affection for the imperial enterprise. After all, what did the Empire ever do for Scotland? Well, it provided the 1938 Empire Exhibition in Glasgow, for one thing, which confirmed that there was still a big economic investment by Scotland in the Union as late as the eve of the Second World War. But after the war, everything changed, even as the surface of things remained largely the same. By the late 1950s, Scots were still part of Great Britain, but it was a Britain that had a limited international footprint; it was a Britain united in a new ideal of collective social security rather than military conquest.

The Empire had been regarded by many Scots as a moral enterprise, a civilising influence on the world as well as a field of economic opportunity, and now it was no more. What took its place was a different kind of moral community – social democracy, government by enlightened technocrats. The man from the ministry looked after the economy using Keynesian tools of economic management, while the man in the white coat applied science to health, agriculture and power generation. It was all about rational planning and doing things the right way, without emotion or Utopian ideas. Academics talked of "the end of ideology", of the new consensus between governments of Left and Right that the economy could be managed for the benefit of all. National Plans would bring all together and make Britain prosperous – all of Britain. There was an instrumental quality to the Union as it emerged after the war. Scots became used to the language of the "levers" of economic management, and when things went wrong, in the 1960s and 1970s, they wondered why those levers were not being pulled in their direction.

THE WEE MAGIC STANE

During the 1950s, in this new Britain, Scottish Nationalism seemed at best an irrelevance, at worst a step into the past. The Left saw it as a reactionary force which divided workers and diverted them away from class struggle. The Scottish National Party remained divided between fundamentalists and home rulers, though this hardly mattered since the movement barely registered in any general election in the 1950s. Arthur Donaldson's claim that the party had 1,000 members in Scotland was optimistic, to say the least. However, the SNP managed briefly to command the attention of the nation when, on Christmas Day 1950, a group of Nationalist students, led by Ian Hamilton, stole the Stone of Destiny from Westminster Abbey, damaging the Coronation Chair in the process.

This Pythonesque caper, and the subsequent police hunt for the "Wee Magic Stane", as it became known, caught the imagination of Scots, who needed something to smile about during the cold, grey winter of 1950. It remains one of the most successful PR stunts in Scottish Nationalist history. The reaction of the British establishment was predictably over the top. "Sacrilege at Westminster!" thundered *The Times*, describing it as "a coarse and vulgar crime". The thieves claimed that the Stone of Scone, on which Scottish kings had been crowned until it was stolen by Edward I in November 1296, should have been returned in 1328 under the terms of the Treaty of Northampton. They were only helping England fulfil its side of the bargain. Unfortunately, the students dropped the Stone as they were trying to get it out of the Coronation Chair, where it had lain for 700 years. They found to their horror that they had two magic stones. Nevertheless, they somehow managed to drive the shattered relic to Scotland, where it was repaired by a Glasgow stonemason.

The stone was returned to Arbroath Abbey four months later with a rather humble letter of apology to King George VI. However, perhaps because of the breakage, there were persistent rumours it was not the real stone that was returned. When I researched a TV programme on the 30th anniversary of the heist, I came across numerous Nationalists who claimed to have fragments of it on their mantelpieces, set in rings and located in paperweights. The First Minister, Alex Salmond, insists it was not the real Stone of Scone that was taken by Edward I in the 13th century, but probably a sandstone block used to cover the cesspit at Scone. That's an attractive idea. But Ian Hamilton, who went on to become a distinguished Scottish QC and write a book about the affair, insists that the stone they returned was the real one. If it had been switched by the Abbot of Scone, as Salmond suggests, then surely the real one would have been produced when Robert I was crowned there in 1306.

The Attorney-General decided not to prosecute the stone thieves – even though they'd broken into Westminster Abbey, caused criminal damage and clearly broken the law. Hamilton says "they were feart to prosecute us".[47] But their "good homes" backgrounds had a lot to do with it, too. If the gang had been working class and had broken into a national monument they might not have got off so lightly. But the Labour Government didn't want to create any martyrs to the cause, even a cause as apparently hopeless as Scottish Nationalism in the 1950s, and preferred not to give the thieves any more of the oxygen of publicity.

The theft of the Coronation Stone was an event of no direct political significance, but it entered popular culture, and has featured in numerous books and feature films, the most recent in 2008 in an Ealing-style comedy starring Robert Carlyle and Charlie Cox. The stone episode was much more popular than the other Nationalist civil disobedience in the 1950s – the blowing up of Elizabeth II post boxes, on the grounds she was Elizabeth I in Scotland. Most Scots regarded that as simple vandalism. But with the stone, the combination of wit and daring had a John Buchan quality to it, which appealed to Scots brought up on books like *John Macnab*. But perhaps it also marked the moment when the allure of monarchy had started to fade north of the border. In a previous age, patriotic Scots, who after all fought for King and Country, might have taken offence at this iconoclasm. The emotional attachment to royalty, like the emotional attachment to the British Empire, was starting to fade along with deference and respect for authority.

History repeated itself as farce in 1996 when, after a letter-writing campaign organised by the Skye Bridge campaigner, Robbie the Pict, the stone was returned to Scotland by Michael Forsyth, the last Conservative Secretary of State for Scotland. I don't know what he hoped to achieve by this faintly ridiculous ceremony in which the stone was piped across the border in an army Land Rover. Presumably, by placing the stone in Edinburgh Castle, next to the Scottish regalia that had been disinterred by Sir Walter Scott in 1818, he hoped to reignite the Tory patriotism of the romantic novelist. If so, it didn't work. In the General Election the next year, the Tories were wiped out in Scotland.

But in the 1950s, Scottish Conservatism (or rather Scottish Unionism, since the Tories hadn't yet changed their name) was in no need of patriotic stunts. The post-war settlement may have been a Labour creation, and the pillars of the modern welfare state established by the Attlee government of 1945. But while Scots voted in large numbers for Labour in 1945, they never fully made the break from conservative Unionism. Labour failed to seal the deal and their post-war electoral achievement was short-lived. Scotland remained a small 'c' conservative country in the 1950s, and the Scottish Unionist Party came roaring back, winning a majority of seats and a majority of votes in the 1955 General Election – the first and last time any party has done that since the Second World War. It looked like the 1930s all over again. A spell of Labour government followed by a reversion to conservative Unionism.

But this was not a return to the politics of the past. This was a very different kind of Unionism in the 1950s, based on a radically different ideological premise – corporatism. The Conservatives had bought into the post-war settlement, the "Butskellite Consensus" as it was called, and Scottish voters clearly felt the Tories could now be trusted to maintain the UK welfare state, nationalised industries and the National Health Service. Harold Macmillan, who became Prime Minister after Suez, boasted of building more council houses than Labour. "Supermac" was the embodiment of one-nation Conservatism. His grandfather, the son of an Arran crofter, had founded the Macmillan publishing company in the 19th century. Many Scots saw him as a reassuring patrician presence after the trauma of Suez.

Why did Scots vote Tory in such numbers in the 1950s when Labour had given them so much after the war? Perhaps many Scots were more comfortable with Conservatism then because they were more comfortable with authority. Scots experience in the home, the schoolroom, the barracks and the Kirk was "know your place", "speak when spoken to", "obey orders" and "fear the Lord". Labour later installed as Shadow Scottish Secretary one Willie Ross, a former army major who spoke like a Scottish headmaster and ran the Scottish Office like a military HQ. He went on to be Labour's longest serving Scottish Secretary.

The Tories also successfully targeted the women's vote, sympathising with the difficulty mothers were having with rationing and playing on their fears of Glasgow gangs and alcoholic husbands that were hyped in Conservative-leaning Scottish newspapers. And Scotland remained a religious country in the 1950s – Church of Scotland membership peaked in the same year that the Conservative and Unionist Party won its greatest-ever election victory. The Kirk in the 1950s still sounded like the Conservative Party at prayer. It was essentially a middle-class institution, though many working-class voters still regarded Church membership as a mark of social progress, and as Protestants, they voted Unionist.

However, the main problem with Labour after the war was the state. The armoury of wartime controls on the economy was largely retained after the war. This meant increasingly that the UK was governed from Whitehall, and while this was a very benign form of dirigisme, there was concern that Scotland was becoming remote from centres of decision-making. Scottish Conservatives warned that Scotland risked being marginalised in the new United Kingdom, dominated by Socialists in London.

Churchill played on this, accusing Labour of "totalitarianism" in its policies of nationalisation and direction of industry. In the 1950 General Election campaign, he said enigmatically, "I would never adopt the view that Scotland should be forced into the serfdom of Socialism by a vote in the House of Commons". This was interpreted by some as a suggestion that Scotland should seek independence rather than have Socialism imposed from England. Churchill had, of course, briefly advocated "home rule all round" before the First World War. But it seems unlikely that the British war leader had turned Nationalist. It was a political tease – an attempt to capitalise on Scottishness at Labour's expense, while playing on fears of Communism.

This right-wing attack on the overbearing Labour state seemed to work at the ballot box, initially at least. But it was a political poisoned pill because it played on suspicions of London domination which could equally apply to Conservative governments in Westminster. Both Labour and the Conservatives were advocates of an undiluted Union in the 1950s. Labour still had a commitment to a Scottish assembly in its constitution, but it was of interest only because of attempts within the party to have it removed. The Conservatives continued to do well in Scottish elections up until and including the 1964 General Election, when Labour finally took power in Westminster. But the writing was on the wall for Tory Unionism in Scotland, though it wasn't easy to read. Instead of switching directly to Labour, the Scottish voters took an eccentric turn and, in November 1967, elected a young woman lawyer, Winnie Ewing, at a by-election in one of the safest Labour seats in Scotland, the mining constituency of Hamilton. The high noon of Unionism was over.

Mel Gibson as William Wallace in Icon Entertainment International's *Braveheart* (1995). Myth-making money-machine or a sense of Scottish spirit? In spite of extensive historical inaccuracies, the film is one of Alex Salmond's favourites.
Photo credit: Herald Times Group

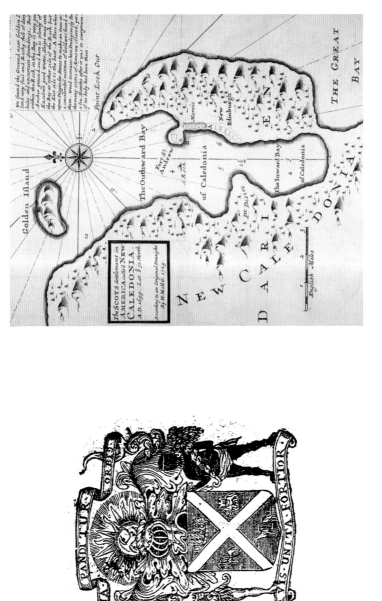

Coat-of-arms of the Company of Scotland Trading to Africa and the Indies (left), whose ill-fated Darien Scheme was an attempt to establish "Caledonia" on the Isthmus of Panama (right) in the late 1690s.

Contrasting portrayals of King George IV's visit to Edinburgh in 1822. The tartan pageantry increased his popularity in Scotland, as Wilkie's flattering painting suggests (right), but contemporary caricatures (left) offer a different perspective.

On the 13th and 14th March 1941, the town of Clydebank was largely destroyed by Luftwaffe raids. Some 528 people were killed, more than 617 seriously injured, and 48,000 lost their homes. *Photo credit: Herald Times Group*

James Keir Hardie (1856 – 1915), the founder of the British Labour Party. Many nationalists lionise Hardie as the father of Scottish home rule, but his work was much more far-reaching, including campaigns for self-rule for India and an end to segregation in South Africa.

Thomas "Tom" Johnston (1881 – 1965), Labour's greatest-ever Scottish Secretary of State. "He introduced rent controls, promoted council housing and even launched a primordial version of the NHS."
Photo credit: Herald Times Group

Andy Stewart and Robert Wilson in 1962 filming the White
Heather Club, the Scottish variety show that ran from 1958 to 1968.
Photo credit: Herald Times Group

Secretary of State for Scotland Willie Ross at the opening of the
Red Road flats in 1966. *Photo credit: Herald Times Group*

May Day rally in Queen's Park, Glasgow, 1974. Prime Minister
Harold Wilson speaks to the crowd.
Photo credit: Herald Times Group

The seeds of power: a younger Gordon Brown (top), former Prime Minister; and Alex Salmond (bottom), First Minister of Scotland.
Photo credit: Herald Times Group | Gordon Brown image from Scottish Media Newspapers Archive

Scenes of jubilation for Scottish football fans at Wembley in 1977
as Scotland beat England 2-1, their first victory in the home of the
"Auld Enemy" in ten years.
Photo credit: Herald Times Group

Tommy Sheridan at George Square, Glasgow, during an anti-Poll Tax demo.
Photo credit: Herald Times Group

1998, Donald Dewar, the first First Minister of Scotland, standing at the site of the Scottish Parliament building before construction.
Photo credit: Herald Times Group | Scottish Media Newspapers Archive

1999, (left to right) Donald Dewar, Queen Elizabeth II and Sir David Steel, the first Presiding Officer of the Scottish Parliament.
Photo credit: Herald Times Group | Scottish Media Newspapers Archive

Henry McLeish, the second First Minister of Scotland,
following his resignation in June 2001.
Photo credit: Herald Times Group | by Graham Hamilton

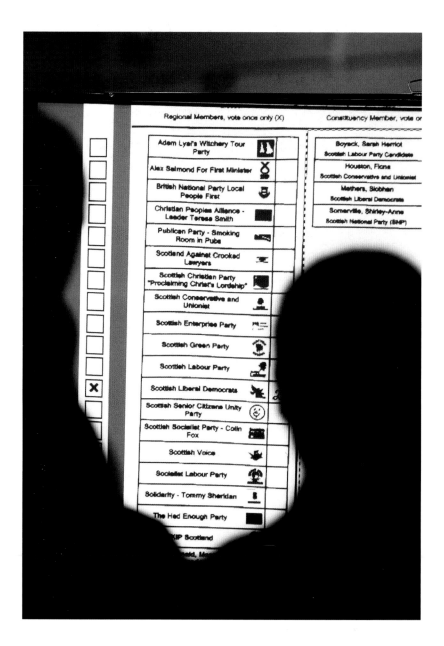

During the 2007 Scottish Parliament election there were many invalid – or "spoiled" – ballots, with around 140,000 votes being discarded due to confusion surrounding the new voting system.
Photo credit: Herald Times Group

15th October 2012, St Andrew's House, Edinburgh – Alex Salmond and David Cameron agree on terms for the 2014 Independence Referendum. *Photo credit: Herald Times Group | by Gordon Terris*

Nigel Farrage, the leader of UKIP, under siege from protestors in Edinburgh, during his visit in May 2013. UKIP's growth in England is at odds with their lack of popularity in Scotland, fuelling the debate around the UK in Europe and Scotland's relationship with the union in the EU.
Photo credit: Herald Times Group

CHAPTER EIGHT
THE 1960S — EXCEPT FOR VIEWERS IN SCOTLAND

GEORGE HERIOT'S School was endowed by the goldsmith George Heriot, banker to King James VI, in the 17th century, as a "hospital" for the "puir, faitherless bairns" of Edinburgh. I was neither poor nor an orphan when I was enrolled there in the 1950s. This charitable institution, which had created a remarkable network of free schools in the city by the start of the 19th century, educating thousands of working-class children, had been captured in 1885 by the Edinburgh middle-classes, who turned it into a fee-paying school. The poor bairns were no longer welcome, though a number of free places were reserved for "foundationers". By the 1950s, Heriot's had become a special kind of fee-paying school that received a direct grant from the local council to keep the charges low enough for the Edinburgh professional classes to afford. So much for the egalitarian Scottish education system. The Scottish middle-classes, in Edinburgh at least, knew how to look after their own.

I arrived aged five years old and was plunged into what seemed to me a dark and threatening environment compared with my green and pleasant time in Finchley, London, where I had attended "Sunshine School" and spent most of my time playing in friends' gardens. It was much too cold for that in Edinburgh, and play was replaced by rote learning and the strap, or "tawse" liberally applied. There wasn't a lot of sunshine at Heriot's at the start of the 1960s and my older brother, Robin, loathed it so much that he ran away at 14 to join an Aldermaston CND march. I stuck it out, cultivating a sullen indifference towards school activities and suspicion of social contact.

Scottish playground culture in those days was almost entirely one of competitive violence, where you established yourself in the pecking order by a willingness to fight and play football, often at the same time. I never "got" football, owing to a genetic deficiency, setting me apart from the male community in Scotland for the rest of my life. But for some reason, I did quite well at fighting – possibly because I was taller than most of my pawky wee Scottish contemporaries. I rose fairly rapidly in the society of the fist until, at the age of about ten, I met my match in the shape of a pug-faced boy called Brian Mackie who was clearly my physical superior. Unfortunately, I didn't realise this until I found myself eating the tarmac on the school playground. The culture of violence didn't appeal so much after that, though it was an ever-present fact of life.

As a teenager, the electricity of violence seemed to be everywhere in Scotland. On the city streets, at football matches, in pubs. Even at the youth club dances in church halls which I started attending when I was about 15, violence could and frequently did erupt spontaneously. There were notorious gangs based on peripheral housing estates that operated a kind of regimental system – Young Gillie, The Inch, Young Niddrie Terror, Young Mental Drylaw – with their own ethos, battle honours and even songs. Given Scotland's martial history and the fact so many working-class Scots had family connections with the armed forces, I suppose this was hardly surprising. Teenage violence was hardly unique to Scotland as the mods and rockers riots in Brighton testified in the 1960s. But even in the most middle-class areas of Edinburgh where I lived it was everywhere. I recall my astonishment when one of my friends casually assaulted a young person at a chip shop for no apparent reason. This was not fertile ground for the Summer of Love in 1967.

THE SECULAR REFORMATION

At the start of the 1960s, Scotland remained a joyless and colourless place where the Kirk still strongly influenced public morality – "sex" famously was something Edinburgh ladies bought coal in, pubs closed at 10, and recreation beyond football was largely non-existent, unless you included Sunday school. But by the end of the 1960s ... well, not a lot had changed, to be perfectly honest. Scotland still looked cold, grey, poor. However, beneath the surface, a revolution had occurred which destroyed the old Scotland of pursed-lipped conformity and undermined the political and moral allegiances that had endured largely intact since the 1707 Union. The British Empire had already crashed and burned after the Suez Crisis in 1957, and now the moral and psychological hegemony of the Kirk was to be challenged. The age of deference was over.

The most obvious sign of this was the decline in church attendance in a society where the Presbyterian Kirk had dominated ordinary people's lives for centuries through the Session and had even occupied the space left by the absence of a national politics. Church of Scotland membership peaked at 1.32 million in 1956 when attendance was as high as it had ever been in the previous 100 years. Then, suddenly, it collapsed in one of the most dramatic secularisations experienced by any country in the world. The Kirk lost 65% of its communicants within 20 years. The divorce rate in Scotland increased by 400% between 1960 and 1974.

Callum Brown, in *Religion and Society in Scotland since 1707*, described the collapse of all forms of religious observance in Scotland in the 1960s as "cataclysmic". Hugh McLeod, Professor of Church History at Birmingham University, has described the "long sixties" between 1958 and 1974 as "a rupture in religious history as great as that brought about by the Reformation". Since Scotland was one of the countries that led the Reformation in the 16th century, this rupture was all the more dramatic here. Scotland has had a history of intense militant Christianity from the Covenanters to the Disruption, and had an education system largely shaped by the Kirk. It is hard to believe that all this could disappear, in historical terms, overnight. And yet it did.

It's not entirely clear why this great secularisation happened so rapidly in the 1960s, though clearly the rise of youth culture, consumerism, the contraceptive pill and the spread of television all played a part. Urban renewal and the growth of new towns in Scotland such as Livingston and Cumbernauld broke up the family networks and the connections between communities and local ministries. Religious dogmatism was challenged by the spread of progressive ideas and education after the war. Competing belief systems like Marxism became influential in universities, even after Soviet Communism had been discredited by the brutal suppression of the Hungarian Spring in 1956.

More directly, people had seen what government could achieve, and social progress undermined the community of faith. A religion that offered consolation in the afterlife, and had tended to blame poverty and ill-health on lack of godliness, had no place in the age of the welfare state. The Rev Thomas Chalmers had been implacably opposed to welfare and economic interventionism, and thought trade unions and even Chartism were the work of the Devil.[48] The Church of Scotland before the Second World War was very different to the emollient, liberal and pacific faith of the Church today, with its multiculturalism, social concern and opposition to war. It was hard and uncompromising in its antisocial certainties and gave moral support to the British imperial establishment. The Kirk only had itself to blame when people turned away from this austere and unforgiving institution.

A large part of Scottish Protestantism's image problem in the 1960s was that the Kirk had become identified with bigotry and sectarianism. In the 1920s, the Church of Scotland's attitude to the Catholic community in Glasgow was shameful and racist. In the 1950s and 1960s, the annual Orange marches thorough Catholic areas of Glasgow were like the occupations of a foreign power. This image of intolerance, also apparent in the Ulster Unionists' opposition to civil rights in Northern Ireland in the 1960s and 1970s did immense damage to the appeal of established religion to the Scottish middle-classes.

When I was a teenager, I associated religion almost entirely with violence at Celtic-Rangers football fixtures. Religious sectarianism has been one of the worst vices of working-class Scotland. As late as 1982, during the visit of Pope John Paul II to Glasgow, after the removal of some trees from Bellahouston Park a Kirk minister interviewed on TV warned: "Trees today; Protestants tomorrow."[49] The comedian Robbie Coltrane satirised the Orange Scot in his character "Mason Boyne". But Pastor Jack Glass and his 20th century Reformation movement managed to be more ridiculous than any caricature as he railed against the Catholic Antichrist in the 1960s and 1970s. The late Pastor Glass even picketed the General Assembly in 2002 when it finally issued an apology for its sectarian past. The General Assembly of the Church of Scotland stopped vilifying Catholics well before the 1960s. Unfortunately, by then no one was listening to it.

Suddenly, people had more things to do on a Sunday. Mostly, I suspect, it was the discovery by Scots that other people didn't live like Scottish Presbyterians, under a kind of moral dictatorship which saturated the personal sphere, and which accelerated the decline in religious observance in the 1960s. The stifling, depressive quality of Scottish life in the first half of the 20th century was captured in a remarkable film, *My Childhood* by the Scottish film-maker Bill Douglas in 1972. Based on his own experiences in a working-class community of Newcraighall on the outskirts of Edinburgh, this is one of the most important films to emerge from Scotland in the 20th century. Filmed in austere black and white, Douglas used silence and long takes to emphasise the suffocating quality of a culture in which "idle chatter" was considered sinful and human warmth was regarded as morally suspect. Unfortunately, the film is so powerful that it's inclined to leave members of the audience feeling vaguely suicidal after watching it.

You only needed to compare this with the upbeat, romantic comedy *Gregory's Girl*, directed by Bill Forsyth little more than a decade later in Cumbernauld, to see the difference the 1960s made. Though it was shot in a new town that became a by-word for civic ugliness, *Gregory's Girl* captured the profound social change in Scotland after the 1960s. This was a classless world, free of slums and unemployment, where even gender stereotypes were disintegrating. (The story turns on Gregory's "girl" being better than he is at football and how he doesn't care.) The background is shopping malls and security, without tyrannical bosses and ranting Kirk ministers. It's a rare portrayal of a Scotland at ease with itself.

For it has long been a literary cliché that Scots are tortured and guilt-ridden individuals, deformed by Calvinism. Scots' reputation for dourness and gloom is generally traced to the Kirk's suspicion of social activities like dancing and music, poetry and song, and even conversation if it didn't have some spiritual dimension. The Kirk certainly was ragin' against just about everything from ice-cream cones to bicycles. Presbyterianism, with its joyless commonwealth, laced with hypocrisy and cant, was lampooned by Robert Burns in *Holy Willie's Prayer* and even the Tory novelist Sir Walter Scott gave the Kirk a hard time in *Guy Mannering*. More recently, prominent figures in the 20th century Scottish literary "renaissance" such as Edwin Muir, who called Calvinism a "culture of erasure", and novelists like Iain Crichton Smith, author of *Consider the Lilies*, mounted a devastating propaganda assault on Calvinism, which they claimed had left Scottish people emotionally and intellectually deformed. Indeed, many blamed the perceived lack of Scottish artistic achievement in Scotland in the Victorian age, and the degeneration of Scottish literature into sentimentality in what became known as the Kailyard School, the malign influence of the Holy Willies.

Presbyterianism was a religion in which public exposure and shame were instruments of social control. The radical Scottish "anti-psychiatrist" RD Laing's *The Divided Self* in 1960 was interpreted by many as a reaction against Laing's repressive Presbyterian upbringing in Glasgow in the 1920s, drawing again on the Scots' antisyzygy. The climate of moral fear and guilt engendered by Calvinism is said to have contributed to the repressed, tongue-tied and socially autistic character of many Scots. The writer Dr Carol Craig in her book, *The Scots Crisis of Confidence*, argues that the Scots have developed a predisposition to negativity largely because of this "Calvinist inheritance".[50] This is marked by conformity, authoritarianism, Utopianism, judgementalism, a fear of personal exposure, and a tendency to see things in strict either/or terms. That is quite a charge sheet.

Now, Calvinism wasn't a lot of fun, certainly, and Presbyterianism was morally oppressive – the influence of the local Kirk Session was strong, especially in rural areas. However, it is not entirely clear that these behavioural rigidities were uniquely Calvinist, or even that the Scots were, historically, lacking in confidence. Those cowering Calvinistic conformists seemed able to run the British Empire. Projects like the Darien Scheme hardly betrayed a lack of optimism; rather the reverse. Scots certainly weren't timid and tongue-tied when they were setting up the international trading companies, establishing missions in hostile lands, or leading armies in colonial wars, and that was in the 18th and 19th centuries when Calvinism really was puritanical.

In fact, evangelical Christianity arguably tended to make its adherents take greater risks because they believed, like David Livingstone, that they had been "chosen" to follow their vocations and therefore had God's backing for their enterprises. Part of Livingstone's problem was that he believed in himself far too much, and seemed to think his manic adventures were divinely inspired and protected by God. Schooling in Presbyterian Scotland was strict and regimented, but that wasn't unique to Scotland. English public schools created a similar emotionally barren and brutal psychological climate, in which were raised the sons of the aristocrats and capitalists, and it didn't do them any harm. Well, it did, of course – but it didn't seem to make the members of the English ruling classes under-confident as individuals or as a social group, and it certainly didn't stop them turning their country into the imperial superpower of the 19th century.

The image of Scottish Calvinism as a dark repressive force has been challenged in recent years by theologians such as Professor Donald Macleod, who claim there are no grounds for believing that the Kirk, certainly by the 19th century, was anti-art or even that it was particularly anti-democratic. Presbyterianism began life in the Reformation as a rejection of Papal authority. Scottish sociologists, like David McCrone, say that Presbyterianism was not only more democratic than other religions, but that the doctrine of predestination promoted egalitarianism because members of the Elect were all equal as individuals before God. The Scottish educationalist George Davie in his book, *The Democratic Intellect,* in 1962, argued that this egalitarianism defined the open and meritocratic Scottish university system in the 19th century, which produced large numbers of generalist graduates rather than languid members of a social elite. The reaction against authoritarian religion in the 1960s might itself be seen as a continuation of the critical and democratic tradition that inspired the Covenanters' revolutionary rejection of bishops and kings.

Yet what we actually saw in the 1960s wasn't an attempt to reform Presbyterianism, but to erase it – a rejection of all forms of conventional religious authority. The 1960s counter-culture had echoes of one of those emotional, evangelical "awakenings" that used to erupt in the Kirk every 30 years or so. However, this wasn't so much an awakening as a shutting down of the old religion, which was left in a coma from which it has yet to recover. Secularisation was so complete and so rapid in Scotland that it can legitimately be described as a cultural revolution. It has created a gulf of understanding that makes it very difficult for modern Scots to make sense of much Scottish history.

I am particularly ill-qualified to comment personally on Scottish ecclesiastical history because to me religion was a closed book: literally. There were Bibles on the stacked bookshelves of my home in Edinburgh but they were never opened. They testified to a history of religious observance in our family, which had been extinguished by the time I came along. My parents weren't actively hostile to religious people, but they both hated the Kirk as an institution and regarded it, like many intellectuals, as a barrier to Scotland's civic evolution and its cultural development. Even as she lay dying in an Edinburgh hospital, my mother refused to be visited by the well-meaning woman minister offering pastoral care.

This had a lot to do with the fact that my grandfather had been thrown out of the Church for being a pacifist in the First World War. Many Scots never forgave the Kirk for urging hundreds of thousands of young Scots men to sign up and die in the trenches in the original "stupid" war. My father remained a pacifist in the 1930s, and was a conscientious objector in the Second World War, earning in the process 14 years of lost promotion in the civil service career structure. The Church was seen by my parents as an instrument of social control and Kirk ministers as at best sanctimonious busybodies, at worst moral tyrants. The irony was that my parents became active members of the peace movement in Scotland, and ended up in the 1960s spending a great deal of time with like-minded Christians and clerics of all kinds.

During the 1970s, the Church of Scotland changed beyond recognition. As its numbers declined, it ceased being the Tory Party at prayer and emerged as the leading voice for social reform and, eventually, political reform in Scotland, taking a leading role in the process of constitutional change. In 1988, the Scottish Constitutional Convention staged its declaration of Scottish sovereignty in the Church of Scotland Assembly Building on Edinburgh's Mound. The Rev Thomas Chalmers would not have approved. His Kirk defended the existing order of things and opposed political Nationalism. How his Kirk became the body that, in 1988, stood against Margaret Thatcher, a politician whose attitudes were very similar to those of the great Disrupter, is a remarkable story. Perhaps if it had made this break 20 years earlier the Kirk might have survived the 1960s. It looked too much like a deathbed conversion for a Kirk that had been a profoundly reactionary force in Scottish politics.

Scotland was simply a different country at the end of the 1960s. Young men like me were growing their hair long, listening to Jack Bruce, Donovan and The Incredible String Band. Working-class Scots who had worshipped violence started smoking cannabis, listening to *Astral Weeks* and talking about peace. A bewildering variety of spiritualisms entered the marketplace of the divine, from Scientology to Zen Buddhism. The New Age arrived in a caravan park in Forres in 1963 as the Findhorn Foundation became a centre for the exploration of a bewildering variety of mystical trends. The Friends of the Western Buddhist Order set up in Glasgow's Sauchiehall Street, there was the Gestalt Therapy movement in Edinburgh, Hari Krishna congas chanted their way along most of the city centres followed by the orange-dressed followers of Bhagwan Shree Rajneesh. The very widespread use of psychotropic drugs like LSD gave a kind of chemical enlightenment to young people whose spiritual horizons had hitherto been defined by pints of Tartan heavy.

It is hard to grasp just what a profound change this represented in the social and cultural climate in Scotland. And people really did "come together", because the youth culture as I experienced it was almost completely classless. I have never known so many people from so many different social backgrounds as I did in my late teens and early 20s. There was still gang violence in Glasgow's streets after the 1960s, but Scottish working-class men, at least for a while, became almost androgynous, wearing exotic clothes and hairstyles that would have been regarded as "pansy" only a few years before. The school authorities couldn't keep track of what was happening and the headmaster at Heriot's, William McL Dewar, who was quite a liberal educationalist, spent most of his time sending home the aforementioned boys like me who had grown their hair long.

The capital city was given a cultural kick up the backside by the Edinburgh International Festival, launched by an Austrian opera manager, Rudolf Bing, with support from the British Council as an attempt to revive European culture after the war. Their first choice had been Oxford, but it lacked the infrastructure. By the 1960s, the EIF had established an international reputation and became a forcing ground for radical ideas in Scotland as Beat poets and authors gathered for events like the seminal Edinburgh World Writers' Conference in 1962. American authors like Norman Mailer and William Burroughs clashed with Scottish literary hoodlums like Alexander Trocchi and Hugh MacDiarmid. That this was taking place in dour conventional Edinburgh seemed scarcely believable. The late-night review, *Beyond the Fringe*, which was actually part of the official festival, launched the careers of Peter Cook and Dudley Moore, and is credited with beginning the satire boom.

Ironically, the festival fringe grew so rapidly in the 1960s thanks to the large number of church halls in the capital city, a legacy of the Disruption when the breakaway Free Kirk launched a church-building boom in the middle of the 19th century. Kirk morality was relentlessly lampooned and excoriated in countless church halls on the Fringe as Scotland discovered sex. In 1963, Edinburgh was shocked and outraged when a nude female model was wheeled across the organ gallery of the McEwan Hall as part of an avant-garde drama event. Town councillors demanded an end to this filth posing as art. But times changed. By 1970, naked nuns engaged in an orgy scene at the climax of a production of the Prokofiev's *The Fiery Angel* couldn't even arouse the ire of the Tory councillors. In the 1960s, many of Edinburgh's citizens still regarded the Festival as an alien presence, but they were inevitably influenced by the climate of new ideas.

We didn't realise at the time that this was an intellectual and moral revolution. Or that it was happening in the most middle-class enclave of one of the most God-fearing cities the world has ever known. My girlfriend, Helen Primrose, the daughter of a Scottish psychiatrist, lived in a solid sandstone house in Dalrymple Crescent, in the south side of Edinburgh, an area which had the largest concentration of churches relative to population of anywhere in Europe. This address became a convention of the weird and wonderful. For a time, it even turned into an ashram of the Divine Light Mission. Edinburgh matrons in hats, on their way to afternoon tea, were accosted by saffron-robed devotees offering instant enlightenment. It was all very superficial and selfish. Young people who had grown up with the security of the welfare state condemned their parents, even though they were the generation that had created all this through their sacrifice in the war. But Bob Dylan had said, in the most influential song of the 1960s, that the Times They Were A' Changing. For Scotland, this was Year Zero.

MIDDLE CLASS RADICALISM

So, what happened to the old Scotland of the pew and pulpit? Where did the Presbyterian ethic go? The religious and sectarian ties that had bound worker, manager and capitalist to the Presbyterian Kirk and had provided the moral basis for the Union and the British Empire seemed to disappear in a blaze of coloured light.

The moral vacuum was filled by feminism, materialism, environmentalism, Marxism and spiritualisms of various kinds. Civic Scotland turned from church-related activities – charities, temperance and Sunday School – to diverse activities, like pacifism, the Campaign for Nuclear Disarmament, the women's movement, therapy and conservation. Somewhere in this cultural maelstrom, Scottish Nationalism emerged as a branch of the non-revolutionary Left. It was a uniquely Scottish form of middle-class radicalism. My mother joined the Scottish National Party after 1964 because she was outraged at the Labour government of Harold Wilson refusing to honour his promise to abolish nuclear weapons, which had been stationed in the Holy Loch on the River Clyde in 1961.

One of my most vivid childhood memories is of sitting in my dad's car in a very long and slow anti-nuclear demonstration somewhere near the Holy Loch when a member of the Empire Loyalists – a right-wing counter-movement of the day – leapt onto the roof ripping off a flag with the CND symbol that was fixed to the car aerial on the roof. My father was a pacifist, but it didn't stop him and our family friend, Dougie Stewart, chasing after them to have a serious exchange of views. I was more bothered about the car, I have to say, and nearly killed myself trying to replace the broken aerial while the car was in motion.

A number of prominent Nationalists like Margo MacDonald also joined the Scottish National Party as a direct result of its policies on nuclear disarmament. The SNP leader in the 1960s, Billy Wolfe, was another prominent supporter of CND. Many of the people who found their way into the SNP were the kind of energetic middle-class idealists who a century before would have become active in the Kirk as missionaries, like Stephen Maxwell, author of *The Case for Left Wing Nationalism*, the founding document of the '79 Group, who went on to become the director of the Scottish Council for Voluntary Organisations. Environmentalists like Malcolm Slessor, Professor of Energy Studies at Strathclyde University, were very influential in the civic Nationalism that emerged from the 1960s.

Scottish people may never have shown much interest in Marxism, but it was a passion that gripped writers, playwrights, musicians, academics and teachers in Scotland in the 1960s especially after the student revolts in Paris – "Les Événements" in 1968. The most successful left-wing theatre group to emerge from Scotland in the 1960s was John McGrath's 7:84 theatre company –

"7% of the population own 84% of the wealth" – and was a proving ground for a generation of Scottish actors including Bill Paterson, David Hayman and Peter Mullan. Broadcaster Stuart Cosgrove recalls the importance of the company: "I think there was no question that the culture was ahead of the politics rather than the other way round. There were all sorts of different dynamics going on there, and 7:84 gave voice to that."[51]

The most successful of its agitprop productions *The Cheviot, the Stag and the Black Black Oil* in 1973, nominally about the predations of the capitalist classes in Scotland through the ages, ended up promoting Scottish Nationalism rather than workers' insurrection. John McGrath, and most of his company, regarded the SNP as reactionary and anti-working class. But as the review toured Scotland, the audiences, especially in the Highlands, saw their grievances over the clearances, landlordism and exploitation, vividly portrayed as a national issue. And the SNP capitalised on it by leafleting and recruiting wherever the production played. "The front rows were packed with kids," Bill Paterson said in *Road To Referendum*. "And the older people were near the front to hear better and the rowdies up the back with their half bottles … it really crossed the board and you could tell that every night."

Cheviot was partially inspired by a series of bestselling books by the ex-Communist journalist John Prebble in the 1960s: *Culloden, The Highland Clearances* and *Glencoe*. Prebble helped create modern Scotland's image of itself, rightly or wrongly, as a country that has suffered from oppression by England. In Peter Watkins's acclaimed but controversial BBC docudrama *Culloden*, broadcast in 1964 and based on Prebble's book of the same name, kilted Scots were depicted being pursued and massacred by English redcoats. The film had a considerable impact, not least because of the graphic violence. It was an emotional and over-simplified account of history, portraying the Jacobite Rebellion as a bit like an England vs Scotland football match that got out of hand. Lowland Scotland's opposition to Bonnie Prince Charlie was glossed over. But Prebble's books and Watkins's film did arouse great interest in Scottish history, as well as resentment of England. Moreover, the idea of Scotland as a persecuted and oppressed country injected a degree of radical chic into Scottish Nationalism, though it has to be said that any comparison between the very middle-class SNP and the anti-imperialist movements portrayed in Frantz Fanon's *The Wretched of the Earth* was fanciful.

Socialists like George Galloway, then a left-wing trade unionist, were not impressed by the idea of the SNP as leaders of a national liberation struggle. "Bear in mind," he says in *Road to Referendum*, "that at this time the Vietnamese people were coming to the end of their victorious revolutionary fight against imperialism. Portugal was throwing off Fascism, Spain was about to. Greece had just done so. Our icons were Che Guevara, Fidel Castro and how anyone could feel any great affinity with this wee Paisley lawyer [Winnie Ewing, the victor of the 1967 Hamilton by-election] beat me at the time, and beats me still."[52]

But a wistful sense of Scotland as an oppressed nation became one of the themes of 1960s popular culture, and was prominent in the folk music revival. The Corries penned *Flower of Scotland* in 1967, a celebration of Scotland's victory over the English at Bannockburn and which is now the unofficial Scottish national anthem at rugby internationals. Ewan MacColl, Hamish Imlach, Phil Cunningham, Jean Redpath and Dick Gaughan were by no means all Nationalists. Indeed, one product of the folk scene, Billy Connolly, who went on to become Scotland's most successful comedy export, was virulently opposed to Scottish Nationalism. But they all contributed to the cultural climate out of which political Nationalism emerged. There is a direct line of descent from the 1960s folk revival to the 1980s folk-rock Nationalism of The Proclaimers, Runrig and Dougie MacLean of The Tannahill Weavers, who wrote Scotland's other unofficial national anthem *Caledonia*. That particular song went on to feature in a Tennent's lager TV advert in the 1980s that looked like an SNP party political broadcast. A young man sick of London, hurls his briefcase in a skip, and takes the first train home – to a pint of Scottish beer. Nationalism had become a marketable commodity to young people.

The symbols of Scottish identity – the kilt, tartan, bagpipes – started to undergo a semiological transformation after the 1960s. They had hitherto been associated with the Tory Right in Scotland – with landowners, military bands and the shortbread-tin Scottishness marketed by the Scottish Tourist Board. But gradually attitudes to the national costume began to change. It became quite cool for men to wear kilts with big boots and XL jumpers at political meetings in the 1970s. The fact that tartanry was almost entirely invented by the Victorians, and bore little relationship to anything Highlanders had actually worn before the Union, made educated

Nationalists scoff at all this revivalism. But people are entitled to do what they like with their cultural inheritance. There has long been an element of self-mockery bound up with the kilt and Scottishness: the White Heather Club, *Donald Where's Yer Trousers*, the speculation about undergarments. So what if the kilt was invented by an Englishman (allegedly). The Scots created a new form of ironic patriotism after the 1960s – not so much "Scots Wha Hae" as "Scots ... Whatever". The gender-bending aspect of men wearing skirts also fitted the tenor of the times.

Tartan became something of a fashion accessory in the 1960s and 1970s largely because of the Tartan Army, the exuberant Scottish football supporters who followed the national team across the world and became an international phenomenon in the days when Scotland still made it to the finals of the World Cup. The relationship between football and Scottish Nationalism is important if vague. A number of Scottish Nationalists will tell you that they found the triumphalism of England's victory in the World Cup in 1966 to be a kind of cultural turning point in Scotland. Even Unionists, like Donald Findlay QC, a leading figure in the No campaign in the Devolution Referendum, says that this was when Scotland started to feel that England no longer cared. "People began to get fed up of being referred to as being English, when we were Scottish," he said. "And we were only British when it seemed to suit the English. The weather stopped at Carlisle, the news stopped at Carlisle."[53]

It might seem facile to trace the emergence of political Nationalism to the football terraces of the 1960s and 1970s, but there is no doubt it was part of the process through which the old Scottish identity was refashioned. Professor James Kellas wrote that "working class Nationalism is generally related to culture and football, not politics". The historian Professor Chris Harvie argued in his ground-breaking *Scotland and Nationalism* that the creation of the Scottish Football Association in 1887 – a declaration of sporting independence from the English league – was more significant than all the home rule motions proposed in parliament by Liberal radicals in the 1880s. He suggests this was where political Scottish Nationalism began. Scots famously read their newspapers from back to front – and Scottish editors to this day are acutely aware of how important sport is to the finances of the Scottish press. The rise of Scottish Nationalism as a political force in recent years has been in inverse proportion to the performance of the Scottish international football team on the field of play. Scotland was consistently gubbed in international fixtures throughout the 1970s even as the SNP started winning elections, and in recent years the Tartan Army has faded with the team's decline into mediocrity. Perhaps Nationalism no longer needed football as a rallying cry.

THE STRANGE DEATH OF THE
SCOTTISH UNIONIST PARTY

The cultural reformation of the 1960s didn't kill the Scottish Conservatives stone-dead, but it was the moment its grip on Scottish politics began to fail. They became the Scottish Conservatives in 1965 – before that they had been the Scottish Unionist Party, which was a very different creature from the English Tory Party. The Scottish Unionists opposed political Nationalism, but it had always traded on its Scottish identity. The novelist and Unionist MP, John Buchan, coined the famous oxymoron that all Scottish Unionists should be Scottish Nationalists.

The Unionist Scottish Secretary in the 1930s, Walter Elliot, played the Scottish card with great skill in the UK Cabinet and installed much of the machinery of administrative devolution to the Scottish Office that was inherited by the Labour Scottish Secretary Tom Johnston during the war. The Unionists were also called the "Progressives" in local government and the Scottish Unionist Party supported a number of progressive policies including social housing. They backed the 1924 Housing Act which had been promoted by the Red Clydesider John Wheatley. This provided subsidies to build 200,000 houses in the 1920s and 1930s – though they tended to go to better-off artisans and the lower middle-classes because of the relatively high rents.

The Scottish Unionists were not just the Tory Party in disguise. This is why they were so successful. In the General Election of 1931, the Scottish Unionists won 58 out of 73 Scottish seats, more than Labour has ever won. However, after the 1960s, the Scottish Unionists became identified with a party that had never been popular in Scotland: the English Conservatives. The name change in the mid-1960s was a colossal mistake and sowed the seeds of the destruction of Scotland's party of the centre-right.

It was understandable that the Unionists should have wanted to modernise in the 1960s – after all, the Union in their name referred not to the 1707 Union with Scotland but the 1801 Union between Ireland and Great Britain. The cause of Ulster Protestantism didn't seem to have much relevance to Scottish politics in the 1960s. However, by changing its name the party severed its connection with a political movement that had steadily become more liberal and progressive since the 1930s and had colonised some of the territory vacated by the Scottish Liberals. Moreover, the Scottish Unionist Party had a distinctively Scottish identity which the Tories lacked. David Torrance, biographer of Alex Salmond, has claimed[54] that the Scottish Unionist Party was "the SNP of its day ... all it lacked was a 1950s version of Alex Salmond". That's as may be. What it got was Teddy Taylor.

Taylor, a right-wing Monday Club politician who won Glasgow Cathcart in 1964, was meant to be the new face of Tory Scotland. He was a hang'em and flog'em populist who campaigned for the return of the birch. He was popular, especially among women and older voters in the Glasgow housing estates who claimed to be living in fear of the gangs and vandalism they read about in the press. But he was very different from the patrician Unionists of the past like Harold Macmillan. Mrs Thatcher had Taylor marked out as the future Scottish Secretary of State after the resignation of Malcolm Rifkind in 1975 over her abandonment of devolution. But Taylor lost his seat in 1979, and like so many Scottish Tories had to look for a constituency in England. The Scottish Conservatives thereafter collapsed in much the same way the Kirk had in the 1960s.

And so, Scotland became a Labour country at last, and the party went on to dominate Scottish politics for the rest of the century. But the Labour Party never quite achieved the same grip on Scottish political culture that the old Scottish Unionist Party enjoyed. This was partly because Labour was, almost from the beginning, divided on the Scottish Question. Devolution had remained on Labour's electoral agenda in the 1950s, but no one in the party took it seriously – indeed, there were many attempts to abandon Labour's manifesto commitment to Scottish home rule, which seemed an irrelevance in the era of the UK welfare state. Labour looked to the Tories as its political enemies, which was one reason it failed to notice the rise of Scottish Nationalism in the 1960s until it was too late. The Labour MP for West Lothian, Tam Dalyell, who had seen the warning signs in his own constituency, insists that Labour in London's "sheer panic" helped to fuel Nationalism by exaggerating its importance. Labour in Scotland was to call out with their leader Harold Wilson. They thought, with cause, that Hamilton was a protest vote and should not be taken too seriously. However, by 1974, the SNP was winning 30% of the Scottish vote.

OF POST-WAR WELFARE UNIONISM

So why did Labour not seal the deal? What went wrong with Labour Unionism in the 1960s? Well, in short, the Scottish economy went wrong. The old industries of shipbuilding and heavy engineering rebounded in the 1950s, but they stumbled into the 1960s and then collapsed in the 1970s. The Scots built the best steam engines in the world in the 1950s, but by the 1960s the world had given up steam for diesel. Scottish yards built magnificent bespoke liners like the Queen Mary and the QE2, launched in 1967, in an age when liners were being replaced by the jet plane. The Clyde wasn't really in the business of building bulk carriers and container ships, and couldn't compete with new production-line shipyards in South Korea and Japan. But this still doesn't explain why there wasn't investment in new technologies and new designs. There remained a world demand for specialist ships, but the Clyde couldn't compete on price.

The attitudes of the Scottish workforce had a lot to do with Scotland's economic malaise in the 1960s. There were endless demarcation disputes on the Clyde, as skilled workers defended their privileges. The electricians and engineers, welders, riveters, and boilermakers were all in different craft unions. Every new job became a battleground. There were literally hundreds of different pay scales. At a Glasgow book event commemorating the UCS leader Jimmy Reid, which I chaired in 2010, a number of former Communist shop stewards spoke of their own regret at the contribution that outdated unionism made to the fall of the Clyde. But it wasn't really the unions that were to blame – after all, when the yards came under threat of closure in 1971, the workers at Upper Clyde Shipbuilders kept on working without pay. There had been an air of defeatism in the industry, at all levels, that spread through management and was tolerated by successive governments. There was a sense that Scotland's heavy industries where outdated and all that could be done was to manage their decline. Yet the Glasgow-Clyde industrial complex had been one of the most advanced engineering centres in the world, with unparalleled skills and technologies built up over generations. Indolent managers, incompetent politicians and fractious workers did what the German bombers failed to do in 1941.

Fashion had a lot to do with it also, and an attitude to industry that was framed by the consumer goods industries in the south – the "sunrise" industries of white goods and motor cars. Labour's regional policy sought to establish "growth poles" in Scotland by implanting factories such as the Rootes car plant in Linwood, Renfrewshire. The government used the new Industrial Development Certificates and an array of grants to strong-arm Rootes into coming north from the Midlands in 1961 to mop up unemployed workers from the Clydebank shipyards. Linwood was chosen because of its proximity to the Pressed Steel Fisher factory, which already provided steel for car bodies. It was a perfectly sensible plan. Unfortunately, the workers didn't take to the boring and repetitive production line and there were perpetual strikes and disputes. Moreover, the parts suppliers were still mostly based in the Midlands, which added to the cost of production. Hillman Imp Engines had to make a 600-mile round trip to the Midlands before being fitted to the finished cars. Scotland's only major car-manufacturing plant never made money. Linwood was taken over by Chrysler in 1967 and then by Peugeot Talbot, but it never recovered.

The electronics industry was a rather better story. Largely through Tom Johnston's direction of industry during the war, firms like Ferranti had set up in Scotland, and in the 1950s US companies such as IBM, NCR and Honeywell started coming to Scotland to service the growing European market. However, many of these factories were essentially assembly plants; there was little indigenous manufacturing, and the decline of the older industries meant that unemployment started to creep up throughout the 1960s. Scots looked to the state to sort it out, and it didn't. The levers didn't work.

Which brings us to another facet of post-war Scotland: the strange death of Scottish capitalism. By the 1960s, Scotland seemed to have lost much of the economic dynamism and entrepreneurial initiative which had made it such a powerhouse of the Industrial Revolution. What had happened to the spirit of capitalism that had created all these mills and mines and engineering works and was supposed to have been the legacy of the Protestant ethic? What had happened to the "animal spirits" of Scottish business? Where were the merchant capitalists like the Jardines, the Mathesons? The financial entrepreneurs like William Paterson who created the Bank of England and launched the Darien Scheme. Where were the inventors and entrepreneurs like James "Paraffin" Young, William Douglas Weir, John Logie Baird? William Lithgow turned a legacy of £1,000 in 1874 into the largest shipbuilding firm in the world in the first half of the 20th century. Why did so few follow that example after the war? Where did they go? To this day, Scotland has one of the lowest rates of business start-ups in Europe.

Some of them had already gone abroad, like Andrew Carnegie, the steel magnate, and David Buick, the car manufacturer – part of the Scottish diaspora that had drained talent and initiative from Scotland for generations. In the 20th century, Scotland lost a net two million people through emigration, and we can assume that many of them were the educated, ambitious and entrepreneurial individuals likely to start businesses. Scotland's loss was Canada's gain. Cities like Montreal were largely built by Scots since the days of the Hudson Bay and North West companies, which explains why there is a thistle in Montreal's civic coat of arms. Scotland's capitalists also tended to invest their profits abroad rather than in Scotland, which starved Scottish industry of investment.

But the "we wuz robbed" theory of Scottish economic decline is something of a cop-out. Scotland lost just as many souls to the diaspora in the 19th century, yet that was the century of the Industrial Revolution when Scotland became the workshop of the world. Emigration alone cannot explain why the huge industrial momentum built up in Scotland during and after the Industrial Revolution simply petered out. Industrial countries like Germany didn't just give up on manufacturing. Richard J Finlay argues[55] that Scotland was not just the country of heavy industry and powerful unions that is portrayed in most modern history books. There were still many small family-run factories that operated in a semi-rural environment until well into the 20th century. This "Mittelstand", as it would have been called in Germany, provided a lot of the bedrock support and finance for the old Unionist Party. Where did it go?

When Margaret Thatcher insisted that "Scots invented Thatcherism long before I was thought of" she had a point. Had post-war corporatism stifled the entrepreneurial drive of the country of Adam Smith?

The Right blames state controls, corporatism and the legacy of class conflict, but again this does not explain why Scotland became de-industrialised at a time when the rest of Britain in the 1960s was powering ahead under Labour governments as well as Tory ones. Social commentators point to the anxious Scottish personality and the docility bred by Presbyterian ministers, suggesting that the Scots were too "feart" to set up businesses. But these psycho-historical generalisations are at best descriptions, not always accurate ones, rather than explanations. The dominance of monopoly capitalism, the Scottish Left's answer in the 1960s, wasn't a satisfactory account either. Monopoly capitalism didn't prevent American entrepreneurs from developing high-end microelectronics and computing industries – sometimes using patents and scientific discoveries from Scottish universities. There was much talk of the branch plant syndrome in the 1960s – multinationals setting up assembly plants in Scotland – which begged the question of why there weren't more Scottish plants in the undergrowth in the first place.

There is an argument that Scotland had become over-dependent on the state in the decades after the war; that Scots had lost, at least for a time, the enthusiasm or the ability to create viable businesses and take advantage of the booming economy and the spread of affluence in the 1950s and 1960s. Scottish wages rose dramatically in the 1950s. Scots engineers had even been involved in the development of many of the new consumer goods, like John Logie Baird and television. Lack of capital had a lot to do with it, along with the economic pull of the south-east of England. Scots with a good idea knew where to take it – London. As the state became ever more significant as an economic agent, the location of the government became that much more important. It was hardly surprising therefore that economic decisions taken in London tended to benefit the south-east.

Prominent figures in the Labour Party in the 1960s like Jim Sillars warned that the party was losing traction because of the failure of the Scottish economy to keep pace with the south of England.[56] Unemployment rose significantly in the 1960s in Scotland, though to levels we would hardly consider problematic today. Labour had complacently assumed that Scotland would reward them in perpetuity for nationalisation, council housing, the NHS and all the other social advances brought about by the benevolent state. They were wrong. It wasn't that the Scots were ungrateful, just that an increasing number of them were worried that Scotland was neglected. Labour's dominance was exercised through the council estates, the trade unions and local government, and what Scottish voters saw in all three was a closed and monolithic party apparatus that seemed bureaucratic and remote.

The lack of amenities on Scotland's housing estates, like the absence of pubs – a legacy of Labour's early alignment with the temperance movement – caused resentment. As did the fact that people weren't allowed to paint their doors or personalise their houses. The trade unions were a great force for social advance in Scotland, but many Scots were uneasy about being enlisted into the great industrial armies. The Scots, truth be told, had never been very comfortable with Socialism. Keir Hardie founded the British Labour Party but couldn't win a parliamentary seat in Scotland. Local government in Scotland in the west at least also became associated, rightly or wrongly, with corruption and sectarianism in the 1960s. As argued by Gerry Hassan in *The Strange Death of Labour Scotland,* these three pillars of Labour's Scottish hegemony were to go rapidly into decline after the 1970s, thanks to council house sales and Tory anti-union legislation. But most of the problems with Labour Scotland had become apparent in the 1960s.

Winnie Ewing's by-election victory in 1967 was short-lived, and Labour recovered the seat in the 1970 General Election. But it led directly to the Kilbrandon Commission on the Constitution, set up by Harold Wilson, which began the move towards limited self-government. Initially, Labour in Scotland refused to support a Scottish Assembly. Labour's Scottish Secretary, Willie Ross, famously remarked: "Why do you need a Scottish Parliament? I'm your Scottish Parliament".[57] Harold Wilson, worried about losing MPs in Scotland, had other ideas. He knew that a Labour government in the UK could not happen without Scottish seats and he was determined to prevent the SNP taking any more of them. He effectively ordered his Scottish party executive to support devolution in the infamous Dalintober Street special conference of 1974.

Labour's shotgun wedding with home rule was partially successful in halting the slide. In the October 1974 General Election, the Scottish National Party returned only 11 MPs out of 72. Labour was relieved, but scared, since they won only 36% of the vote, the party's lowest share since 1931. The Nationalists had won 30% of the Scottish vote, and in 35 of Labour's 41 seats, the SNP were in second place. The Nationalist threat had not gone away. It took the SNP's own self-destructive behaviour in the latter 1970s to succeed where Labour failed in the 1960s.

The 1960s were the great political and cultural fault line in Scottish history. Scotland was transformed as the Kirk collapsed and the Tories went into steep decline. Labour established itself as the national party of Scotland, but found itself harried by a new upstart Nationalism after Hamilton in 1967. The British Empire, which had bound Scotland morally and economically to the Union, disintegrated and the industries that had made Glasgow the Second City of the Empire went into catastrophic and unexpected decline. A dramatic imbalance emerged between economic growth in Scotland and England, despite attempts by the state to direct industry north of the border. The state had become a key player in the economy, and Scots were beginning to fear that it had been captured by the south-east of England. A sense of grievance emerged in Scottish popular culture as historic injustices were re-examined by agitprop theatre, books, television.

The 1960s were an age of huge uncertainty and confusion at all levels in Scottish society. Class divisions were becoming blurred as deference evaporated and new political movements crowded onto the stage. One of them was Scottish Nationalism. However, it was never clear whether this political Nationalism was a significant political movement or just another 60s fad. The course of the 1970s suggested it might just have been the latter.

CHAPTER NINE
THE REFERENDUM OF '79
AND THE COLLAPSE OF
INDUSTRIAL SCOTLAND

$$\times$$

IN THE WINTER of 1979, I was a post-graduate student at Edinburgh University, going nowhere. I had become a victim of an austere and abstract theoretical Marxism, which was fashionable in university circles in the 1970s and which had about as much to do with revolution as the study of Aramaic text. This was strange considering that this was the most intense period of overt class conflict since the 1920s: the Winter of Discontent, when bodies were supposedly piling up in the graveyards and rubbish was lying uncollected in the streets. I didn't see the bodies, but I remember watching army Green Goddesses trundling around the city in place of striking firemen and fantasising that the country was on the brink of martial law. Gerry Hassan remembers it too: "You've got to remember the politics of the 1970s. Politics of the 1970s are fractious, divisive, nasty. They're about the concerns about Britain's economic decline. There was even talks at the sides of would we have to have a military coup or something."[58] But I was lost in the impenetrable intellectual constructs of French Marxist structuralism, and finding that even I couldn't understand what I was writing.

Then, curiously, I was offered a job as a political researcher in the BBC's Referendum Unit for the March 1979 Devolution Referendum. I'd done some work for the BBC on elections before, but this was different. The unit was housed in a Portakabin perched on the edge of the River Kelvin next to BBC Scotland's then-headquarters in Queen Margaret Drive in Glasgow's west end. Like the referendum, it was precariously balanced. Queen Margaret Drive in those days was a hotbed of cultural self-loathing, saturated with alcohol, perpetually complaining and feuding with itself. But it was a pleasant change from the zombie intellectualism of university.

My job was to collate the news coverage, digest the issues, brief correspondents and – most importantly – keep track of where the action was so that it could be covered by a thrice-weekly campaign report programme. I rapidly discovered that there was very little action anywhere in February 1979. Apart from the indefatigable Labour MP Tam Dalyell, author of the West Lothian Question, and his opposite number, Jim Sillars, who had recently left Labour to form the Nationalist Scottish Labour Party, the campaigns were almost non-existent until the last week or so. If it hadn't been for the Jim and Tam roadshow, I think they might have just decided to cancel the referendum owing to lack of interest. There was scarcely a village hall they didn't visit, and they became great friends. Sillars recollects that he even took to carrying Tam's suitcase for him, until he found that it was filled with No campaign leaflets.

I was burdened by a personal crisis of confidence because I thought I must be missing something. Others did too, because a cabin of reporters, cameramen and directors were waiting on me to tell them what was happening because they couldn't just film the Tam and Jim show three times a week. There was no internet of course in those days – no web pages, Twitter or blogs. Only the phone and a list of numbers that often rang out since offices didn't yet have telephone answering machines. I knew that Gordon Brown was intensely active ,as only he can be, in the Yes campaign. The future Prime Minister was then a college lecturer and unsuccessful Labour candidate in the General Election-that-never-was in 1978. I had a meeting with him in the Abbotsford Bar in Edinburgh to try to work out what wasn't happening. He gave me a long list of his future engagements and little else. I don't know if he was deluding himself or if he was just trying to spin me, but he seemed to think the Yes campaign was coasting to victory.

It was abundantly clear it was not. Apathy was the dominant mood in Scotland, even as we in the media tried to pretend otherwise. Scottish voters could arouse little enthusiasm for an assembly that sounded like a new and superfluous layer of local government, except that it didn't even have the power to raise its own revenues. Scots had other things on their minds in the 1970s. There was industrial chaos, hyperinflation, the IMF, factory closures, a sense of social disintegration – the proposed Scottish Assembly didn't even have primary law-making powers. It seemed like a pointless exercise in constitutional tinkering, totally out of tune with the times. The Celtic revivalism of the 1960s had faded. Punk rock was the protest music of the 1970s, but the Sex Pistols appeared to have no views on the merits of constitutional reform. Worst of all, Scotland had been humiliated in the 1978 World Cup in Argentina when manager Aly MacLeod's Tartan Army lost to Peru in the first round.

I took to driving around some of the peripheral housing estates of Glasgow looking for signs of electoral life – posters, pictures, canvassers, anything. But this wasn't like any general election, where the parties know how to put on a show. In this campaign all the parties were divided within themselves and didn't think it was worth the effort. Scottish Labour was intensely unhappy, having been forced to adopt devolution after the "Battle of Dalintober Street" in 1974. They had effectively been ordered by Harold Wilson to support a Scottish Assembly which many in the party believed was an over-reaction to the Hamilton by-election. Others felt that focusing on the constitution diverted attention from the real enemies: the Tories. They complied in the end. But they were damned if they were going to waste their money and effort campaigning for it. Rumours circulated of stacks of Yes campaign leaflets piling up in Labour constituency offices with no one to deliver them. The Scottish Secretary of the Labour Party, Helen Liddell, announced that Labour would not be "soiling its hands"[59] by joining any umbrella campaigns, so no one else could deliver them either. The Labour-supporting journalist, Brian Wilson, set up a Labour No campaign which had articulate support from Labour MPs like Robin Cook.

The SNP was equally divided. Many Nationalists believed that devolution was a Labour trap, a toothless talking shop, and that they should have nothing to do with it. The party officially supported a Yes vote, and individuals like the MP for Clackmannan, George Reid, were energetic in their campaigning for the Scottish Assembly. But there were few like him. The SNP was in a state of incipient civil war between the headstrong MPs in Westminster, who mostly sat for former Conservative seats, and the party back in Scotland, under its social democratic leader, Billy Wolfe. There was a further rift on the far-left with Margo MacDonald, winner of the Govan by-election of 1973, and Stephen Maxwell, the press officer, urging the party to become explicitly Socialist and republican. A relatively obscure Alex Salmond was a member of this "'79

Group" as it came to be known. The SNP was not a happy ship in 1979 and was heading for electoral oblivion, though it didn't realise how soon.

The Tories, who were still a force in Scottish politics in the 1970s, were also divided over devolution. The former Conservative leader, Edward Heath had arguably launched the devolution process in his "Declaration of Perth" in 1968, when he proposed an elected assembly for Scotland and upstaged Harold Wilson. This was what caused the Labour leader to fall out with his devo-sceptic Scottish Labour Party in 1974. The Tory Shadow Scottish Secretary, Malcolm Rifkind, was a supporter of devolution as was the popular Tory Shadow Agriculture Minister, Alick Buchanan-Smith. They at least had an understanding of the complex dynamics of Scottish Unionism, and the importance of identity. But the new leader of the party, Margaret Thatcher, did not.

Malcolm Rifkind is unrepentant. "I actually have in my possession," he told *Road to Referendum*, "a letter I received from Margaret Thatcher after she had become leader of the Conservative Party, in which she said the Conservative Party remains committed to a Scottish Assembly and that is our policy." But Conservatives in Westminster didn't see it that way and, like their leader, were instinctively hostile to the whole concept of devolution, which they regarded as anti-British. When Mrs Thatcher finally made clear she was not going to support the Scotland Bill, and would campaign for a No vote in the referendum, Rifkind and Buchanan-Smith resigned. This robbed the Yes campaign of two top-rank politicians of the Right, though Buchanan-Smith made clear his support for a Yes vote. Scottish business was universally Conservative in those days and wanted nothing to do with devolution, though it could never quite explain why. They suspected that the Scottish Assembly would be hostile to business – which in the late 1970s was probably correct, though it would have been powerless to do anything about it.

It was becoming difficult to find anyone who really supported the Scottish Assembly, other than Gordon Brown. The turning point in the campaign came when the former Tory PM Lord Home, who'd been put in charge of devolution by Ted Heath in 1968 and was supposed to be a devolutionist, declared that Scots should vote No. He argued that the assembly proposed under the Scotland Act of 1978 lacked tax-raising powers and was not elected under proportional representation. It would lead only to expensive bureaucracy, he said, promising that the incoming Conservatives would come up with a "better devolution bill" – which, of course, they never did. Lord Home's name has lived in infamy ever since for queering the pitch. However, he had a point about the assembly. The Scottish Parliament that finally did arrive in 1997 had tax-raising powers and was elected under proportional representation. Mind you, by then, Conservatives were opposed to it for precisely those reasons.

The No campaign was better organised and better funded than the Yes side. The "Scotland Says No" campaign had strong business support and outspent "Yes for Scotland" by at least two to one,[60] though in those days there was no funding limit and no accounting of campaign spending, so no one knows exactly how much was spent. Jim Sillars paid for the first Yes leaflet out of his own pocket.[61] But it wasn't really about the funding. As so often in Scottish history, fear was the key to the outcome of the 1979 referendum campaign. The No supporters said that devolution would mean higher taxation, even though the assembly had no tax-raising powers, and that businesses would be discouraged from coming to Scotland. It claimed that Scotland would lose influence and that the assembly would be at best a costly irrelevance, at worse the beginning of the break-up of Britain. It was pretty thin stuff, but at least they had a common hymn sheet.

The Yes campaign was more seriously flawed because no one could explain convincingly what the Scottish Assembly was for. The SNP regarded it as a stepping stone to independence, while Labour saw it as an electoral expedient, a device to frustrate the Nationalists. Neither of these attitudes lent itself to positive campaigning. The argument that an elected assembly would bring better governance seemed dubious. The proposed Scottish Assembly had little legislative responsibility and no economic powers to speak of. What had devolution to offer a country that was in chaos as a result of UK-wide industrial conflict. Why pay for another layer of bureaucracy and 142 elected politicians? One of the few politicians who could talk with real passion and conviction about legislative devolution was Labour MP and academic John P MacIntosh, and he unfortunately had just died in summer of 1978. It was left to the young, but admittedly capable future Labour leader, John Smith, Devolution Minister in the Callaghan government, to put the case for devolution – a voice in the wilderness.

At the climax of the campaign, if one could call it that, the BBC in London decided it would be a good idea to film the Oxford Union debate on devolution, on Sunday 25th February. We rounded up the key supporters – the SNP's Margo MacDonald, Jim Sillars, the leader of the SLP, and John Smith, the Labour Minister with Responsibility for Devolution, and flew them to Oxford in a chartered plane. It felt like being with a band going on tour, the only difference being that no one was buying tickets and the band members weren't playing together.

There was much banter, and I recall Jim Sillars being ribbed because he had ironed his own shirtsleeves, as if this was some concession to the English establishment. The real reason was that Jim had been in the navy and dressing properly was second nature to him. The debate itself was a curiously lacklustre affair in which the star turn was a long-haired Brian Wilson, his open-neck shirt and cord jeans contrasting with the glittering evening dress of the students, who argued with considerable passion that devolution was divisive and reactionary. At that stage I more or less agreed with him. However, I found the debate, in this bastion of English privilege, to be strangely offensive. Unsurprisingly, Oxford decided that devolution was not a good idea.

As the campaign hurtled towards the buffers, I discovered that I was more sympathetic to devolution than I'd realised. I'd intended to abstain on the grounds that devolution was a crushing irrelevance, but the dismal conduct of the campaign made me think again. Quite a few Scots seemed to feel the same, which is why, against all the odds, the Yes campaign won in the end by 52% to 48%. In the circumstances, given the weakness of the Yes campaign and the half-heartedness of the Scotland Act, this was a minor miracle. I believe the Scots made this decision very late in the day, within the final 72 hours, and the Oxford debate may well have played a significant role in turning opinion in favour of devolution.

But, of course, this Yes vote was not recognised because of the infamous 40% rule – the amendment tabled by the Labour MP for Islington, George Cunningham, during the committee stage of the Scotland Bill. This required that 40% of the Scottish electorate had to vote Yes for the Scottish Assembly to be delivered. The result was well short, since only 33% of Scots had voted in the affirmative. Nationalists were furious at the cheating, gerrymandering, double-dealing English, even though Cunningham was a Scot. Cunning-ham recalls receiving voluminous hate mail advising him to: "Go and do what Judas did, but take a nice strong rope." Many said that the dead had been given a vote, the sick had a vote, people who weren't registered had a vote and people who didn't vote had a vote – and they'd all effectively voted No.

Scottish Labour politicians reacted, on the whole, with in-difference, because most never really wanted the assembly in the first place. Their main focus was the forthcoming General Election when they knew they had a serious fight on their hands from Mar-garet Thatcher, and the referendum campaign was for most a diver-sion of energy. Some Labour people took it personally – the former Labour MP, George Galloway, recalls returning to party headquar-ters on election night and finding Gordon Brown in tears. "It was an act of gross treachery," says Galloway today.[62]

In the wider Scotland, few tears were shed over the loss of the Toom Tabard Parliament. But Scotland was left discontented and with a vague sense of having been robbed, even though the stolen goods were considered largely valueless. In the week of the vote, the much-loved Turnbull cartoon in The Glasgow Herald de-picted the Scottish lion rampant cowering with its tail between its legs saying "I'm feart". It wasn't so much fear of the unknown as discontent at the known – the feeble devolutionary offering seemed to answer none of the pressing questions facing Scotland. Scots had been given a choice they hadn't asked for between tokenistic home rule and a status quo that was turning Scotland into an industrial wasteland. What had devolution to do with saving failing industries like the Linwood car plant and the Ravenscraig steelworks? What about Scotland's oil, which by 1979 was flooding the UK Exchequer with vast wealth, very little of which would come Scotland's way? What had devolution to say about the power of the trade unions, which had long been regarded as important democratic institutions in Scotland, but seemed to have turned into vehicles of industrial self-destruction. Could the Scottish Assembly have done anything about hyperinflation, which had been running at between 12% and 25% through the 1970s? The answer in all cases had to be no.

Scots didn't want an ornamental parliament. Many felt pa-tronised by the cosy constitutionalism of the Kilbrandon Report and Scotland Act, with its dodgy amendments, circumscribed powers and phoney promise of greater democracy. As Enoch Powell said:

"Power devolved is power retained." But Scotland in 1979 didn't have anywhere else to turn. To the left of Labour was a collection of Trotskyite factions that spent their time arguing with each other; "vicious microbes dividing and multiplying in a drop of water" as one former Leftist put it. Jim Sillars's attempt to revive the old Scottish Labour Party that Keir Hardie had founded with RB Cunninghame Graham in 1888 failed, as it too disintegrated into factionalism and farce after 1979. As co-founder Alex Neil observed: "We should probably have taken more time. We didn't think we had the time at the time."[63]

Scots weren't used to thinking of themselves as a separate nation, and anyway the SNP seemed to be as argumentative as the Trots. Labour had presided over hyperinflation, mass unemployment, the IMF rescue, and, despite being the political representatives of organised labour, seemed unable to control or reason with the trade union barons. Lord Home's cynical promise of a better devolution – he must have know Margaret Thatcher would never deliver – fuelled Scotland's growing antagonism towards the Scottish Tories. They may have been the most successful political party in Scotland, but by the 1970s, the Scottish Tories had acquired a death wish.

The consequences of the referendum debacle were immediate and profound. In a fit of pointless self-destructiveness, the 11 SNP MPs in Westminster withdrew their support from the faltering Labour administration of Jim Callaghan. "Turkeys voting for an early Christmas," as the PM put it when it became clear they would not side with Labour in the Tory confidence motion in the Commons on 28th March 1979. Callaghan lost by one vote, and announced an immediate general election. The SNP didn't bring him down on their own – David Steel's Liberals also played turkey with the Tories that night. But Nationalist votes secured Callaghan's downfall and allowed Labour to claim that the SNP were responsible for bringing in Margaret Thatcher and 18 years of Tory rule. As Jim Sillars ruefully remarked, it made canvassing for SNP in the 1980s a high-risk occupation. "There was pure hatred on the doorsteps," he recalls, "for letting the Tories in."[64]

Why did the SNP walk into this bear-trap? The former leader, Gordon Wilson, says they believed that they had much greater support in Scotland than they really had, because of all those good second places in the October 1974 election.[65] He also says that the Nationalist MPs were exhausted, and there is no doubt that the most active members, like George Reid, had driven themselves to the edge. Their self-immolation, like some millennial sect seeking an early afterlife, probably had more to do with the inherent weakness of the SNP as a party. It had no firm ideology, an amateur organisation and very little history to fall back upon, having only recently emerged from the eccentric fringes of political life in the 1960s. It was a collection of elected members who didn't have a lot in common except a vague desire to bring about an independent Scotland. When they realised that the Scotland Act was a Unionist set-up, they decided to pull the temple down around their ears because they couldn't think of anything better to do. If they'd stuck it out, the SNP might well have fared rather better in a general election in October 1979 than the one they precipitated in May, once the Scots had reflected on the referendum result. Then again, they might not.

In the May 1979 General Election, the SNP lost nine of its 11 MPs – back to the drawing board. The SNP was left confused and at war with itself. Labour was in a bad way, too, out of power and out of ideas – but at least they had the consolation of winning 44 Scottish seats in the 1979 election against the SNP's two. Many disappointed devolutionists, like journalist and author Neal Ascherson left Scotland in despair. The clear message taken from 1979 by the Thatcher government was that Scotland was no longer a problem. The Scottish bluff had been called. There was no need to keep pouring money into Scotland to keep alive its crumbling manufacturing sector, and no need for Westminster to offer any concessions in exchange for oil. There had been a deliberate attempt, as confirmed by recently released government documents, to conceal from Scots the true extent of the hydrocarbon wealth in the North Sea.[66] Nor did Thatcher pause to worry about her party in Scotland, which had been on the winning side. Surely, it was only a matter of time before Scotland, too, became enamoured of the Iron Lady. Big mistake.

WHERE DID MY JOB GO?

While Scottish Nationalism became a joke, the continuing industrial closures were anything but. The Singer Sewing Machine factory at Clydebank closed in June 1980. This brought an end to a century of sewing machine production in a plant which at its height had employed 16,000 people. In the same year, the Corpach Pulp Mill closed in Loch Linnhe. Half a century of tyre production at Dunlop's plant at Inchinnan ended with closure in 1981 with the loss of 2,000 jobs. Then it was 1,500 at Massey Ferguson at Kilmarnock; 13,000 at Coats Patons; 9,000 jobs disappeared at Peugeot Talbot car plant at Linwood. Burroughs Computers, Hoover, British Leyland all followed. It was as if a decision had been taken to wipe industrial Scotland off the map. Scottish Tory grandees like the Scottish Secretary, George Younger, did their best in Cabinet to protect Scotland from the worst of Thatcher's economic policies, and repeatedly saved the Ravenscraig steel plant in Motherwell, which had become an industrial totem in Scotland. But the economic scorched-earth policies continued.

I had somehow been kept on at the BBC despite my indifferent performance in the Referendum Unit, and moved on to presenting half-hour television documentaries for the *Current Account* series. In the early 1980s, these programmes charted the end of Scotland as a manufacturing nation. This was one of the most traumatic periods in Scotland's history, an industrial revolution in reverse, the effects of which are still being felt today, not least in the appalling health statistics of west central Scotland. If the 1960s saw the end of the British Empire and the Kirk, the 1980s drew a line under Scotland's industrial history. It was as if the supports of the Union were being kicked away one by one.

In some respects the recessions of the early 1980s were more devastating to the communities affected than war, which at least had the consolation of solidarity in the face of a common enemy. Between 1979 and 1981 alone, 11% of Scottish manufacturing jobs disappeared. Scottish manufacturing lost 31% of its capacity by 1987 as a result of the Thatcher industrial recessions, and much of what was left was sold off to foreign buyers. The Scottish economy recovered marginally in the 1990s thanks to the influx of electronics companies, attracted by government incentives and access to the EU. By 1993, Scotland was producing 10% of the world's PCs. But critics warned that this was transitory investment, a "branch plant syndrome".

Hugh Aitken, the chief executive of the Scottish operation of computer company Sun Microsystems, famously described Silicon Glen as a "screw-driver shop", providing essentially blue-collar jobs. Since 1997, Scottish manufacturing industry has lost 100,000 jobs, replaced by low-paid service occupations and public sector employment. Of the 200,000 jobs created in Scotland between 1995 and 2008, 85% were in three sectors: health and social work; education and administration; and defence and social security.[67] Between 1951 and 2001, Scotland lost 70% of its manufacturing employment, most of it in the 1980s.[68]

There was, of course, solidarity, bucket loads of it in the early-1980s, among Scottish working-class communities, who put up a spirited resistance to the destruction of their livelihoods, but there was no chance of victory in this war. There were only casualties. Professor Phil Hanlon of Glasgow University's Department of Public Health has demonstrated that Scottish health deteriorated relative to other industrial areas of Europe since the 1980s. Scotland has had disproportionately high levels of coronary heart disease and cancer, and life expectancy is shorter than in comparable areas like Silesia in Poland or Moravia in the Czech Republic.[69] When people lament the poor state of health of the Scots, they are actually talking about the consequences, not of diet, but of industrial policy.

Women played a prominent role in the shop-floor resistance, staging work-ins at plants such as Lee Jeans in Greenock in 1981 and at Plessey Electronics in Bathgate in 1982. In the winter of 1982 we got wind of the forthcoming factory occupation by the 300 women employees at Plessey and decided to make a film of it for *Current Account*. It was a rare opportunity to follow an industrial confrontation from the very beginning. We were inside the plant with the cameras at 6am to film the workers locking the bosses out of their own factory as they arrived for work. The women, with enormous good humour, organised the running of their workplace, making improvements that the indifferent male management had never thought about because they never spoke to their own workers. It was great television, and the Plessey women, hilarious and heroic, were natural television stars. There appeared to be a greater degree of determination among the Scottish female workforces than among the men. In fact, most of the male workers at

Plessey refused to take part in the occupation.

The men at the neighbouring British Leyland truck plant at Bathgate were also taking action against the closure of their factory, so we got two occupations for the price of one. But though they dutifully raised money for the Plessey occupation, and gave them as much support as they could, the Leyland workers clearly didn't have a fraction of the fight that the women appeared to possess. This was probably down to realism as much as defeatism. The male dominated trade unions had been on the losing side too often. They'd seen the work-in at Upper Clyde Shipbuilders, and had no illusions about the ability of a local workforce to take over and run companies – especially when they were branch plants of multinationals. The trade unions understandably focused on getting the best redundancy deals for their members, and tried not to get carried away with syndicalist psycho-dramas.

Labour was leery, too, of factory occupations, which looked like Trotskyism. I recall George Galloway, just elected the youngest chairman of the Labour Party in Scotland, arriving at Plessey one day, impeccably turned out in a banker's coat with a velvet collar, and being greeted as if he were a professional footballer. A young Nationalist lawyer also turned up to help the Plessey workforce, by the name of Kenny MacAskill – now the Scottish Justice Secretary – to give pro-bono legal advice. With his help, the women achieved a limited victory when Plessey accepted a takeover offer from the firm Arcotronic, which saved 80 jobs – at least for a while.

But in the end, it didn't matter. The workers were all thrown out of work eventually, whether they fought or not. Plessey, Bathgate, all the occupations went the way of UCS and were ghosts within 18 months. The sense of powerlessness that gripped central Scotland in the recessions of the 1980s was almost palpable – you could feel the spirit disappearing from the people as their livelihoods were taken away. Men and women appearing to shrink physically during the course of a bitter industrial dispute, as if they'd been hit by accelerated ageing syndrome. Scotland was one long story of industrial decline in the early 1980s, and I had the misfortune to witness it all at very close hand, experiencing the guilt of the voyeur. In the early 1980s I made films at Inchinnan, Plessey, Bathgate, Polmaise Colliery and Ravenscraig. I was still relatively young then, had only been out of university for a year or so, and I found it emotionally harrowing. I hadn't had time to develop the hard skin of the seasoned journalist, and too often I found myself on the "wrong side" of the camera.

Film-making is very personal. To cover a factory occupation you almost end up living with the workforce, which makes it all the more uncomfortable when it collapses and you go onto the next story, while they go onto the dole. I worried that we were unintentionally manipulating the workforces, egging them on to make shows of defiance for the cameras. We were middle-class freeloaders playing at solidarity with the workers, and our jobs weren't on the line. Worse, the soup kitchens, the defiant singing, the rattling collection tins, the braziers eventually became horrible television clichés and we could tell that the viewers were beginning to switch off. There is only so long that you can be interested in watching a corpse decompose.

We tried to be constructive, interviewing academics, trade unionists and politicians. Tories blamed Socialism and Labour blamed the bosses, but no one seemed to be able to do anything about it. We kept being told that Scotland was just "too far from the centre of things" which really didn't make sense. Scotland wasn't "remote" – it was ideally located as a land-bridge between the Atlantic Ocean and Continental Europe, as the Scottish Council for Development and Industry had long argued. We kept being told that "metal bashing" was a thing of the past. Yet, at that very moment, some of the greatest steel structures ever built were being constructed on the other side of Scotland – oil platforms to extract oil from the North Sea.

There was a problem with industrial relations in Britain – self-destructive union militancy and a propensity to strike. In Scotland, defence of the craft traditions of the skilled workers certainly contributed to the collapse of the Scottish shipbuilding industry. But this was no excuse for what happened in the 1980s. As we will see in later chapters of this book, social democracy and entrepreneurialism worked perfectly well together in the Nordic countries like Denmark, Finland and Norway where a co-operative approach and judicious public investment delivered viable economies with the highest standards of living in the world, even without oil. This could have worked in Scotland, had there been the political will. In countries like Germany, "Mitbestimmung", or co-determination, brought the workforce into the running of companies. What struck me most spending time in the condemned factories of west central

Scotland was the intelligence of the workers in these industries, who often seemed to know more about their business than the management did.

Ravenscraig was one of the most advanced strip steel plants in Europe, and one of the most efficient, and everyone at the plant was bewildered that no one seemed to know this. They knew that their industries were viable, and in many cases could prove it. The Scottish Trades Union Congress produced numerous reports indicating how the Scottish economy could be modernised, and, like the SCDI, avoided crude class politics. But prejudice against making things meant that Scotland's industrial infrastructure was considered expendable in the war against organised labour. This economic vandalism would have been inconceivable in countries such as Germany, where it would have been regarded as irresponsible to let the skills of the workers go to waste and valuable industrial plants rust.

Perhaps too much state bureaucracy had stifled entrepreneurial initiative and undermined the will to succeed, though I find that a poor explanation. Corporatism wasn't unique to Scotland. There was something uniquely morbid about the executive cadres in industrial Scotland in the 1980s. The managers we spoke to in these emerging industrial wastelands seemed to face closure with a listless resignation, as if there wasn't any point bothering. Most of the ambitious ones had left for England, Canada and Australia, and those who remained felt they were simply managing decline, waiting for their pensions. Even among the metropolitan Left, there was a widespread view that what happened in Scotland in the 1980s was in some way inevitable. And this is how the history of the period is taught in Scottish schools as if industrial entropy was unavoidable. It has been seen as a form of industrial romanticism to question why this decline happened.

But there was nothing inevitable about it; the deindustrialisation of Scotland was the result of conscious political decisions taken predominantly in London. Regional policy was abandoned to the free play of market forces – except of course that there was nothing free about it. Government policies of privatisation, deregulation, tax reduction, trade union reform all served to enrich the upper and middle-classes of the south-east of England. That was where the new economy of finance and services was concentrated. Mrs Thatcher's answer to the decline of manufacturing was the Big

Bang in the City of London in 1986 which created the bonus-driven banking economy that finally imploded in the crash of 2008. London finance houses earned fees from the privatisation of the utilities and speculated on the share prices of former state assets. The sale of council houses provided further profitable work for the banks who supplied the mortgage loans, often with questionable endowment policies attached to them. Britain became a nation of property speculators. House prices rocketed in the south-east,which allowed the London middle classes to pocket substantial capital gains merely by sitting in their homes. The UK became one of the most unequal societies in the developed world, thanks to the Howe/Lawson tax cuts, which reduced the top rate of tax from 83% to 40%.

It was considered slightly indecent to portray the industrial clearances in this way, at least in media circles in the 1980s, because it sounded a bit, well, "Nationalist". But I wasn't a Nationalist and I couldn't see any other way of accounting for what had happened. The strategy of lowering inflation through cuts in public expenditure, privatisation and destroying the power of the trade unions was a policy that damaged all industrial areas of Britain, but hit Scotland particularly hard. Mass unemployment was used as a political tool by the UK government in the 1980s to combat organised labour. Scotland was collateral damage in Margaret Thatcher's class war. It all culminated with a grim inevitability in the miners strike in 1984 which brought the long history of Scottish industrial militancy to a close.

It was the easy access to coal that helped spark the Industrial Revolution in Scotland, and it was coal that sustained the great heavy industries of the late 19th and 20th centuries which made Scottish engineering world class. Now the pits were closing and the industrial communities of west central Scotland were being dispersed. Some Scots left to join the army, but the demand for Scottish soldiers wasn't what it was, and even emigration had ceased to be a significant safety valve for Scots. At this time, my older sister, Julie, died after a long struggle with that very Scottish disease, multiple sclerosis, in which the body's nervous tissue rejects itself. And Scotland has the highest rates of MS in the world. I wanted out of broadcasting altogether, but then I'd have been out of work too. So I moved initially to radio and then, like so many Scots, took the road to London – the "noblest vista for a Scotchman on the make".

CHAPTER TEN
FROM '79 TO '97

✕

" W E   M U S T be prepared to hear the sound of cell doors crashing behind us," declared Jim Sillars, now with the SNP, as he launched what was called the "Scottish Resistance" against Thatcher's economic policies in 1981. Unfortunately, the only doors that crashed were those of the Scottish voters in the faces of SNP election canvassers. After the debacle of the referendum and the election that brought in Mrs Thatcher, the Scottish voters didn't want to hear about Nationalism in the early 1980s.

The '79 Group of Socialist and republican Nationalists, so named after the abortive referendum, tried to gain working-class support through a grandiose campaign of "political strikes and civil disobedience on a massive scale", as Sillars put it. But the revolution never quite took off. In October 1981, when he and five other '79 Group members broke into the Royal High School building on Edinburgh's Calton Hill, which would have housed the Scottish Assembly had enough Scots voted Yes in the 1979 referendum, the resistance collapsed in farce. Sillars injured his arm breaking a window to gain entry; the activists were arrested before they could make a statement; and a mass demonstration planned for the next day was cancelled in embarrassment. The Easter Rising it wasn't.

This dismal episode only served to confirm the Scottish National Party's political irrelevance in the 1980s. After bringing upon itself the blame for letting Thatcher into Number Ten, and losing all but two of its MPs in the process, the SNP dissolved then into acrimonious factionalism. In 1982 the leader of the SNP, Gordon Wilson, expelled the '79 Group. That led to the departure of the SNP's greatest asset, Margo MacDonald, one of the most famous Scottish personalities in Britain after Billy Connolly. A woman who had an extraordinary effect on normally reserved Scotsmen, like Stuart Cosgrove. "This woman with her blonde peroxide hair, buxom lady, very bright, capable of speaking, [would] literally stand up on the soapbox and speak to the working class, but also could walk into a university chamber and debate with the best of them. Bright, articulate, charismatic, I mean just the woman of your dreams."[70] It also led to the departure from the SNP of a young man of 28 who seemed to be inordinately sure of himself. His name was Alex Salmond.

Both of them were to return to the fold in due course. But the national question largely disappeared from the political agenda after the 1979 Referendum. Labour in Scotland retreated into its local authority fastness, trying to fight off Tory caps on council spending and the 1980 Tenants' Rights Act which introduced council house sales. Scots may not have been keen on Mrs Thatcher but they rather liked some of her policies. "The policy of council house sales was even more popular in Scotland than in England," recalls Malcolm Rifkind.[71] Indeed, within 20 years, Scotland's Hungarian levels of home ownership had been reversed as Scotland became an owner-occupier nation.

But in 1982, following the deepest economic recession since the Second World War, few expected Margaret Thatcher to survive. She was at one point the most unpopular Prime Minister of the 20th century. Labour was waiting for Mrs Thatcher to follow her predecessor, Edward Heath, and abandon "punk monetarism", as the former Labour Chancellor Denis Healey had called it. Few had taken her at her word when she announced that "the lady's not for turning". UK unemployment rose to two million in 1981 and three million by the time the recession ended in 1982. In those days it was considered inconceivable that a government could survive the return of mass unemployment on a scale unseen since the 1930s. But she did, with a little help from General Galtieri.

The Falklands War in 1982 aroused little enthusiasm in Scotland. A few patriotic Scots cheered when Mrs Thatcher told the Scottish Conservatives in May that it represented "a triumphant reawakening of British pride" – mostly because of their unquestioning support for the Scottish regiments. But the Church of Scotland was left divided over the Falklands War, and only supported the invasion reluctantly and after a heated debate at the General Assembly. To many Scots, the Falklands adventure seemed like a parody of British imperialism, history repeating itself as farce. At least, that was, until HMS Sheffield was sunk, the first British warship to go down since the Second World War. But victory at Goose Green boosted Margaret Thatcher's popularity – and allowed her to win a triumphant victory over Labour's Michael Foot in the 1983 General Election. Labour's manifesto – "the longest suicide note in history" – helped. The call for a siege economy backed by nationalisation, did not appeal to the British electorate, who still blamed Labour for the Winter of Discontent. Labour's election campaign was an organisational disaster, led by Michael Foot, a brilliant orator and intellectual who was ill-equipped for the television age. It was Labour's worst result in a UK general election since the 1931. The party returned 28% of the vote, just 3% ahead of the SDP-Liberal Alliance. Out of touch and out of time, it looked as if Labour could be heading for the same fate as the old Liberal Party in the 1920s.

After taking on General Galtieri, and burying Labour, Mrs Thatcher finally felt able to take on Arthur Scargill, the leader of the National Union of Mineworkers. "We had to fight the enemy without in the Falklands," she told the 1984 Tory conference. "Now we are fighting the enemy within." The miners had brought down her predecessor Edward Heath in February 1974 when, amid industrial chaos and a three-day week, he had gone to the country asking: "Who runs Britain?" – and got the wrong answer. She wasn't going to make the same mistake. The miners' strike of 1984/5 was a disaster that everyone could see coming, except, apparently, the leader of the NUM, Arthur Scargill. Mrs Thatcher had prepared for the strike for three years, and only announced the savage round of pit closures when she was confident she had the coal stocks, the alternative energy sources and the legal protections, to fight off Arthur Scargill's flying pickets. Private road hauliers had been hired to move coal, power stations converted to run on oil. The police were given generous financial incentives to remain loyal – officers at the battle of Orgreave coking plant in Rotherham used to wave their overtime slips at the striking miners.

In Scotland, the dispute was particularly bitter, not least because there was a widespread feeling that it should never have taken place, and that if it had been left to the leader of the Scottish miners, Mick McGahey, it wouldn't have. Without the full support of the TUC or the pit overmen's union NACODS, and without a strike ballot or significant support from the public, the strike was doomed from the start. I had made a half-hour film profile of the Scottish miners' leader, Mick McGahey, called *Scargill's Left Hand Man*, before the strike, and got to know the hard-drinking Communist quite well. Many in the Labour Party believed that he would have exploited the weaknesses of the National Coal Board's chief executive, Ian MacGregor, an expatriate Scot from Kinlochleven who was appointed by Mrs Thatcher to perform open-heart surgery on the mining industry. MacGregor was a poor media performer who had been wobbling before and during the action. He showed signs of instability when he turned up to supposedly secret talks with the NUM at the Norton House Hotel in Edinburgh in September 1984 and emerged from his car with a green plastic bag over his face. This was in full view of the TV cameras. Mick McGahey was a realist who understood that Thatcher was a class warrior who would never give in to Scargill; there was a widespread belief in Scottish political circles that McGahey would have settled for the compromise that was offered by MacGregor at Norton House. But Arthur Scargill was determined to fight to the finish.

After 1985, when the defeated miners returned to work behind their brass bands, industrial resistance crumbled and trade union membership went into steep decline with 13 pits closing within the next five years. Before the First World War, there were 140,000 miners in Scotland; after the last deep mine pit, Longannet, closed in 2002 there were barely 500. In 2013, even open-cast coal-mining collapsed in Scotland. In Dalkeith, where my children attended the local King's Park primary school, the only reminder of this district's 300-year history of coal mining was a miner's lamp on the school football shirts.

NEW TIMES

In the late-1980s, the intellectual climate on the Left was dominated by what the Communist Party theoretical journal, *Marxism Today*, called "New Times" – the theory that we were entering a new post-industrial era of capitalism. This was based on a lecture delivered by the Marxist historian EJ Hobsbawm in 1978 called *The Forward March of Labour Halted?* in which he argued that the age of mass politics based on the manual working-class was over. Hobsbawm advised that the Left would have to widen its appeal if it wanted to remain relevant to relatively affluent white-collar workers, women voters and public-sector employees.

Marxism Today's editor, Martin Jacques, then proclaimed that

"Thatcherism" was a radical new "hegemonic" project, which could appeal to individualist, non-unionised voters who didn't think of themselves as "working class" any more and didn't like benefit scroungers. This theory – largely a recognition of political reality – migrated rapidly to mainstream Labour politicians through the Labour leader Neil Kinnock, who took over after Labour's comprehensive rejection in the 1983 General Election. From Kinnock, the theory progressed rapidly to Tony Blair, who was to go on to make it the intellectual foundation of the New Labour "Project".

But the future Labour Prime Minister thought he was only following his argument to its logical conclusion and abandoning Clause 4, the trade unions, and "monolithic" public-service provision. *Marxism Today* – its job done – decided to end it all, and the magazine liquidated itself in 1992. Perhaps the irony of a Marxist organ giving birth to Tony Blair was just too much to take. Before he died, Professor Hobsbawm made clear that he thought Blair had taken him rather too literally and that he had never intended Labour to abandon social democracy altogether. Nor does Martin Jacques accept collective responsibility for New Labour.

But the point about this analysis for Scottish politics was that New Labour was largely a response to the altered material circumstances of Labour voters south of the border. In his pamphlet, *Southern Discomfort*, the Labour MP Giles Radice argued that Labour would never win again unless it allied its "objective of social justice to the individualistic aspirations of voters in the south of England". Working-class *Sun*-reading voters in the south wanted nothing to do with old Labour, with its council housing and union mentality. This was the age of "Loadsamoney", the Essex-lad character played by Harry Enfield on the TV show *Saturday Night Live*, who boasted about the size of his "wad" and threw money around like confetti.

Scots didn't find this particularly funny for the obvious reason that their wads were getting smaller, and many were beginning a career on benefits that would last for the rest of their lives. The theory that being working class was old-fashioned was small consolation for manufacturing workers who'd lost their livelihoods. They felt increasingly abandoned by Labour, a party they supported in the sincere belief that it wanted to improve the lives of working people – or at least keep them in work. Scots saw the welfare state, which had been the basis of the Unionist bargain after the Second World War, being intellectually challenged by UK politicians of the Right and the Left in the 1980s and 1990s.

The UK was becoming two political nations and this was clear in voting patterns. In the 1983 General Election, Labour won nearly one million votes in Scotland and 41 seats against the Tories' 21, even though it was under severe pressure from the breakaway SDP-Liberal Alliance. In England, by contrast, Labour won only 148 seats against the Conservatives' 362. Labour's defence policy was regarded as a large part of Labour's problem in 1983. The Soviet Union still seemed to pose a real threat and unilateral nuclear disarmament looked like dangerous defeatism to many English voters. The Tories ran newspaper ads showing a British soldier with his hands up under the catchline: "Labour's Defence Policy". But here again, a north/south divide was opening. Scots clearly didn't find unilateralism to be a sufficient reason to stop voting Labour. In fact, in Scotland, partly as a result of the SNP's campaigning, many voters wanted to see the removal of nuclear weapons from the Clyde.

The Scottish dimension was becoming more apparent in the 1980s. The trouble was that the Scottish Nationalists weren't benefiting from it. They returned only two seats in 1983, attracting a dismal 12% of the vote. The SNP, it seemed, had become almost as irrelevant, politically, as it had been in the 1950s. The cultural commentator, Stuart Hall, argued in *Marxism Today* that one of the consequences of "New Times" would be that the politics of class would give way to the politics of identity. Clearly, the politics of identity wasn't making much progress in Scotland.

Or was it? Commentators perhaps made a mistake in the 1980s in measuring the impact of Scottish Nationalism purely in terms of the electoral returns of the SNP. In fact, identity politics was very much a feature of political life in Scotland, it just didn't take place in political parties. Stuart Cosgrove, believes that the national question migrated to popular music in the 1980s.[72] If you wanted to know what was happening in Scotland the best place to look was in the lyrics and comments of bands like Hue and Cry, The Proclaimers, Runrig. That the Scottish National Party failed initially to capitalise on this growing sense of political Scottishness is perhaps understandable because it was registering in popular culture rather than opinion polls.

Scottish rock music developed its own intelligentsia in the

1980s, with the irrepressible Pat Kane of Hue and Cry, Ricky Ross of Deacon Blue, Craig Reid of The Proclaimers. These performers were able to speak to people of all classes, using their popularity to canvas for social and political change. But it wasn't so much what they said as the way they said it, according to Stuart Cosgrove: "When The Proclaimers appeared on Channel 4's The Tube in January 1987. It was an unbelievable critical moment in Scottish popular culture history," he says. "And one of the reasons it was that big was to do with their voices. It was the first time ever that I had heard Scottish accents like that on mainstream TV."[73]

But their lyrics were worth a listen too. Never before had Scottish industrial history made it into the pop charts. Their most famous song, *Letter from America*, which paraphrases the 19th-century poem *Lochaber No More* and charts the factory closures in Linwood and Bathgate, reached number three in the singles charts. Deacon Blue's anthem, *Dignity*, about a dustman who saves up to buy a boat, was seen as a rejection of Thatcherite values in an age of mass unemployment – though on examining the lyrics I'm not sure Mrs Thatcher would entirely have disagreed with its message.

When Sir Nicholas Fairbairn, the bibulous Tory Solicitor General described Annie Lennox and Simple Minds as "left-wing scum" for appearing at a Nelson Mandela concert, many Scots were outraged. At the very least, Scottish popular music represented a cultural antidote to the go-getting, power-dressing ethos of the 1980s, which Scotland never bought into, even thought Scots were buying their council houses just as enthusiastically as people in England. In the 1980s, this cultural self-confidence arguably provided the foundation for the constitutional changes in the next decade. At a time when the unions were defeated, universities had retreated into scholastic irrelevance and the political parties were all over the place, the minstrels returned to mediate Scotland's national conversation, just as the Scottish bards had done in earlier times – from Blind Harry to Robert Burns.

Pop music also created a space in which Scots could keep thinking politically without getting caught up in the tribalism and factionalism of the established parties, which had failed Scotland in the 1970s and 1980s. The parties seemed to be more concerned about attacking each other rather than mobilising a serious resistance. Most Scots refuse to be placed in a Labour or SNP pigeon hole, still less a Tory pigeon hole. I felt this very strongly myself, not least because, as a BBC journalist, I was supposed to be independent of any political allegiance. And I was. The only party I have ever been a member of was Labour, and even then, only very briefly. However, that didn't stop me being accused by one side or the other of being a member of the "other lot".

Scots turned away from the political parties in the 1980s in much the same way they turned away from the Kirk in the 1960s. By the early 1990s, the active membership of all Scottish parties had more than halved. Labour had about 15,000 members; the SNP around 10,000. Political parties were no longer mass organisations. There were more members of the National Trust for Scotland than all the Scottish political parties combined. The existing party political system no longer was fit for purpose. At the very moment, when Scots were rediscovering their national political identity, even the Scottish National Party was anathema to most Scots.

Scotland's cultural awakening predated the Poll Tax, but as soon as Margaret Thatcher announced at the Tory conference in Perth in 1987 that the community charge was to be introduced in Scotland a year ahead of England, it erupted onto the streets. Scots from all parties, including some Conservatives, were morally outraged at a tax in which a "dustman paid the same as a duke". This included many hundreds of thousands of middle-class Scots in Edinburgh who stood to gain financially from the "community charge", as it was officially called. "It was a pretty dumb political decision, in retrospect," says Malcolm Rifkind ruefully, "but the reasons for it were nothing to do with guinea pigs, it was to do with trying to deal with the controversy over the rating system as soon as possible."[74] Guinea pigs or no, the perception in Scotland was that this abominable tax was being imposed by a government which had been rejected by the vast majority of Scottish voters.

In the 1987 General Election, the Tories lost 11 of their 21 Scottish MPs, and Scotland realised that it was entering a constitutional crisis. It was called the "Doomsday Scenario" by the Scottish press. A neo-Nationalist grouping called Scottish Labour Action erupted from the ranks of the Scottish Labour Party. Led by the youthful lawyer, Ian Smart, and the future Labour health minister, Susan Deacon, who looked more like a rock singer than a Labour politician, SLA called for a campaign of non-payment of the Poll Tax. SLA's founding statement demanded "the right of the Scottish people to self-determination". This was not the kind of language that anyone had heard from Labour politicians – at least not since the days of Keir Hardie and the ILP. And more importantly, in the television era, they all looked good.

But non-payment was not a position that the Labour Shadow Scottish Secretary, Donald Dewar, was prepared to endorse, because it meant breaking the law of the land. Dewar was a Scottish lawyer first and a politician second. Scots took to the streets in huge numbers to protest against the hated tax. Writers like the novelist William McIlvanney condemned Thatcherism's assault on "the very fabric of Scottish life". But it took direct action to frustrate its implementation, though not the kind of pointless vandalism of the SNP's aborted Scottish resistance.

Tommy Sheridan, the militant leader, who also looked and behaved more like a rock-star than a politician, organised well-publicised demonstrations to prevent warrant sales – the process of debt recovery used by some councils which involved the debtor's possessions being brought onto the pavement and sold to the highest bidder. "We made the Poll Tax unworkable in that first year", he claims in *Road to Referendum*, condemning the established parties. "Labour councils that said they were against the Poll Tax but were sending out sheriff officers to working-class families to collect it. Disgraceful."[75] Sheridan ended up going to prison for his views. But the campaign went on, even after the Poll Tax was abolished. To this day, £435m remains uncollected across Scotland.[76]

Those institutions loosely called "civil society" – the churches, trade unions, parties and charities found common cause in the Poll Tax in a way that had eluded them in 1979. Here was a moral issue that could unite Scots in the way abstract constitutional issues could not, and the discontent was made abundantly clear to Mrs Thatcher when she came north to address the General Assembly of the Church of Scotland in May 1988. In her Sermon on the Mound, as it was called, she tried to argue that the Good Samaritan was only able to be charitable because he had been able to become rich. "Christianity is about spiritual redemption," she said, echoing the Rev Thomas Chalmers, "not social reform." The Kirk responded by handing her a stack of Church and Nation reports calling for social reform on poverty, housing and unemployment. The next day, Margaret Thatcher attended the Scottish Cup Final between Celtic and Dundee United. The fans expressed their discontent at her Conservative sermonising in their own unique way. They came equipped with red cards which they raised when the Prime Minister entered, while singing, as George Galloway recalls, "Mrs Thatcher, Mrs Thatcher, stick the Poll Tax up your arse".

The two most salient facts about the Scottish anti-Poll Tax campaign of 1987 to 1990 was its peaceful character – there were no riots – and its complete failure to prevent it happening. It was only after anti-Poll Tax riots in Trafalgar Square in 1990 that the UK Government took note and moved to scrap it – and ultimately its author, Margaret Thatcher, resigned in November 1990 after her Cabinet revolted against her. "We were certainly involved in breaking the law," recalls Tommy Sheridan, "but we did it a lot more civilly than breaking shop windows, and rioting and stealing sunglasses."[77] The message could not have been clearer: it didn't matter that Scots had made peaceful and eloquent rejection of the Poll Tax, through some of the largest peaceful demonstrations in Scottish history – chuck a few fire bombs in central London and the Government listens.

A CLAIM OF RIGHT

If Scotland votes for independence in 2014, then Alex Salmond may be tempted to raise a statue to Thatcher outside the Scottish Parliament because the recovery of the Scottish National Party in the late-1980s couldn't have happened without her. The Poll Tax suddenly injected a national dimension into Scottish politics as Alex Salmond turned the party's fire firmly on the Tory's "lack of a mandate" and led a broad-based campaign for non-payment.

Then, in 1988, Jim Sillars, now with the Scottish National Party, destroyed a 19,000 Labour majority to win the Govan by-election, winning back the seat that his now-wife Margo MacDonald had lost in 1974. Govan was a family affair for the Nationalists.

The journalist Fiona Ross recalls ringing Donald Dewar three days before polling day at 7pm. "To my astonishment he answered the phone. He was at home. That told me everything I needed to know because normally he would have been out knocking doors." The doors that had been slamming in Nationalist faces since 1979 suddenly were opening again.

Jim Sillars attributed his victory to a televised debate in

which he had asked the rather lumpen Labour candidate, Bob Gillespie, what his view was on "additionality" – the principle that EU subsidies should not replace existing public spending in member states. "Bob didn't have a view on additionality, indeed, he hadn't a clue what it meant," Sillars recalls.[78] That was a significant moment in Labour's decline. Bob Gillespie's pitch was that he was "Clyde-built" – a genuine member of the industrial working-class. But working-class voters were no longer prepared to have their votes taken for granted. They were no longer content to support any old "numpty" – to use the Glasgow vernacular – just because they happened to wear a red rosette.

Govan was the moment Scotland embarked in earnest upon its journey to self-government. The Poll Tax debacle condensed all the grievances that had been building up since the 1960s and forced Scotland to reassess its place in the Union. The shabby machinations over the referendum, the industrial vandalism, the loss of Scotland's oil-wealth, all came together in a resolution which was never written down anywhere, or voted on, or debated, but became the mission of almost every politically aware citizen of Scotland. First destroy the Tories; then restore the Scottish Parliament.

Unfortunately, this being Scotland, things didn't quite work out as planned. Indeed, the 1992 General Election, when chattering Scotland expected the Tories to be wiped out, turned into a stay of execution as they gained two seats north of the border. This result was more painful to many Scots than the fact that Neil Kinnock failed to win the election for Labour. The absence of the Thatcher factor, combined with the vagaries of the electoral system, gave the Tories an illusory recovery. In fact, their share of the vote, in 1992, reached an all-time low of 24%.[79]

I was in London presenting political programmes for BBC2 in Westminster, but I felt the shock waves from 400 miles away. Jim Sillars, deprived of his Govan seat, and on his way out of active politics, condemned Scottish voters as "90-Minute Patriots". There also was a flurry of cross-party activity, and the convening of various umbrella groups, such as Scotland United. A non-party coalition of MPs, novelists like William McIlvanney, councillors and trade unionists, Scotland United organised a Democracy Demonstration in December 1992 coinciding the European heads of government meeting in Edinburgh, which attracted around 40,000 people. But Scottish political tribalism was not dead, even in this setback, as one of its leaders, the then Labour MP George Galloway recalled: "The late Donald Dewar described me as a collaborator, because I was standing on platforms with Alex Salmond. And my riposte was, We're not collaborators, we're the resistance".[80] There was a sense of desperation among home rule voters at the inability of the Scottish political parties to realise the aspirations of the Scottish people.

But they needn't have worried because, thanks to a small, wrinkled ex-civil servant called Jim Ross, the fuse had already been lit under the British state, and it was primed to go off in 1997. The Yoda of Scottish home rule, he was the lead author of Scotland's Claim of Right, the document prepared for the newly convened, or reconvened, Scottish Constitutional Convention in 1987. It looked back to Scottish history in order to take Scots forward to self-government. It was basically an attempt to repeat the success of John MacCormick's post-war Constitutional Convention with its National Covenant, which had been signed by two million Scots by 1951.

In the early 1980s, the Campaign for a Scottish Assembly was a threadbare organisation run by a handful of self-styled "inveterate troublemakers" like Alan Lawson, editor of neo-Nationalist magazine *Radical Scotland*. It had no organisation or funding to speak of, but it kept the faith. I first came across Jim Ross, a member of CSA, addressing a sparsely attended fringe meeting at a Labour conference in the mid-1980s and I was amazed at the confidence with which he outlined his plan to restore sovereignty to the Scottish people. It seemed utterly ridiculous – this little man taking on the British state. But he did it – with a little help from his friends.

He called it *The Claim of Right* to chime with Scottish history, even though the 1689 original had been more of a declaration against episcopacy than a demand for popular sovereignty. The more recent Claim of Right drawn up by the breakaway evangelicals led by the Rev Thomas Chalmers, who walked out of the Church of Scotland in the 1843 Disruption, had even less: that was a rejection of the rights of landowners to nominate Kirk ministers and represented, perhaps, an assertion of ecclesiastical independence from the state but had nothing to do with setting up a Scottish Parliament. But the Claim drafted for the Scottish Constitutional Convention in 1988 struck the right historical note at the right time, and was signed on 30th March 1989 in the General Assembly building (built by the Rev

Thomas Chalmers's Free Kirk on Edinburgh's Mound) by most of Scotland's MPs, MEPs, councillors and an array of civic organisations including trade unions, small business representatives and charities.

The fact it was signed by all but one of Labour's predominantly Unionist Scottish MPs suggests some divine intervention may have been involved because the document read like the Declaration of Arbroath. The sovereignty pledge stated that: "We, gathered as the Scottish Constitutional Convention, do hereby acknowledge the sovereign right of the Scottish people to determine the form of Government best suited to their needs, and do hereby declare and pledge that in all our actions and deliberations their interests shall be paramount." It didn't promise to resist English rule so long as but a hundred of them were left alive, but it was a pretty *Braveheartish* pledge nevertheless. It also called for a referendum, though it didn't suggest who would organise it.

"And what if that voice we know so well says, 'We say no and we are the state'?" asked Canon Kenyon Wright, the Episcopalian clergyman who chaired the Constitutional Convention, in the most famous rhetorical question of the devolution era. "Well, we say yes – and we are the people." In fact, Mrs Thatcher, then still in office, completely ignored the event, and may not even have known it was taking place because she had other things on her mind, like her government's divisions over Europe. The *Claim of Right* document had no legal or constitutional standing whatever, and was dismissed by Tories and much of the press as a PR stunt.

The Labour Shadow Secretary, Donald Dewar, was initially reluctant to get involved with the Constitutional Convention at all on the grounds that it looked like "an unelected talking shop". And he was right – that's exactly what it was – initially. But somehow, Jim Ross's advocacy, the Kirk's endorsement and the sight of Scottish MPs actually co-operating with each other lent a dignity and sense of history to the campaign for a Scottish Parliament, and demonstrated that, in the right circumstances, the pen really is mightier than the sword. The Claim captured the imagination of the Scottish people, by appealing over the heads of the discredited Scottish political parties and by reinventing Scottish history in Nationalist drag.

Perversely, the only opposition party that wasn't there to take the sovereignty pledge was the Scottish National Party. The

Convention was boycotted by the Nationalists, on the advice of Jim Sillars, the SNP vice-convener and victor of Govan. He claims that this was because the SNP was only to be allocated three seats on the cross-party body, and because the Convention wouldn't support the idea of a multi-option referendum that included independence. It is a matter of record that Alex Salmond believed this boycott to be a mistake at the time, though he now says in *Road to Referendum* that it probably "didn't make any difference in the long run".

Actually, I think it did make a difference. The Convention wouldn't have been nearly as successful had the SNP been involved. This is because the Labour MPs would never have put their name to the sovereignty pledge with Nationalists in attendance. The two tribes of Scotland would have spent their entire time arguing with each other and seeing who could walk out first. The SNP, which despite Govan was still an insignificant force in the late-1980s, benefited enormously from the Convention, but only because it wasn't a part of it.

The Nationalists were still on the sidelines as the Convention went on to draw up a blueprint for a Scottish Parliament elected on proportional representation with revenue-raising powers, called *Scotland's Parliament; Scotland's Right* in 1995. This proposed an elected Scottish Parliament with the power to vary income tax by 3p in the pound, and the authority to legislate on a wide range of domestic areas including education, criminal justice and health. The UK Parliament in Westminster would primarily be responsible for defence, foreign affairs, immigration, social security, taxation and broad economic policy.

By now, the Constitutional Convention was under the joint chairmanship of the Liberal leader David Steel and the former Labour minister Harry Ewing. Under the new Labour leader, John Smith's devolution had been accepted as "the settled will" of the Scottish people, an unquestioned commitment from Labour, to be implemented within the first year of coming to office. This was the same John Smith who I had flown down to Oxford for the fatal debate on the eve of the 1979 referendum. It had been a long time coming, but the former Devolution Minister was completely confident that the Parliament would happen. The Tories under John Major were divided over the Maastricht Treaty and Europe in general, and it seemed only a matter of time until Labour took over and Scottish hopes were fulfilled. Unfortunately, John Smith died in

1994, and under Labour's new leader, Tony Blair, devolution was the settled will no more.

NOT SO SETTLED

Tony Blair didn't oppose devolution; he just didn't really care much about it either. He was dedicated to the New Labour/*Marxism Today* "Project" of abandoning the politics of the manufacturing age and making Labour attractive to those individualistic, home-owning aspirational voters who had abandoned Labour for Thatcher in the 1980s. His idea of constitutional change was to scrap Clause 4 of the Labour Constitution, the one committing the party to nationalising "the means of production distribution and exchange". He inherited the devolution commitment from John Smith and assumed that it was not worth the political risk of trying to abandon it. As Gerry Hassan puts it, "We know that Blair wasn't a home ruler. We know that Blair was a British Nationalist. We also know, from all the briefings of the New Labour era, that Blair in the run-in of 1996 and 1997, looked hard at whether he could drop the Scottish Parliament proposals, but he knew he couldn't."[81] But, like Harold Wilson before him, Blair realised the importance of securing a contingent of Scottish MPs if Labour were to win a comfortable majority in the House of Commons.

Blair had been brought up in Edinburgh and went to Fettes, but he was never entirely comfortable with the Scottish party, nor it with him. The Islington set of Labour intellectuals, of which Blair was the most prominent member, regarded the Scots as a powerful if somewhat primitive force, a kind of Labour id, that had to be placated rather than led. Tony Blair's press spokesman, Alastair Campbell, was also a Scot and played the bagpipes, but he had serious problems with the Scottish press as did his boss, who reportedly called them "unreconstructed wankers". Campbell wrote in his diaries about his leader's difficulties with the Scottish media[82]: "TB said he'd had a day full of whingeing jock journos saying they wanted devolution and they wanted no tax and they wanted Scotland to get more money and they wanted to win the World Cup and why was I stopping them ... I said he [Blair] should try to hide his antagonism." While Alastair Campbell claimed to loath the "jocks" as he called the political press corps, he was close to a number of Scottish journalists in the press gallery in Westminster. I was not one of them. My relations with the great spin doctor were poor because he had been informed by Scottish Labour MPs that I was a slippery Nationalist, working undercover, and got my orders direct from Alex Salmond.

This was odd because in the early 1990s I, like many Scots, had very little interest in the politics of independence. I thought Alex Salmond was a clever and combative politician who did a good job as a guerilla opposition leader, but I never imagined that the SNP was anything other than a protest organisation. Unlike many Scots in Westminster, I didn't go to Burns Nights or bore on about Scottish literature, antisyzygys and football. I was married, had children, lived in a Victorian terraced house in Battersea and even had a cottage in Dorset. As a non-football supporting Anglo-Scot, who didn't care about religion, I'd always had difficulty fitting in with certain elements of Scottish male society because a lot of them regarded me as, well, English. However, in London, where I had been born, I discovered that I was assumed – certainly in the Westminster village – to be a bit of a Scottish Nationalist hard man, which couldn't have been further from the truth at the time. I had gone down to London, not to take on the English establishment, but to become a BBC presenter on one of the raft of TV programmes which were launched on the back of the televising of Parliament which began in 1989. But I found there to be what I can only call an impatience with Scotland among many in the Westminster village in the 1990s. I kept finding myself embroiled in heated discussions over obscure issues like the West Lothian Question and the Barnett Formula. A lot of London journalists and politicians seemed to resent the idea of Scottish MPs voting on English affairs in the Commons. I always regarded Tam Dalyell's West Lothian complaint – first raised in the debate over the Scotland and Wales Bill in the 1970s – as constitutional pedantry.

I didn't feel particularly strongly about it, but I still argued the case that it was a bit rich to complain about Scots having a say on English affairs when English Tory MPs had an inbuilt majority on Scottish parliamentary committees. There was not what I would call prejudice against Scots, but there was an increasing wariness. I was a card-carrying member of the Parliamentary Lobby for nearly ten years, the Westminster freemasonry of "insider" hacks who are permitted access to the Members' Lobby of the House of Commons, but there was an air of suspicion there, too. When Peter Mandelson slipped into the lobby to give his off-the-record briefings to the hack pack, I was often told that I was not entitled to listen in. No reason given – just a feeling on his part that I couldn't be relied upon not to betray confidences. Mind you, he was probably right.

With hindsight, it's clear that tensions were building up because of the more assertive political culture that was emerging in Scotland in the years up to the Devolution Referendum. After 1992, when John Major described devolution as "the most dangerous proposition ever put before the British people", there was a reassessment of the relationship between Scotland and England. UK politicians who had not really thought very much about how Scotland fitted into the UK constitutional machinery started to question what they perceived as unfairnesses in the funding arrangements. Around this time, the controversy over public spending in Scotland surfaced. In 1995, the Scottish Office produced the infamous Government Expenditure and Revenue Scotland tables that appeared to show that Scots received £1,400 more per head in public spending than the UK average. This ignored various forms of 'non-identified' public spending in the south, such as the Jubilee line extension and London's Cross Rail projects. Anyway, oil revenues were not included in the calculus and any spending disparity was more than covered by hydrocarbon taxes. However, some English journalists and politicians became convinced that Scotland was taking England for a ride, and the hoary old West Lothian Question was exhumed to challenge Labour's plans for devolution. In Labour, this came right from the top.

BETRAYAL

As the Conservatives became embroiled in the various sleaze scandals that followed John Major's "back to basics" initiative in 1994, it became clear that Labour was on the way back to power. While Tony Blair was not thought to be actively opposed to devolution, he was clearly no enthusiast. This was Gordon Brown's territory, and in the division of responsibilities at the top of the Labour Party after the Granita deal on the leadership, Blair left Scotland well alone. The Shadow Cabinet was anyway practically a Scottish government in exile, with Donald Dewar, Robin Cook, Derry Irvine,

George Robertson and other Caledonian luminaries in prominent roles. Devolution was an article of faith among the Scottish barons, and Blair initially avoided heresy.

However, this was to change. The New Labour leader was emboldened by the discovery that the Scottish Labour Party was not as hostile to the abandonment of Socialism as everyone had told him it was. The Scottish Labour conference in March 1995 was the first significant Labour body to endorse the scrapping of Clause Four, after Blair had announced it, theatrically, in the very last lines of his first speech to the UK Labour conference in October 1994. Blair recognised that devolution was unfinished business, but as the possibility of a Labour victory turned into probability, he began to worry it might create a degree of unnecessary destabilisation of the British state at a time when Labour was trying to be ultra-patriotic. This was around the time that Blair, or rather his communications chief, Alastair Campbell, was writing articles in *The Sun* about how much the New Labour leader "loved the pound" and wanted "Britain to be great again". Splitting the nation up through constitutional change didn't connect.

At this stage, Labour was committed to legislating for a Scottish Parliament without a referendum in the first year of a Labour Government. This was no longer acceptable to Tony Blair. In his diaries, *Prelude to Power*, Alastair Campbell, claims that Labour's abandonment of the "settled will" policy was taken by the Labour leader alone, without consultation with Gordon Brown, the then Shadow Chancellor. He recounts: "[Tony Blair] wanted to limit the tax-raising powers. He wanted to promise a referendum before the Parliament is established and he wanted to be explicit in that 'power devolved is power retained at Westminster'".[83] Campbell quotes Pat McFadden, the Scottish MP who advised Blair saying: "There would be Hell to pay in the party, not least from Gordon Brown." According to Campbell, Tony Blair replied: "They'll just have to live with it." I'm not entirely sure of the accuracy of this account. It seems inconceivable to me that Tony Blair would have made this dramatic U-turn had he not cleared it in advance with Gordon Brown, the godfather of Scottish Labour. One of the drawbacks of learning history through the memoirs of press officers is that they're inclined to think the political world revolves entirely around them. Campbell may not have been as far in the loop as he thought he was. It seems that Brown had been persuaded by the

experience of the Constitutional Convention that a form of democratic consultation might entrench the Scottish Parliament and that
it could deliver a better Scottish Parliament than the "empty suit" of
1979.

Tony Blair's discomfort with devolution grew ever greater
the nearer he came to the General Election. In June 1996, according to Alastair Campbell, he even contemplated abandoning tax-
raising powers and dropping the primary law-making powers of
the Scottish Parliament altogether. But he realised that would be
too explosive so he looked for other ways to curb the ambitions
of the devolutionists.[84] A Labour committee under the Shadow
Lord Chancellor, Lord Derry Irvine, a close friend of Blair, had
been looking into the practicalities of devolution during 1995, according to the Scottish journalist Peter Jones.[85] It concluded that the
best way to ensure the legislation actually happened, and was not
amended-to-death, like previous devolution bills in the 1970s, was
to make absolutely sure that this was indeed the "settled will" of the
Scottish people before putting it before Parliament. And the only
way to ensure that, said Irvine, was a pre-legislative referendum.
The alternative might be to end up in with a succession of failed
bills, as happened to the Liberal Prime Minister William Gladstone
over Irish Home Rule in the 19th century. Blair later claimed he had
his referendum epiphany after reading Roy Jenkins's biography
of Gladstone, and decided that he wasn't going to end up like the
grand old man.

The Shadow Scottish Secretary George Robertson was the
fall-guy here. It's not clear whether or not he knew about the Derry
Irvine committee, but it certainly came as a shock when he was
informed that he had to give a speech in June 1996 saying that
devolution wasn't quite the settled will any more, and that there
would have to be another referendum, like in 1979. Only months
previously, he'd told John Humphrys on the BBC's *On the Record*
programme, commenting on the Constitutional Convention blueprint, that "no referendum would be necessary". Now, after years of
arguing that the only mandate needed for devolution was a general
election victory, he had to explain why Labour would only legislate for a Scottish Parliament if there was a clear demand for it in a
referendum. And worse – there would have to be a separate ballot
over tax powers.

The U-turn was condemned as betrayal. The Labour co-chair

of the Convention, Lord Ewing, resigned in disgust. *The Scotsman* declared that "this referendum is not needed and not wanted". It seemed, to many in Scotland, like a modern version of the Cunningham amendment. Memories of the 40% rule and Labour's conduct in the 1979 referendum campaign were still fresh in the mind of political Scotland – 18 years of hurt, as The Lightning Seeds might have put it. This was the year of the Euros, everyone was using football metaphors and the referendum was regarded a foul play by Tony's England team. The Scottish National Party leader, Alex Salmond, said it was confirmation that Labour could never be trusted to deliver devolution. The Scottish Executive of the Labour Party then confused matters by proposing, in July 1996, a two-stage referendum with three questions. It began to look as if the entire devolution project was crashing to the ground.

But with hindsight, Tony Blair was right to call for the referendum, though perhaps for the wrong reasons. By moving early and holding a pre-legislative referendum in 1997, Tony Blair didn't impede devolution, he ensured it would definitely happen. Had Blair not gone for a referendum before putting the Scotland Bill through Parliament, the House of Lords would probably have blocked it and demanded a referendum anyway, citing the precedent of 1979. There would have been parliamentary deadlock. The referendum wouldn't have taken place until much later in the Labour parliament, by which time it would have become vulnerable to backbench revolts and voter disillusion with Labour. There were many Labour MPs, from the north of England especially, who were still deeply unhappy about Scottish devolution and thought that the Labour government was far too heavily influenced by Scottish MPs.

The referendum was a gamble by Blair because it could have undermined Labour's electoral chances in the 1997 General Election – at least in Scotland. But it was a measure of the continued weakness of the Scottish National Party that Blair did not consider them to be a significant threat. What was more important in his mind was answering the West Lothian Question – about Scottish MPs voting on English affairs when English MPs have no voting rights in devolved Scottish affairs. It remains unanswered to this day. One of the consequences of the political storm that erupted in Scotland in the summer of 1996 was that Tony Blair had to accept the Constitutional Convention's blueprint for a Scottish Parliament with its proposals for primary legislative powers. According to Alastair Campbell, Blair did not agree with this at all. He wanted to ensure that power rested unambiguously in Westminster after devolution. But as a condition of incurring the wrath of the Scottish media over the referendum U-turn, George Robertson insisted on no more changes to the Constitutional Convention blueprint. So by a quirk of Unionist fate, Jim Ross's plan to restore Scottish sovereignty slipped under the wire.

A FAREWELL TO THE SCOTTISH TORIES

The most bizarre event of that frenetic pre-election year was yet to come. On 30th November 1996, an army Land Rover accompanied by a detail of the Royal Company of Archers, trundled up the Royal Mile in Edinburgh taking the Stone of Destiny, the block of sacred sandstone that had been stolen from Scotland by King Edward I exactly 700 years previously, to its last resting place in Edinburgh Castle. The Tory Scottish Secretary, Michael Forsyth, realising that his party was facing doom in Scotland persuaded John Major to make a final desperate bid to make the Tories sound Scottish. Caledonian mystics claimed that this was a confirmation of the Latin prophecy that when the stone returned to Scotland, so would sovereignty. There's enough Arthurian nonsense bound up with the "Fatal Stone" to fill a dozen Dan Brown books.

Scots were left bemused and amused at this bizarre gesture by the leader of the Scottish Conservatives – a party which had no future in Scotland seeking to mobilise the past in a desperate attempt to stave off the inevitable. Saving the Scottish Tories would take more than the Wee Magic Stane. The General Election of 1997 was the end for the Tories in Scotland, a dead stop. They lost every one of their Scottish seats. Scottish voters made up for their miscalculations in 1992 and used tactical voting to leverage every non-Conservative vote. Since the 1980s, Scots had developed an almost telepathic ability to use their votes tactically to eliminate Conservative representation in Scotland – now they had wiped the slate clean.

The Scottish Tories actually won 18% of the vote in 1997, but it was so dispersed that it didn't deliver a single Scottish seat in the House of Commons. The Tories had been opponents of devolution and of proportional representation – but in the end that was their lifeline, because it was only PR in Holyrood that revived the corpse of Scottish Conservatism. On election night, the outgoing Scottish Secretary, Michael Forsyth, looked devastated as well he might, for this wasn't just a change in government, but a transformative event in Scottish history. The Tories had been – to repeat – the most successful political party in Scotland throughout most of the 20th century. Far more successful than Labour, which only wrested control from the Unionists for brief spells in the 1920s and in 1945 and didn't come fully into its own until the 1980s. Now, Michael Forsyth – Margaret Thatcher's apostle in Scotland – had brought that auld Unionist sang to a close.

I was in London covering the UK General Election but you could almost hear the cheering all the way from Westminster, just as I had heard the echoes of Scottish despair in 1992. The result led to an outpouring of equally irrational optimism and almost eclipsed the anxieties about Tony Blair's jiggery-pokery with the Scottish referendum. But the Nationalists had little to celebrate in the 1997 result. The SNP had made modest gains and doubled its seats from three to six, though they only increased its share of the vote by 0.6% up to 22.1%. This was undoubtedly Labour's night, and though it didn't match the Tory Unionists in 1955 and win a majority of votes, it returned its largest number of seats – 56 seats in Scotland out of 72. Scotland was united: behind Labour. It is not hard to understand why Scottish Labour MPs feel aggrieved when they are told that they are a spent force in Scottish politics and that the SNP is "Scotland's party". Labour was clearly Scotland's national party, at least as far as general election politics is concerned – and, to some extent, this remains the case today. Labour won more than one million votes in Scotland in the 2010 General Election.

The new Scottish Secretary, Donald Dewar, and his irrepressible special adviser, Wendy Alexander, went to work immediately drafting a white paper on devolution – with a little manic assistance from the Chancellor Gordon Brown. This document *Scotland's Parliament* was published in July 1997, and briefly became a bestseller in Scotland, uniquely for a government publication. Though when Dewar boasted about this in parliament, the Scottish Tory MP, Michael Ancram, wasn't impressed. "I should remind him that some bestsellers are horror stories and that nearly all are fiction." A good line that – but the fact that Ancram sat for the English seat of

Devizes, there being no Tory seats left in Scotland, blunted his barb. Tony Blair, had he had the time to read the white paper, might also have taken fright. Power devolved was not power retained in this document. It went far beyond the 1970s devolution white papers by specifying that only the powers reserved to Westminster should be spelled out in the legislation. Everything else would be assumed to be devolved to the 129 members of the Scottish Parliament. They would be elected by a hybrid electoral system, the additional members system, which elected 72 MSPs by first past the post, and 56 drawn from party lists. It was generally agreed that AMS was the best way of ensuring the constituency link remained, while ensuring that no party – and especially not the Scottish National Party – would win an absolute majority.

This would be a parliament with primary legislative powers – by a popular mandate of the Scottish electorate. The white paper declared that sovereignty remained "ultimately" in Westminster. The idea was that Westminster had demonstrated its sovereignty by handing primary legislative powers to the Scottish Parliament. But this was constitutional sophistry since it raised the question of whether and under what circumstances this chunk of sovereignty could or would ever be taken back by Westminster. The whole point about sovereignty is that – in constitutional theory – it is supposed to be unitary and indivisible. Yet here sovereignty was being chopped up and, parts of it, handed over to another legislature. And, in a further constitutional innovation, the Scottish Parliament was to be given automatic power on all the areas on which the Scotland Act was silent. Only specified powers such as defence, overall economic policy, foreign affairs, broadcasting and abortion were to be "reserved" exclusively to Westminster. Anything not specified would be assumed to be in the remit of the Scottish Parliament.

This was more than even the Scottish Constitutional Convention had asked for. It was a Scottish Parliament in every sense of the word, even though it called the new Scottish administration the "Scottish Executive" rather than a Scottish government. Had anything like this been proposed by the SNP, it would have been dismissed as Nationalism – and in many ways it was. Some might call it federalism – and I certainly did – though federalism presupposes the creation of a new federal level of government with an explicit division of powers between the states and the federal executive. This had a division of powers, but no central federal authority.

Perhaps only in Britain, with its unwritten constitution and long history of improvisation and "muddling through", could anything like this have been introduced. It was no exaggeration to say that Britain would never be the same again. The British state was no longer unitary. There was a competing seat of legislative authority, a rival sovereignty, to be located in Scotland. The white paper didn't begin to address the West Lothian Question; it just ignored it. Here were 56 Scottish Labour MPs, many of them in the Labour Cabinet, who would be having a decisive say on English affairs through their votes in the Westminster Parliament, when English MPs – predominantly Conservatives – would have no say on domestic affairs in the Scottish Parliament.

Where was the outcry at this inequity? Well, since there were now no Scottish Tory MPs sitting in the House of Commons, there was no legitimate Conservative voices to raise objections. English Tory MPs had other things on their minds. They realised that the Scottish party had no choice now but to adopt devolution in Scotland. You couldn't argue with a complete political wipe-out. A number of Conservatives I spoke to then thought that the Scottish Tories would break away, or would at least change their name, since "Tory" was a toxic brand in Scotland. Unfortunately for them, they didn't.

The devolution white paper was a landmark document and the Scottish Parliament we see today is a direct result of Donald Dewar and Wendy Alexander's intellectual coup d'état under the very eyes of Tony Blair, the arch Unionist. But it took the SNP Government to realise the potential of the devolution settlement. Salmond had several private meetings with Donald Dewar in 1997 at which he was asked what his terms would be for joining a cross-party campaign. In the course of these meetings, they constructed a form of words which Salmond believes led directly to the 2014 referendum. In Westminster, on 21st May, 1997, Dewar said: "I should be the last to challenge the sovereignty of the people, or deny them the right to opt for any solution to the constitutional question they wished. For example, if they want to go for independence I see no reason why they should not do so. In fact, if they want to, they should. I should be the first to accept that." This was duly agreed during the Scotland Bill debate, and is why even today Salmond insists that the Scotland Act is the "best piece of constitutional legislation ever".

DON'T THINK TWICE

After the publication, events moved fast. The Referendum Bill was tabled almost immediately and passed with hardly any time for Tory critics like Michael Howard to point out that Scots were about to vote in a referendum without any idea what they were voting for. This was a serious argument. A pre-legislative referendum was a leap in the dark. But it was one leap that the Scottish voters were clearly prepared to take. The referendum was set for 11th September 1997, the anniversary of the Battle of Stirling Bridge.

This campaign could not have been more different to 1979. For a start, the SNP under Alex Salmond was fully on board with the Yes campaign – called Scotland Forward – even though some internal party critics still argued that the SNP should be demanding a multi-option referendum, including independence. Salmond was not interested in taking the Sillars's route of splendid isolation and pressed ahead. The campaign was largely dominated by set-piece events featuring the three party leaders – the Three Tenors as they were called – Alex Salmond, Donald Dewar and the Scottish Liberal Democrat leader, Jim Wallace, all singing from the same hymn sheet. It was a sight that inspired confidence in the Scottish people because, for the first time, the three non-Conservative parties were actually working together. The shambles and sectarianism of 1979 were forgotten.

Meanwhile, the No campaign, called "Think Twice" (borrowed from a Celine Dion song of the same name) barely got off the starting blocks. Led as it was by Conservatives, like the former Scottish Secretary Michael Forsyth, who had just been humiliated in the General Election, it struggled to get a hearing. Unlike in 1979 when Scottish business came out strongly against devolution, this time it was largely silent – though this may partly have been because there wasn't much big business left in Scotland. Even the death of Diana, Princess of Wales, on 31st August 1997, failed to derail the campaign. The bouquets of memorial flowers were still stacking up outside Kensington Palace as Scotland embarked on a truncated four-day referendum campaign after the funeral. It was the constitutional equivalent of speed dating, and none the worse for that since Scotland had already made up its mind to vote Yes.

Was the result a foregone conclusion? Not everyone thought so. *The Scotsman* newspaper, for which I had been writing a weekly column from Westminster, was not convinced that this "settled will" stuff really held any water. The paper had recently been taken over by the reclusive Scottish businessmen the Barclay brothers, who had installed the conservative commentator, and former *Sunday Times* editor, Andrew Neil, as Editor-in-Chief. His view, often robustly expressed, was that devolution was a preoccupation of the Scottish chattering classes – a body of about 1,000 people – and was not an issue the Scottish public really cared about. *The Scotsman* thought, even on the eve of the referendum, that the result would be inconclusive. In fact, the devolution proposals were endorsed by a massive three to one majority and tax-raising by two to one.

The 1997 Devolution Referendum was the closest I had come to revolutionary change in my lifetime. This was a practical democratic revolution; without barricades; without fighting in the streets; without Utopian ambitions; and without any retribution afterwards. The result was decisive, democratic and everyone accepted it without quibbling or prevaricating. The Scottish people acted quietly but decisively to alter the British constitution fundamentally and irrevocably, and to restore popular sovereignty to Scotland. The Scots had every right to be proud of themselves. It was a great achievement.

Devolution would open up a new democratic space in the UK in which it became possible to envisage a different kind of politics to that of Westminster. The Scottish Parliament would be proportional, open, accessible and would deliver, as Donald Dewar put it, "Scottish solutions to Scottish problems". This was the end of a long history of failures: the home rule bills of the Gladstone Liberals, the National Covenant of 1950 and the abortive 1979 referendum. But it had got there in the end. The Scots had found themselves with a genuine Scottish Parliament, a legislature, for the first time in 300 years.

The people of Scotland were quietly rejoicing. But they weren't rejoicing for long.

CHAPTER ELEVEN
NIGHTMARE ON HOLYROOD

$$\times$$

THE VETERAN Nationalist Winnie Ewing seemed to be lost for words, fumbling with her notes. Had she forgotten her lines? Eventually, voice cracking with emotion, Mrs Ewing finally found her voice: "The Scottish Parliament, which adjourned on March 25, 1707, is hereby reconvened." It was 12th May 1999 and Scotland had a national legislature for the first time in more than 300 years. Then, all Hell broke loose.

Within a year, the "father of the nation" Donald Dewar would be dead; Enric Miralles, the Catalan architect, would be dead; Alex Salmond, who had staked his political career on devolution, had resigned in disgust and sought refuge in Westminster. The parliament building was a national scandal and there were calls for the repeal of the Scotland Act. From day one, the press attacked the Scottish Parliament, and the MSPs in it, with a ferocity that was almost pathological. It was a cathartic moment for Scotland, as the nation came face-to-face with the reality of self-government – even the qualified self-government delivered by the Scotland Act. Creating a parliament from scratch is not easy, especially in the goldfish bowl of a hostile media. "All of a sudden," recalls Alex Salmond, "they have this wonderful parliament that many of the titles had campaigned for, many for generations, and so the first instinct was to kick it as hard as possible."[86]

It was, above all, the image presented by the infant parliament that offended Scots – the inarticulate MSPs, the feeble debates, the unimaginative legislation, the preoccupation with minority rights and identity politics. I had the dubious privilege of presenting all this to the nation, having returned to Scotland in 1999 to present the thrice-weekly *Holyrood Live* programmes on BBC TV, and to help launch the *Sunday Herald*, the paper I still write for today. It looked like the perfect job. Bright confident morning. In the next seven years, I presented nearly 1,000 hours of live television from Holyrood, and had to write about it at length every week for the *Sunday Herald*. It was like delivering the last rites three times a week and then having to write an obituary every weekend.

Why were the early years so bad? There were a number of very good reasons, by no means all to do with the cost of the Holyrood building project. This was a parliament largely composed of parliamentary neophytes, of rookie MSPs. Few of the big names in Scottish politics – Gordon Brown, Robin Cook, George Robertson – deigned to serve in the parliament they had campaigned for so vigorously – they were sitting comfortably in the UK Cabinet of Tony Blair. It was the same for many Liberal Democrat home rulers, such as Charles Kennedy and Sir Menzies Campbell, unable to resist the magnetic pull of London. Westminster was where the political action was, where the big jobs were and where the media focused its attention. This has been Scotland's story since the Middle Ages when Robert the Bruce couldn't decide whether to be Edward's man in Scotland or Scotland's man in London.

From the outset, the Scottish Parliament had a provincial, second order status and everyone in the political world knew it. This was compounded by Labour's Stalinist candidate selection procedure, which was designed to root out potential rebels, like the Labour home ruler Dennis Canavan, the MP for Falkirk West, a capable and charismatic politician who had every right to expect to be allowed to stand for the parliament he had worked hard for over many years. It also rooted out anyone with independence of mind.

Even experienced parliamentarians, like the Falkirk East MP Michael Connarty, were blackballed, along with Scottish Labour action figures like Ian Smart, a sharp young version of Donald Dewar, a number of capable women like Esther Robertson, co-ordinator of the Scottish Constitutional Convention and SLA luminary, Susan Deacon, though the latter managed to scrabble onto the candidates list through the heroic lobbying of Dewar. The result was a parliament composed largely of biddable politicians who didn't know what they were doing.

They didn't do themselves any favours in those crucial early weeks by awarding themselves medals for just being there, voting themselves a "family-friendly" three-day week with evenings off, debating their own salary and expenses at inordinate length, and then promptly going off on two months' paid leave. It looked as if Scotland's new parliamentarians were only concerned with their pay and conditions. On the day of the state opening, a cartoon in the *Edinburgh Evening News* depicted an MSP as a pig lounging on a deckchair in the sun, with a medal round its neck, counting its expenses. Unfair? Certainly, but they should have seen it coming. Some MSPs approached their new jobs with a shop steward mentality, which may have been acceptable in the classrooms, quangos and council chambers whence most of them came, but not in Scotland's national Parliament, serving in which was supposed to be a privilege.

It wouldn't have been so bad if they had been any good at their jobs. Few of the 129 MSPs were competent speakers, and now under intense scrutiny their shortcomings were cruelly exposed. Debates became shorter and shorter as backbench members stumbled through their prepared briefs. It didn't help that the Parliament didn't appear to have very much to do. The first legislative programme, unveiled by Donald Dewar in June 1999, was condemned by the press and opposition as unambitious, dry, plodding. Among the dreary bills on traffic congestion, financial auditing and educational standards, one stood out. The Incapable Adults Bill was designed "to protect the rights and interests of those people who, for whatever reason, are incapable of managing their own affairs". "You mean like the members of the Scottish Parliament?" said the nation in unison.

The only time the parliament really raised its game was during the state opening ceremony on 1st July, which went off smoothly and with a degree of dignity, largely because of the presence of Her Majesty the Queen. The SNP's unofficial monarch, Sean Connery, was there, too, and said it was the greatest day of his life. The parliament scrubbed up well and the celebrations were modest without being subdued. There was just enough Robert Burns, and 1,600 schoolchildren who didn't seem very sure why they were there. And, for reasons best known to the organisers, a fly-past by Concorde which had not yet gone out of service. Donald Dewar – after accompanying Her Majesty down the parliamentary steps with his hands in his pockets – delivered the speech of his life.

"In the quiet moments today, we might hear some echoes of the past: the shout of the welder in the din of the great Clyde shipyards; the speak of the Mearns, with its soul in the land; the discourse of the Enlightenment, when Edinburgh and Glasgow were a light held to the intellectual life of

Europe; the wild cry of the Great Pipes; and back to the distance cries of the battles of Bruce and Wallace ... honest and simple dignity are priceless virtues imparted not by rank or birth or privilege but part of the soul."

In that single passage of a short speech, Dewar had summed up Scotland's enduring communitarian image of itself – flattering in many ways but deeply felt. It really did echo down the ages.

It is very hard to read that speech and not regard Donald Dewar as a nationalist, at least with a small 'n'. Alex Salmond would happily have delivered it word-for-word. The Queen seemed to like it, too, and appeared uncharacteristically cheerful throughout the day, perhaps out of surprise at the warmth of her welcome in Scotland. Alex Salmond watched it all intently – noting the anachronistic presence of royalty and the Queen's obvious popularity. It was as if the Scots needed a reassuring presence to give them confidence in their new parliament. The SNP leader – a former republican – may have concluded here that retaining the Queen as head of state could help rather than hinder the progress to independence.

After giving the press all summer to recycle stories about lazy MSPs, the Parliament finally got back to business in September in its temporary home in the Assembly Building on the Mound. In 1843, this building had seen the Disruption of the Church of Scotland, the defining event of 19th-century Scotland. Now it provided the setting for the disintegration of the Scottish Parliament's reputation and moral authority just in time for the new millennium. Scots expected better. The cries of Bruce and the discourse of the Enlightenment had been replaced by the whimpers of the MSP from Numptyshire.

The essential problem was that Labour didn't know what it wanted to do with the Parliament it had created, devolution having essentially been born as a political device for undermining the popularity of the Scottish National Party. Tony Blair never wanted it in the first place, and regarded it all as Gordon's "thing". The Chancellor had other things on his mind after 1997, like making the Bank of England independent and compiling lists of reasons for not joining the European Monetary Union. Nothing happened without Brown's say-so in Scotland – but he had curiously little to say. The Scottish Executive was adrift. It was an administration without a purpose, leading a Parliament without a clue.

Donald Dewar was an exhausted man, having spent three

years fighting an election, winning a referendum, delivering a masterly white paper, and then wrestling Derry Irvine and Jack Straw, line-by-line, clause-by-clause, through the Cabinet committee examining the Scotland Bill. He was also trying to cope with the deepening scandal over the new Parliament building, the costs of which were now mounting alarmingly. Had it not been for the Scottish Liberal Democrats, Labour's partners in the first Scottish coalition, the Parliament might as well have stayed on permanent gardening leave. At least the LibDems, under their energetic leader, Jim Wallace, had plenty of policies – like abolishing university tuition fees (the policy the LibDems reneged upon ten years later in Westminster), proportional representation for local government elections, and free personal care for the elderly. Landmark policies that were shelved in the coalition negotiations with Labour to form the first partnership agreement.

The Scottish Liberal Democrats had also been historic supporters of land reform since the days of Gladstone and the Highland Land Wars in the 19th century and they succeeded in persuading Dewar to abolish Scotland's feudal system of land tenure. The community right-to-buy land, a rural version of council house sales, later became quite successful, allowing communities in Assynt and other parts of the Highlands to repossess some of the land taken from them by the Scottish nobility hundreds of years ago. Parliament also legislated to set up a university for the Highlands and Islands. But few Scots lived in crofts, and the rest of the agenda sounded legalistic and abstract, if not plain boring. Dewar was accused of failing to "hit the ground running" in the way that Tony Blair had seized the moment after the 1997 General Election and delivered eye-catching measures like the national minimum wage, Bank of England reform, the windfall tax on the utilities and the New Deal.

Dewar's defence was that Holyrood had to learn to walk before it could run. The new parliament was the UK's most important constitutional innovation, arguably, since the creation of the Irish Free State in 1922. Britain was no longer a unitary state – it had a subordinate parliament with primary legislative powers and Dewar, a lawyer, felt an onerous responsibility to make new arrangements work effectively. Moreover, this was a parliament of minorities led by a coalition in a political culture used to the winner-takes-all principle of Westminster. Scottish voters found the coalition horse-trading between Labour and the Scottish Liberal Democrats slightly shabby. They saw policies being adopted from a party that had lost the election, while policies they had voted for were ditched. Dewar believed that "co-operative government" was going to take time to sort out, and it seemed reasonable to rein back on controversial legislation in the first few years. Much of the parliament's work was supposed to be done anyway in cross-party committees, away from the glare of the debating chamber. Then there was all the institutional machinery to set up – a Minister of Justice, Freedom of Information Commissioners, a reformed civil service, a Civic Forum, Equal Opportunities Units, etc. Many well-paid jobs were created for the winning parties and their supporters, but the Scottish voters didn't get a piece of that action. What they got was the Parliament building.

THE HOLE IN THE GROUND THAT ATE HOLYROOD

Most high-profile public procurement projects go wrong. When politicians are in charge there is no incentive to underspend, and every incentive to interfere, adapt, change, revise. When I covered the work of the National Audit Office in Westminster in the early 1990s I saw many similar disasters; for example, the British Library in Paddington, which ended up costing half a billion pounds and was 16 years late – and that was in the days when £1 billion was still serious money. From the moment Donald Dewar promised in 1997 that the new Scottish Parliament building was going to cost £10m to £40m, anyone could see there was going to be trouble. It was pure fantasy. Holyrood ended up three years late at a cost of £414m, which is probably par for the course for prestige projects like this. But that was little consolation for Scottish taxpayers. To them, £414m was ten hospitals, 40 schools, 100 day-care centres.

What most infuriated Scots was that there was already a splendid Parliament building lying empty, which had been fitted out with a debating chamber before the abortive Devolution Referendum of 1979. The Royal High School building on Calton Hill was a fine example of Scottish neoclassical architecture, based on a Greek temple in Athens, and designed by Thomas Hamilton in 1828. It could have been combined with the equally substantial Scottish Office across the road to create a parliamentary precinct in an underused corner of the city, which had excellent transport links and was only ten minutes' walk from Princes Street. But Donald Dewar regarded New Parliament House, as it was then called, as a "nationalist shibboleth". There had been a vigil by home rulers outside the building since the failed 1979 referendum which he didn't like very much. Plus it was too small, too traditional.

Dewar wanted to endow the Parliament with a unique piece of contemporary architecture, rather than a musty piece of Victoriana. It would be Donald's Guggenheim Bilbao. Moreover, he believed, probably correctly, that if he didn't get the building underway before the Scottish Parliament met it would probably never happen at all, because an ambitious costly project would unite the opposition parties against him. But that hardly justified ploughing ahead into the unknown. Henry McLeish, his junior minister, who had also spent many long hours in committee getting the Scotland Bill through Westminster, urged caution. "Leave it to the parliament, Donald," he pleaded.[87] But the FM wasn't listening. Dewar used his powers as a temporary dictator to promote what many regarded as a vanity project.

At the end of 1997, Dewar had convened a special Design Selection Panel, with a remit to come up with, not a "shed", but a piece of art. And to do it as quickly as possible. The panellists were captivated by the ideas of a radical Catalan architect, Enric Miralles, whose pitch involved throwing an armful of twigs and leaves on the table before the committee members and telling them that his parliament was going to grow out of the natural environment of Scotland. Upturned boats, Charles Rennie Mackintosh flower sketches, skating ministers were all enlisted to create a conceptual work which was at the very limits of building technology, and seemed far too small.

By early 1999, the cost was escalating fast and Miralles was AWOL in Barcelona proving harder and harder to pin down. The project manager, Bill Armstrong, had resigned in despair at the delays and the doodles he was receiving instead of proper technical drawings. After an interview for a BBC programme, I put it to Donald Dewar that, from what I was hearing, the building was going to cost £200m. He guffawed and said "there would be a revolution" if that happened. There almost was. Parliament nearly scrapped the project altogether after it was elected in June 1999, and only narrowly voted to proceed after the First Minister and his civil servants assured MSPs that it would cost more to scrap than to continue. This claim was hard to justify. Work had scarcely begun and the prime site at the foot of Edinburgh's Royal Mile could have been sold into the burgeoning commercial property market. Before the crucial vote Dewar promised that the final cost would be £109m. In fact, the cost had already escalated to more than £130m. Did Dewar lie to Parliament? We don't know. He always insisted that he had not been told of the latest cost escalation by civil servants.

As the Scottish Parliament Corporate Body, a cross-party committee of MSPs, took over the project in the summer of 1999 they pointed out that the floor space was inadequate, the debating chamber wasn't round enough, access was poor and a listed building on the site, Queensberry House, could not after all be demolished and had to be incorporated into the ultra-modern design. It fell to the newly elected Presiding Officer of the Parliament, the former Liberal leader, Sir David Steel, to try to reconcile Miralles's poetic vision with the practical requirements of a working parliament, and also the conflicting demands of the political parties. As he admitted himself, this was not a task with which he felt well-equipped to deal. "It was a bit of a nightmare," he recalls in *Road To Referendum*. "We had to increase the size of it because the size of it was wrong and the costs were going up, and Donald said to me, 'David we mustn't play pass the parcel with this project,' and I said, 'But Donald, you have already played it.'"

As the plans grew and changed by the week, communications with Barcelona became more fraught. There had been an understanding that Miralles would move to Scotland to oversee the project, which he never did. Indeed, he was never to visit his magnum opus ever again. In July 2000, Enric Miralles died of a brain tumour aged 45.

The parliament was stunned. His wife, and fellow architect, the glamorous and strong-willed Benedetta Tagliabule took over the Holyrood project as a memorial to her late husband. The parliamentary authorities were hardly going to deny her wishes that the building should be worthy of his memory. They did everything in their power to accommodate her demands. Unfortunately, it wasn't clear if she knew entirely what her late husband had intended. Prince Charles, on his annual visits to the Gothic Holyrood Palace across the road, said nothing – he didn't need to because his silence was eloquent enough. This was another monstrous carbuncle, located in the middle of Edinburgh's Old Town. How it was supposed to harmonise with the medieval streets of this World Heritage Site was always a mystery. But Prince Charles was the least of their problems as the project ran completely out of control. Costs doubled and doubled again – £100m, £200m, £400m – progress became slower and slower.

The Holyrood building was formally opened by the Queen on 9th October 2004, three years late and ten times over budget. An inquiry into the scandal, by the former Conservative Lord Advocate, Lord Fraser of Carmyllie, in 2004, concluded as such inquiries do, that everyone was to blame and therefore no one was to blame. The press pointed the finger of blame at a soft-spoken civil servant, Barbara Doig, who had had the misfortune to be nominally in charge of the project when the construction contract was awarded to Bovis Construction, without apparently reviewing cheaper bids. That led to legal action against the Parliament's corporate body from the disappointed tenders.

But none of those directly involved in the fiasco from the Permanent Secretary Sir Muir Russell down, paid any legal penalty, suffered any censure or lost their jobs. In true bureaucratic tradition, the people responsible for the defining financial disaster of the new Scotland received pensions or promotions instead of punishment.

The real problem was that no one had been in charge of the project in its early days and the open-ended construction management contract, which had been agreed by the UK Cabinet before the Scottish Parliament had even been elected, turned out to leave all the risk with the public purse and very little with the contractors. It was a classic public procurement cock-up. If it hadn't been for the tough Nationalist Deputy Presiding Officer, George Reid, who took charge in 1999 and knocked heads together on a daily basis for three years, it might still be uncompleted today. The damage to Parliamentary morale was immense. This appeared to confirm what some MPs in Westminster had privately been saying: that the Scots were incapable of running a national Parliament. It became another stick with which Scotland could beat itself, and the MSPs in Holyrood.

Yet there was nothing uniquely Scottish about the Parliament building fiasco. Far worse scandals happen in defence procurement all the time. At least Scotland got a decent building which won the prestigious 2005 Stirling Prize for architecture, and much praise from critics like Jonathan Glancey in *The Guardian*, who called it "a rich, complex and crafted design as much landscape as architecture". My own view is that it looks a bit like a provincial airport. This is largely because the original complex organic design – the upturned boats – had to be jacked up on towers to provide twice the original accommodation. To cut costs, the parliamentary authorities dropped Miralles' idea of a sensuous, wavy roof over the entrance foyer, replacing it with what looked like, in this writer's opinion, a large bus shelter. The Scottish Parliament looks beautiful from the air – which is fine for airline passengers but not for the man in the street. Defenders of the Holyrood building point out that it has turned into one of Scotland's biggest tourist attractions and has a current asset value much in excess of £400m on the government's books – though it's not quite clear what this means since it can never be sold.

THE ROOF FALLS IN

The protracted row over the Parliament building drained confidence from an already underpowered Scottish Executive and a parliament that couldn't find its voice. Everything that could go wrong did go wrong in the 17 months that Donald Dewar was the first First Minister. A sting operation by *The Observer* newspaper revealed that commercial lobbyists with Labour connections appeared to be selling access to ministers. Donald Dewar's office needed a revolving door to cope with the rapid departure of members of his staff caught with prostitutes, making allegations of death threats against ministers, and generally finding it impossible to work with each other. Questions were raised about the First Minister's judgement. Then, in October 1999, the Communities Minister, Wendy Alexander, a former Labour researcher and close confidante of Dewar, agreed to speak at a gay rights conference in Glasgow and detonated a neutron bomb under Holyrood.

Alexander told the conference that the Scottish Executive intended to scrap Section 2A of the local government legislation that outlawed the "promotion" of homosexuality in schools. This was the Scottish version of Clause 28 that had been introduced by the Tories in a fit of homophobic populism in the 1980s. There was a furious reaction from Scottish Church figures, led by Cardinal Winning, the leader of Scotland's 600,000 Catholics, who took this to be an assault on the institution of marriage. He forged an alliance with the millionaire businessman, and SNP supporter, Brian Souter, of Stagecoach fame, to launch an anti-repeal campaign called "Keep the Clause".

At the campaign's launch in November, an incandescent Souter declared of the repeal: "Scotland didnae vote for it, and we're no huvvin' it." His campaign claimed that Scottish children would be taught gay sex education in the classrooms. Souter provided £500,000 for a private referendum in which more than one million Scots voted to keep Section 2A. Then, the American TV evangelist, Pat Robertson, who had been working on a telephone banking project with Bank of Scotland, intervened saying that Scotland was a "dark land" over-run by homosexuals. A chastened Wendy Alexander told Parliament: "Repeal is not and never has been about the promotion of homosexuality in our schools. Nor is repeal about political correctness or even marriage. It is about building a tolerant Scotland." But tolerance appeared to be in short supply in Scotland on the eve of the new millennium.

For the liberal intellectuals who had campaigned for Scottish home rule, this was the most painful of all the crises to hit the infant Parliament. Dewar and Alexander had hoped to show their Labour colleagues in the south that the Scottish Parliament could provide a lead in ending discrimination against sexual minorities. But Scotland remained a country with many conservative attitudes, the pace of Scottish opinion had perhaps not kept abreast of political conscience. Nor had ministers reckoned with the fury of the press. The Scottish tabloids – the *Record, Sun* and *Daily Mail* which between them had over one million readers – united in their own campaign to force Dewar to change his mind. It was a power struggle between the elected politicians and self-appointed guardians of public opinion, with Cardinal Winning leading the charge. It is a measure of how much the climate of opinion has changed in Scotland that many of the comments uttered by supporters of "Keep the Clause" in 1999 and 2000 might today be considered hate crime. Cardinal Winning's successor, Cardinal Keith O'Brien, resigned in 2013 after admitting to inappropriate behaviour with priests.

It was a particularly delicate moment for Alex Salmond,

leading an impoverished party that depended on donations from Brian Souter – the "homophobic bus-driver", as he was portrayed in a Steve Bell cartoon in *The Guardian*, over which Souter threatened to sue for defamation. Salmond was painfully aware, too, that perhaps a quarter of his parliamentary party agreed with the Stagecoach magnate. But the SNP leader didn't back down on his commitment to abolish Section 2A – though he sought a compromise by including in the legislation various affirmations of the virtues of wedlock. Salmond became a kind of marriage guidance counsellor from Hell trying to mediate between Souter and the Scottish Executive. Dewar also offered various semantic compromises, including specific guidance for teachers to promote marriage, which they were already supposed to do in the guidelines for sex education in schools.

The affair raged on through 2000, largely because ministers in Dewar's Cabinet refused to stay in line. Labour politicians in west central Scotland have long been close to the Catholic Church, since the days when Labour defended Irish immigrants against Protestant bigotry a century before. A number of Labour ministers took to briefing the tabloid newspapers – apparently in an effort to bounce Dewar into abandoning repeal of Section 2A. Had it not been for this disloyalty, the issue would not have been nearly so damaging to the Scottish Executive and to the Parliament. Writs began to fly, as a kind of moral civil war erupted in the Scottish media between papers which supported repeal, such as the *Sunday Herald* and, well, the rest, who didn't. Billboards went up over Scotland warning Scots about the dangers of gay propaganda in the classrooms.

Then in April, Tony Blair arrived at the Scottish Labour conference and attacked the lurid advertising of "Keep the Clause". "They're told we're going to make kids have homosexual roleplaying," he said. "Kids are going to be force-fed gay sex education. And it's Donald who's doing it. What utter nonsense." The issues seemed to die after that. On 21st June 2000, Section 2A was abolished and nothing more was heard of it.

Looking back, I don't know which was worse – the light this affair shed on the prejudices of some Scottish public figures, or the fact that it took the UK Prime Minister to come north to knock some sense into them. The resonance of the Section 2A affair indicated an aversion to homosexuality among many Scots that was unattractive but hardly unexpected in a society that, until very recently, had been under the strict moral guidance of an unforgiving Calvinist Church. Homosexuality is a sin against God, according to the Bible, and while most Scots stopped going to church in the 1960s and 1970s, their morality was still conditioned by it. Working-class Scotland in the 1990s was still, on the surface at least, a macho, martial culture, where men are men. They demonstrate their masculinity by wearing a "skirt" at weddings, but they weren't ready to embrace metrosexual culture.

The Section 2A affair was primarily a function of the weakness of the new Scottish political leadership, and of the new Parliamentary democracy which had been undermined by a succession of scandals and mishaps. Dewar's Cabinet was deeply divided, the press were out of control and Scottish voters lacked confidence in their domestic politicians. They needed someone to come up from London to reassure them that everything was OK. The stabilisers had yet to come off Holyrood.

Two months after Tony Blair kicked "Keep the Clause" out of the park, Donald Dewar was taken into hospital for heart surgery. Four months later, the "father of the nation", as he was affectionately known by the press corps, was dead from a brain haemorrhage. His funeral in Glasgow Cathedral was the biggest ever seen for a politician in the city, and was attended by Tony Blair and half the British Cabinet. It was a highly emotional event – laced with some hypocritical eulogies from political colleagues who had been fighting Dewar in private for years.

"He was a statesman, he was a national figure," said Henry McLeish. "So to lose someone like that in the new Parliament in Scotland was devastating."[88]

The Scottish Parliament was plunged into a deep depression – but life went on. After a snap leadership election, Dewar was replaced by his junior minister; a progressive and hard-working Labour politician, totally unsuited to the task of salvaging the credibility of Scotland's battered Parliament.

A MUDDLE NOT A FIDDLE

"Henry", as everyone called him, had a number of unfortunate physical tics and a habit of letting his words run away with him

– "McCliché's" as they came to be known. "There is only one party in this coalition," he announced to the bemusement of the Liberal Democrats during a session of First Minister's Questions. Then there was the unfortunate "my best wishes go out to those who were killed". And the positively surreal "I am like a stock, solid to the rock". McLeish's malapropisms added to the gaiety of the nation, but it didn't help restore confidence in the new Scottish democracy.

To give him due credit, the second First Minister of Scotland was considerably more radical than his predecessor. To the surprise and consternation of many Labour MPs, McLeish decided to press ahead with the Liberal Democrat plan for free personal care for the elderly, as recommended by the Sutherland Report on long-term care in 1999. This became one of the landmark measures of the Scottish Parliament and is usually attributed wrongly to Alex Salmond's SNP. Labour in Westminster was furious at McLeish's decision to implement this, which had been ruled out for the wider UK on cost grounds, and ministers did everything they possibly could to frustrate it. The UK Work and Pensions Secretary, Alistair Darling, refused to allow the Scottish Parliament to recycle the £22m in attendance allowances that had been provided for elderly care under the previous system. But McLeish persevered. He regarded "progressive universalism" as a part of the Scottish communitarian tradition and central to cementing Labour's political support in Scotland. His political instincts told him that to thrive in Holyrood, Labour had to distance itself from New Labour in Westminster and had to deliver on those "Scottish solutions to Scottish problems".

Then the curse of Holyrood struck again. Henry McLeish had hardly got his feet under the table at Bute House than he became embroiled in a farcical scandal over the subletting of his parliamentary constituency offices when he was an MP in Westminster. This had all taken place before he became a member of the Scottish Parliament; he hadn't benefited personally; and the matter had apparently been resolved to the satisfaction of the House of Commons Fees Office. On the face of it, this had nothing whatever to do with Holyrood. It was, according to the BBC's seasoned Scottish Political Editor, Brian Taylor, "A storm in a tea cup." But McLeish drowned in it nevertheless. A relentless press campaign, and an inability to account for himself on BBC's *Question Time* under interrogation by David Dimbleby, destroyed the First Minister's confidence and undermined his authority. It was, he famously said: "A muddle not a fiddle," but the muddle became a quicksand. The second First Minister of the Scottish Parliament resigned in ignominy on 8th November 2001, after less than 12 months in office.

After Henry's fall, even the Scottish press appeared to tire of beating up the Scottish Parliament, and his successor, Jack McConnell, the former Finance Minister and an ex-Stirling Council leader was given reasonably favourable coverage – despite persistent rumours of irregularities in his own Motherwell constituency party's finances. His first move was to sack half his Cabinet, in what became known as the "Night of the Claymores" or "Night of the Short Knives". It was an unsubtle and frankly brutal way of imposing discipline on his wayward ministers that appeared to work. Holyrood fell from the front pages as ministers toed the line and got down to work. McConnell believed that above all Parliament required stability. He promised to "do less better", which invited the response: "well, doing something would be a start".

Fond of foreign travel, the new First Minister devoted much of his time to promoting Scotland abroad under the slogan: "The Best Small Country in the World". This infuriated many Scots, especially the literary-minded, who quoted back the poet Hugh MacDiarmid's rhetorical answer: "Scotland, small? Our multiform, our infinite Scotland, small?", which is one of the quotations chiselled into the stonework of the Canongate Wall of the Scottish Parliament building.

McConnell caused further controversy when, during Tartan Week in New York, he appeared in a pin-striped kilt and blouse *sans* sporran and looking, as Scots put it in those non-PC days "like a right jessie". It was, he admitted, the "fashion crime of the century", and tried to laugh it off. However, he says the image has "haunted" him ever since. This is intriguing because wearing a kilt, even a pin-striped one, was normally seen as a patriotic gesture and not in any way remarkable. Perhaps there was still some sensitivity in male Scotland about its masculine self image, following Pat Robertson's "dark land" remark and the Section 2A row.

Back home, with the 2003 Holyrood Election in mind, McConnell sought to demonstrate his machismo to voters by promising to be tough on crime and antisocial behaviour. He proposed tagging for ten-year-olds, street curfews for teenagers, and on-the-spot fines for louts. He also chastised the judiciary for handing out lenient sentences. It was a case of "tough on crime; tough on the judges of crime". At one stage he even suggested taking the children of Scotland's 50,000 hard drug addicts into care.

Antisocial behaviour was certainly a perennial grievance on the housing estates of Scotland, but this law and order populism left a rather sour taste in the mouths of Scotland's liberal establishment, who knew perfectly well that crime had been falling during the previous decade. But there was worse to come. The assault on crime also involved Executive backing for the 2002 Dog Fouling Bill. This was real street-level politics, which invited, and received, ridicule and contempt. Had Scotland restored its Parliament after 300 years in order to deal with dog shit?

The 2003 election was approaching and McConnell worried. "I had three big worries about the 2003 Election campaign," he remembers in *Road To Referendum*. "One was that it would be completely overshadowed by the Iraq War and the general perception of Labour in Westminster. The second was that there was a very, very clear feeling amongst the population of Scotland that the Parliament had underperformed under Labour. And the third was the building."

ENTER THE RAINBOW

The Scottish electorate registered their discontent at the Dog Dirt Parliament in 2003 by using their second votes to lever into Holyrood a variety of smaller parties and independents. Five far-Left Scottish Socialists were elected from party lists and joined their leader, the anti-Poll Tax campaigner and former militant leader, Tommy Sheridan. Seven Green MSPs entered Holyrood also – the first Green parliamentarians in Britain – including the irrepressible Robin Harper, leader of the Scottish Greens complete with multicoloured Dr Who-style scarf. There was also an array of independent MSPs, including Margo MacDonald who had been expelled from the SNP, and Dennis Canavan, the former Labour MP who had been excluded by Labour's candidate inquisition in 1998. Also elected was Britain's first grey party parliamentarian, John Swinburne, of the Scottish Senior Citizens Unity Party.

There was much talk of a rainbow coalition of minority parties, green, grey, red, yellow – though the SNP weren't keen on having their colours added to the spectrum of minorities, since they regarded themselves as the official opposition. But the SNP under their new leader John Swinney had a poor election in 2003 returning only 27 seats, down from 35 in 1999. Labour were also down, but with 50 seats they could claim to have nearly double the strength of the Nationalists and McConnell declared himself to be the Hammer of the Nats. The SNP began to worry that they might be heading back to the outer fringes of Scottish politics. Clearly, they had not benefited from the scandal of the Parliament building, which they had attempted to pin firmly on Labour, or from the chaotic and incompetent management of the first Scottish Executive. If they couldn't prevail against Labour beset by scandal and resignation, when could they?

But 2003 was, first of all, a plague on all their houses from the Scottish voters, who were fed up with the established parties and wanted to punish them. It was also a logical progression for a proportional parliament. The whole point of PR is to allow minor parties, normally excluded by the first-past-the-post voting system, to achieve representation, and in this sense the Scottish Parliament did its job. It gave organisations that could never have won seats in Westminster a chance to show what they were made of.

There was a real sense of excitement among the Scottish chattering classes at what had happened in 2003. This was new democratic ground being furrowed by the Scottish Parliament – and folk started talking about the "New Politics". Between them, the independents and the small parties had as many seats as the Liberal Democrats, who were in the coalition executive. They could have been a formidable "third force", had they been able to work together. Unfortunately, this was the one thing they were temperamentally and ideologically ill-equipped to do.

The behaviour of the Scottish Socialist MSPs rapidly discredited talk of a New Politics. The party had ridden to success on the strength of Tommy Sheridan's performance in the first Scottish Parliamentary term, where he made a significant impact as a passionate speaker and campaigned, successfully, to abolish warrant sales – a uniquely insensitive Scottish form of debt recovery. But the five new MSPs didn't have much time for the legislative process, and it turned out that they didn't have a lot of time for their leader either. They staged a number of pointless, attention-seeking parliamentary disruptions and then disintegrated into bitter internal factionalism.

This involved party members telling tales of their leader Tommy Sheridan's lurid sex life to the tabloid press. Instead of giving a parliamentary voice to the dispossessed, the SSP succumbed to the vice of personality politics. A gaggle of brittle egos jostling for the attention of the *News of the World*, it did little to honour the memory of Leon Trotsky. Sheridan resigned in November 2004 and left the party in 2006, starting a long-running legal battle with the *News of the World*, which would end with his imprisonment for perjury. All of the SSP MSPs lost their seats in the 2007 Holyrood Election.

The Scottish Greens did rather better and became a significant force in the Parliament keeping environmental issues like renewable energy and climate change to the fore in constructive ways. Their co-convener (the Greens didn't have anything as conventional as a formal leader), Patrick Harvie, became an eloquent champion of human rights and civil liberties, and fought vigorously against Labour's proposals for identity cards in Scotland. Intelligent and disciplined, the Greens have continued to punch well above their weight in Holyrood and have become in a very real sense the Parliament's environmental conscience.

The Independent MSP Margo MacDonald became a massive presence in the Parliament, in every sense of the word, and almost constituted a party of her own, championing causes from prostitute tolerance zones to assisted suicide. She has demonstrated just how effective and influential an individual MSP of conscience can be in a parliament of minorities. Free from party discipline, she has been able to speak her mind in a manner that appeals to Scottish voters. The SNP's loss was Holyrood's gain and she deserves credit for her contribution to dragging Scottish democracy out of the moral pit it had dug for itself in the early years.

After the 2003 election, Jack McConnell returned to Bute House, once again in coalition with Jim Wallace's Liberal Democrats, and with his authority greatly enhanced thanks to his apparent besting of the Scottish National Party. He was able to be "his own man" – though it was never entirely clear who that man was, since McConnell's approach to politics had always been essentially managerial. He passed his promised Young Offenders Bill and persevered with his attempts to promote Scotland's image abroad. McConnell established a partnership with David Livingstone's old stamping ground, Malawi, through which the Scottish NHS could help tackle problems like AIDS and infant mortality. This was a perfectly sensible initiative, designed to prepare the ground for the Make Poverty History demonstration that was scheduled to coincide with the G8 summit set for Gleneagles in July 2005. But McConnell was ridiculed by many in his own party for attempting to set up his own foreign policy, especially after he was feted by the Malawian government, which provided a motorcade for his arrival in Lilongue.

In July 2005, Make Poverty History encircled the city of Edinburgh with some 150,000 demonstrators entirely dressed in white. It was a remarkable exercise, even if the point of surrounding Scotland's capital was lost on many of its citizens. But as world leaders, led by the Chancellor Gordon Brown, agreed to "drop debt" of developing countries (or at least some of it), tensions were rising behind the scenes. The Westminster Government initially refused to pay for the policing costs at the Gleneagles summit and McConnell had to threaten to go public to get them to stump up. Around this time, the First Minister became increasingly angry at Labour MPs in Westminster briefing against him in the press. "I was always aware of a whispering campaign against me when I was First Minister that I was too big for my boots, that I was too outspoken and was saying things that were nothing to do with me."[89] He felt undermined by the Westminster leadership and insulted when Tony Blair, in his address to the Scottish Labour conference, made jokes about McConnell's gaffes while in office. This lack of empathy between numbers 10 and 11 Downing Street and the First Minister was extremely damaging. There was a widespread feeling in Scotland that the Scottish Executive was being held in check by "London Labour". This was probably more apparent than real, since it is difficult to identify actual policies of McConnell's that were sat on by Blair or Brown. The perception was damaging enough. In diminishing McConnell, Labour in Westminster appeared to be diminishing Scotland.

Matters came to a head over the abolition of smoking in public places, when McConnell found himself on the wrong side of the pugnacious UK Health Secretary, John Reid. A west of Scotland hard man of the old school, and a smoker himself, Reid believed that smoking was "one of the few pleasures left to the working man". A lot of people in the Scottish Labour Party agreed with him, and they worried that McConnell was going to introduce a well-meaning policy that pleased the BMA but would alienate working-class voters north and south of the border. McConnell was also up against the Scottish tabloid press, which formed an anti-parliamentary alliance reminiscent of "Keep the Clause".

There were forecasts of riots in the pubs if Scottish men were denied the right to a puff with their pint. Did the nanny state have any right to tell people what to do with their own bodies? But McConnell persevered in the face of vocal opposition from John Reid, and in the event the abolition of smoking in public places took place with scarcely any resistance . There was no need for the special "smoking police" that were deployed strategically to preserve public order. Only one establishment has ever been fined for defying the ban, and that was on the day of its introduction.

The smoking ban demonstrated that radical legislation could be introduced by Holyrood with consent, provided the arguments had been aired, and the Scottish people understood the reasons for change. Scotland's desperate health problems, with the worst record for coronary heart disease in Europe, clearly demanded action. In 2005, male life expectancy in certain Glasgow constituencies was recorded as only 56 years – meaning that most of the constituents wouldn't live to collect their old age pensions. The ban on smoking in public places was an infringement of personal liberties, but justified in the interests of the greater good.

At first, health researchers couldn't believe their results when there was a 17% reduction in hospital admissions for heart attacks in the 12 months of the ban. But subsequent research has confirmed not only a reduction in heart attack admissions, but a reduction in asthma and premature and underweight child births. The abolition of smoking in public places has been the single most beneficial piece of health legislation since the Clean Air Acts of the 1950s. It improved the health of the Scottish Parliament, too. Jack McConnell had introduced a ground-breaking piece of legislation that demonstrated finally to Scots that Parliament could change their lives for the better. This was a turning point for Holyrood.

Yet the SNP claimed it was their policy first. The bill to outlaw smoking in enclosed public spaces had first been introduced by Nationalist MSP Stewart Maxwell in February 2004, and the Scottish Executive, at first, opposed it. The SNP wisely chose not to play party politics with the nation's health and avoided the temptation to set up needless obstructions to the legislation, or seek cheap publicity in the press. This bipartisanship by the SNP was noted by the Scottish voters, as it had been over the Section 2A affair. The Nationalists' conduct under John Swinney, and their avoidance of tribalism – well, most of the time – in these lean years helped position them to become the first minority government in Scottish history. The SNP had finally realised that the Scottish voters really disliked adversarial politics, and wanted to see the political parties working together.

The Nationalists also had cause to welcome a remarkable act of un-sectarian politics by Jack McConnell, who in the face of fierce opposition from his own party, pushed through what was arguably the most important constitutional reform since devolution: the introduction of proportional representation for local government elections. Sold to Labour as a necessary evil to seal the second coalition deal with the Scottish Liberal Democrats, this apparently technical change served a death sentence on Labour's "rotten burghs".

In many Scottish local authorities, particularly in the west, there was no serious opposition to Labour. In Glasgow, Labour had 94% of the seats on less than half of the vote. In Midlothian, there was only one opposition councillor. Labour councils in the "Lanarkshire badlands" had become a by-word for bureaucratic inertia, corruption and factionalism. PR broke up Labour's one-party states, and improved accountability by introducing opposition to Scottish council chambers. But it also allowed the SNP to overturn Labour's dominance of the local state. In the first elections under the new system in 2007, the SNP returned more councillors than Labour for the first time ever. Labour's post-war hegemony had been built on three pillars: the trade unions, council housing and the local state. The first two were destroyed by Conservative legislation, but it was Labour that kicked away the third leg.

The Scottish Parliament was winning back some of the public support it had squandered in the early years. But parliamentary madness had not entirely been stamped out. At the Politician of the Year Awards in November 2004, in Edinburgh's Prestonfield House, well-lubricated members of the press became aware that Lord Watson of Invergowrie, a Labour peer and MSP appeared to be tired and emotional. At 2am, closed circuit television recorded a man setting fire to the curtains in the reception area of the 17th-century hotel. Lord Watson, the Firestarter, as he was inevitably dubbed after The Prodigy song, ended up in Saughton Prison for this moment of madness, probably the most bizarre of the tragicomic episodes of the Holyrood years. I had known Mike Watson as an energetic left-wing MP in Westminster in the 1990s and had considerable respect for him. What was it with the Scottish Parliament – was there something in the water that turned perfectly normal, intelligent and responsible MPs into arsonists?

Then, the leader of the Scottish Conservatives, David McLetchie, resigned over his taxi expenses. It emerged in the *Sunday Herald* that he had been claiming for taxi fares to destinations to which he was not entitled under Parliament's expenses rules. This seemed like a worryingly minor offence to cause to the downfall of the leader of a political party. Imagine Ed Miliband being forced to resign because he took a taxi to his lawyers and charged it to Westminster's Fees Office? Unfortunately, Henry McLeish's departure had set the bar to resignation in Holyrood so low, almost anyone could trip over it.

A Liberal Democrat MSP, Keith Raffan, also departed, under a cloud, after revelations of extravagant expenses. It looked as if the parties were vying with one another over who could provide the daftest political resignation.

At the time, it looked to many, this commentator included, that the rules were being applied a little too strictly and that the Scottish Parliament and the Scottish press had lost a sense of proportion over the expenses scandals. Can a serious legislature function when every expense account is being minutely scrutinised for irregularities, and when First Ministers and party leaders can be forced out over transgressions which should never have become resignation issues in the first place? David McLetchie was a serious political figure, whatever your views on his politics, and made a valuable contribution to the Parliament and public life. Apart from anything else, this kind of scrutiny was liable, surely, to deter any normal person for standing for office.

The plus side was that these scandals did at least communicate to the voters that the Scottish Parliament took issues of conduct, especially financial conduct, extremely seriously. The Scottish Parliament had been founded in the wake of the Westminster sleaze scandals of the 1990s, when lobbyists had been found to be crawling all over the Palace of Westminster and MPs were hiring themselves to people like Mohamed al-Fayed of Harrods on a taxi rank basis. Part of Holyrood's mission was to clean up politics. Neither McLeish, McLetchie nor Raffan would have been forced to resign over their misdemeanours had they been in Westminster. None of it would have come to light, because the only reason Scottish journalists were able to investigate the McLetchie taxi chits was because they were made available under the Freedom of Information Act, which had come into effect in January 2005. MPs in Westminster saw it all as further confirmation that the Scottish parliamentarians couldn't run a whelk stall. But the Scottish parliamentarians were to get the last laugh.

In 2009, when the Westminster expenses scandal broke showing how MPs had been financing duck houses, moats and second homes out of their parliamentary expenses, the Scottish Parliament stood immune from public obloquy. Thanks to its rigorous policy of disclosure, Holyrood suddenly looked like a paragon of virtue compared with Westminster, where MPs had been lining their nests at public expense, flipping homes like London estate agents, and committing fraud, as in the case of the Rotherham Labour MP, Denis MacShane, who resigned for charging expenses to an organisation that didn't exist.

What few MPs in the Commons realised at the time was that this Westminster expenses scandal originated in Scotland. In 2006, Heather Brooke, a sharp-eyed freelance investigative journalist, based in London, had been reading with interest the reports by Paul Hutcheon, the *Sunday Herald*'s investigative sleuth, about how he exposed the McLetchie taxi scandal through use of FOI requests. She wondered why this hadn't been tried in Westminster. So she started making applications to view Westminster MPs' expenses, which were blocked by the Speaker of the Commons, Michael Martin. Brooke persisted. She took the issue to the Information Commissioner, and eventually forced the infamous redacted accounts into the public domain. The public were outraged and demanded to be given uncensored details of what their elected representatives had been doing with their hard-earned cash. *The Daily Telegraph* got hold of the files from a former Commons employee, and published them in a series of stories through May and June 2009.

All Hell broke loose – much as it had in Holyrood ten years previously. By 2010, the moral reputations of the two parliaments, Holyrood and Westminster, had been reversed. It was now the

House of Commons that was in the dock of public opinion, reviled by an electorate outraged at parliamentary misconduct by MPs who seemed to care more about personal enrichment than good government. Holyrood meanwhile stood vindicated as a true Freedom of Information Parliament. Devolution was leading parliamentary reform in Britain, though not in ways that MPs in Westminster could possibly have anticipated. MPs even stopped being quite so patronising about the Scottish Parliament – at least for a while.

At the close of 2006, bonsai scandals aside, the Scottish Parliament appeared finally to be getting its act together, at least in a legislative terms. The row over the building project had largely died down and Holyrood was behaving more like a proper professional legislature, though there were still many Scots who believed it to be an expensive waste of space. You might have thought that this would be to the benefit of the First Minister who had stabilised the Holyrood ship, Jack McConnell, but you would be wrong. As the 2007 parliamentary elections approached it became clear that Labour had a real fight on its hands. An ICM opinion poll in November 2006 put support for independence at an historic high of 51% against 39% for the status quo. What was going on? This wasn't in the script. Nationalism was supposed to become less popular when Parliament was working properly.

Westminster was one reason for McConnell's failure to capitalise on the improvement in the standing of Holyrood. Relations had deteriorated between Tony Blair and Gordon Brown and it was looking like war between Number 10 and 11 Downing Street at the end of 2006. Then there was the "cash-for-honours" scandal over the revelation that a number of peers had been ennobled after donating large "loans" to the Labour Party. A number of Labour staffers were helping police with their inquiries. Meanwhile, the real war in Iraq was dragging on and on, leading to increasing numbers of coffins arriving at RAF Brize Norton. Alex Salmond gave voice to the continuing opposition to the war and seemed to strike the correct note – unlike in 1999, when he had lost public support by his condemnation of the bombing of Serbia as "unpardonable folly".

Between 2004 and 2007, the SNP leader was located in Westminster and was waiting for a safe seat in Scotland to allow him to return to Holyrood. In his absence, his deputy, Nicola Sturgeon, received plaudits for her performances at First Minister's Questions.

She also developed the policy agenda that would help win in 2007 – the council tax freeze and the abolition of prescription charges. In doing so, she established herself as Salmond's successor, even before the "absentee landlord", as the SNP's Mike Russell called him, had returned from London.

The SNP had also been getting more professional before 2007. John Swinney may have been no election winner, but he had pushed through reforms in the Scottish National Party, centralising the membership structure, introducing effective fundraising and generally turning the SNP into a modern political party. He was, if you like, the nationalist moderniser, turning the SNP from a campaign of romantic individuals into a professional party that aspired to government. Overtures had been made to Scottish businesses led by the SNP MSP and businessman Jim Mather who, for some years, had been taking a Powerpoint presentation to practically every boardroom in Scotland arguing that Scotland's historic low growth and falling population could only be addressed by independence. This was a distant echo of the former Labour Shadow Chancellor John Smith's "prawn cocktail" offensive in the City of London in the late-1980s. On his return to the SNP leadership in 2004, Alex Salmond had stepped up this "smoked Salmond" offensive. He wanted to scrap the image of tax and spend – the "penny for Scotland" in the 1999 campaign – and become hard-headed and businesslike. The infamous Laffer Curve was invoked by the SNP leader in his arguments, that lowering business taxes and corporation taxes in an independent Scotland could increase tax revenues as well as promote economic dynamism. The SNP became a party of contradictions, at once the most left-wing party in Britain and also one of the most business friendly.

Nationalists, as radical outsiders, had always tended to be rather suspicious of businesspeople, who they assumed were either all Tories, or too preoccupied with retaining access to English markets to be interested in Scottish independence. They were wrong. Almost as soon as the SNP started making serious overtures to the business community in Scotland they discovered that they were pushing at, if not an open door, then certainly not one that was being slammed in their face. This was confirmed by the continued support given to the SNP by the bus magnate Brian Souter. Despite being poles apart politically from Nicola Sturgeon, on issues like Section 2A and sex education in schools, the author of

"Keep the Clause" was still the source of most of the SNP's funds. Sir George Mathewson, the former chairman of the Royal Bank of Scotland and a pillar of the Scottish financial establishment who had long been quietly sympathetic to nationalism, suddenly came out as a Salmond man in the run-up to the 2007 election. Crawford Beveridge of Sun Microsystems was on board. The hotelier, Dan Macdonald of Macdonald Hotels, and "Scotland's richest man", Jim McColl of Clyde Blowers, began to move in a decidedly nationalist direction, though McColl did not become a full convert to independence until some time later.

Before very long, the SNP had a list of 100 business supporters ranging from Kishorn Seafood to Tom Farmer's Kwik-Fit. The money started to pour in with Farmer's £100,000 adding to Souter's £600,000. Soon, the SNP were millionaires, and could start planning the kind of sophisticated election campaign they had always dreamed of. Social democrats in the movement worried about the party's soul; but the election campaign director, the Moray MP Angus Robertson, just worried about winning.

Labour had long ridiculed the Nationalists for their desperate appeals to wealthy expatriates, like Sir Sean Connery who, they pointed out, loved Scotland so much he didn't live here. But they began to realise that they were going to be seriously outspent in 2007. The SNP unveiled their slightly scary voter database, Activate, which sorts all of Scotland's voters in consumer types cross-referenced with voting history and allowed canvassers to communicate with the SNP's "super brain" through smartphone apps. I'm always a little suspicious of claims made for computers, social media and marketing methods in elections. Without actual feet on the ground, they are of limited use. But there is no doubt that the SNP ran the most professional campaign in 2007, completely outspending and out-canvassing Labour, and it provided the basis for their landslide win four years later.

Labour was finding that its main anti-nationalist theme, "divorce is an expensive business" which had been so successful in previous Holyrood election campaigns, was no longer resonating with the voters. Labour's manifesto for the 2007 Scottish parliamentary elections was competent enough, promising to increase the school-leaving age to 18 and reintroduce trams to Edinburgh – but it lacked any stand-out policies. Jack McConnell's attempt to reform the council tax system of local government finance, by extending the bands, came to grief in a rather confused press conference at the height of the campaign. The SNP replied with an offer to freeze council tax indefinitely before replacing it with local income tax. The nationalists also promised to abolish the graduate endowment (after-graduation student fees) and bridge tolls, and promised to keep open threatened hospital A&E units. The Nationalist campaign turned on the cult of personality with huge pictures of Alex Salmond, with the legend, "It's time." The Nationalists placed "Alex Salmond for First Minister" at the top of the regional-list ballot papers, much to the annoyance of the other parties who thought this was unfair. But of course there was nothing in the rules that said parties could not play the personality card, if that's what they wanted. And the SNP were prepared to bet their future on their leader's name.

CHAPTER TWELVE
ENTER THE NATIONALISTS

T H E   N I G H T of the 2007 Scottish parliamentary election was the most chaotic in British electoral history. There was widespread confusion among voters at the new three-part ballot paper, and around 140,000 Scots were effectively disenfranchised. The electric counting machines proved to be unreliable, ballot boxes went missing, one was even attacked by a man wielding a golf club. The result was incredibly close, and counting dragged on all through Friday 4th May until after a recount on the Highland list when a sharp-eyed SNP candidate noted that Labour had been given two more seats than they deserved given their share of the vote. At 5.17pm, when the last result was declared, the announcer on BBC Radio initially suggested that Labour had won the election. But this was quickly corrected, and Scotland discovered that the Scottish National Party had won its first ever election by a margin of 47 seats to 46.

Even then, it wasn't completely clear who had won since it was still theoretically possible for Labour and the 16 Scottish Liberal Democrat MPs to form another coalition executive. There is nothing in the Holyrood rules that says the largest party has to form the government. In a parliament elected on proportional representation, all that is required is that the coalition has a stable majority and is able to get its leader elected. This was what Gordon Brown had urged Jack McConnell to consider, for the sake of the continued unity of the United Kingdom. But McConnell argued that it would look to Scottish people as if the losers were trying to defy the democratic will of the people by fixing the result. So he sat on his hands. McConnell also calculated that if Salmond could not form a stable government, then he might be able to ride to the rescue at a later date. But Alex Salmond, who helicoptered onto the lawn outside Edinburgh's Prestonfield House – even before the final declaration had been made like the leader of an invading army

– was not prepared to allow one second's doubt about who was going to form the next Scottish government. He simply spoke and acted as the First-Minister-in-waiting, and let the media do the rest. The SNP celebrated late into the night, fingers crossed that it wasn't all a dream. For the Unionists, it was a nightmare. The hated Alex Salmond leading the Nationalists to victory in Holyrood.

Was this a vote for independence? No, it was not – the SNP had assured Scots that there would have to be a referendum before any Nationalist administration sued for separation. The Scottish voters had tried Labour coalitions, they had tried the rainbow parliament in 2003, and they were still struggling to find some political leadership that they could respect. After eight years of incompetence, scandal, vanity politics, ultra-leftism and legislative mediocrity, they wanted someone – anyone – who would make the Holyrood parliament work and justify the £400 million spent on it.

As is so often the case, it was the incumbents who lost the 2007 election rather than the opposition who won it. Jack McConnell was given some credit for still being there in Bute House, unlike his predecessors, but the voters clearly did not feel inspired by his "do less better" message, or the idea of Scotland being "the best wee country in the world". Scots were perplexed by New Labour and Tony Blair's marketplace rhetoric of public sector reform in the NHS and education, which was a language Labour in Scotland had started to speak with ideas such as private sector involvement in the clearing of NHS waiting lists. Nor did Scottish voters like Labour breaking its promise on university tuition fees.

There was also, in Scotland, an unease at New Labour's "war on terrorism" with its identity cards, detention without trial – and most Scots were opposed to the war in Iraq. "Alex Salmond's consistent opposition to the Iraq War," concedes Jack McConnell, "started to become the accepted public opinion, and left what we were doing on the inside pages of the papers rather than the front."

Had McConnell been prepared to denounce the Iraq War and create a distance between himself and New Labour, he could probably have won in 2007 – it was incredibly close anyway. If he had told Westminster MPs to get their tanks off his lawn, and let him pursue a more independent line, like the Welsh Labour First Secretary Rhodri Morgan in Cardiff, perhaps the SNP would not have edged it into government. But McConnell worried that if he took an independent line it would antagonise Gordon Brown and split the party. That was something he wasn't prepared to risk.

MINORITY GOVERNMENT

4th May 2007. The world woke up to discover that the National-ists had won the Scottish parliamentary elections. But what did it mean? No one knew – least of all the SNP, who had vaguely assumed that they would form a coalition with the Scottish Liberal Democrats. Since there was scarcely a cigarette paper between their manifestos – on matters like local income tax, free personal care, nuclear power, powers for the Scottish Parliament and Iraq. It was a match made, if not in heaven, then certainly in Holyrood. But by 6th May, Scotland remained without a government and without any clear sign of one.

The BBC's parliamentary offices in Edinburgh are in the Tun building in Holyrood Road opposite Arthur's Seat on what used to be the site of an old brewery. It is a curious pistachio-coloured building that leans out into the road, as if it's trying to overhear what's being said in the Parliament down the road. The BBC has always had a difficult relationship with devolution and Nationalism. Caught between the two nations, it has had the hard job of trying to reflect the distinct political culture of Scotland while not being seen to foment or succour Nationalism. I was stumbling into the Tun to speak to BBC World Service early that Sunday morning, I bumped into the SNP deputy leader, Nicola Sturgeon and her future husband, Peter Murrell, the party chief executive. Sturgeon was mystified. "We offered them everything they could possibly expect," she said, "short of making Nicol Stephen [the Scot-tish Liberal Democrat leader] First Minister. Alex spoke to him on Thursday night, but then the phones just went dead. We just don't know what's going on in there." Murrell thought the Liberal Demo-crats were committing political suicide, which it transpired was not far from the truth.

What had happened was a revealing insight into the difficul-ties faced by parties with split personalities and divided leadership. The Scottish Liberal Democrats are supposed to be a federal party – meaning that the UK party does not necessarily have any say in the affairs of the Scottish LibDems. That wasn't quite the reality. On the

evening after the May election, the UK leader, Sir Menzies Campbell, invited Nicol Stephen and his deputy, the finance spokesman
Tavish Scott, to his home in Edinburgh's New Town to discuss the
future. The discussion was brief. In the time it took to consume a
couple of Domino's pizzas, extra large with added pepperoni, Nicol
Stephen had been persuaded not to hold any discussions with the
SNP unless Alex Salmond agreed to drop his party's commitment
to holding a referendum on independence.

This was an extraordinary condition, tantamount to telling
the SNP to abandon any hope of independence through democratic
means, because at this stage no one believed that any party could
win an overall majority in Holyrood because of the PR voting
system. It was clearly unacceptable. It was also unnecessary. There
was no prospect of the SNP getting their referendum bill onto the
statute books in this Parliament since the parliamentary arithmetic
was against them. It was also faintly disreputable since the Liberal
Democrats were famously keen on referendums, and were calling
for one on UK voting reform and a referendum on continued membership of the European Union. About the only issue they thought
should not be put to the people was Scotland's constitutional future.

The Scottish LibDems were adamant. There would be no
discussions about coalitions, not even discussions about discussions. That Sunday lunchtime, Tavish Scott, who clearly considered
himself the future leader of the Liberal Democrats (though he was
not elected as such until the next year) announced that there would
be no third coalition executive, and I was dragged back into the Tun
to talk about it. And so the Scottish Liberal Democrats laid down
their political lives for the Union – an act of futile self-sacrifice. The
Liberal Democrats were later to form a coalition with the Tories in
Westminster in 2010, which rather made their refusal to deal with
the SNP in 2007, a party most of whose policies they largely agreed
with, seem perverse.

The Liberal Democrats opted out of government in Scotland in 2007. No more ministerial Mondeos. No more smart offices
with researchers and civil servants. No more opportunities to put
forward hallowed LibDem policies like local income tax. They were
out of office and out of power, and, seemingly, were not to return. It
is possible that Scott, like McConnell, believed that Alex Salmond's
attempts to govern alone with no majority in the Parliament would
fail, and that the LibDems would be able to return to power within

a year. After all, it seemed inconceivable that the SNP would be able to get its legislation through a hostile Holyrood on its own, since it only had 47 out of 129 MSPs. But they hadn't bargained for Salmond's staying power.

The SNP leader struck a somewhat cynical deal with the Tory leader, Annabel Goldie, to abstain in the vote for First Minister. The SNP constitution rules out coalition with the Conservatives, but Salmond won their tacit support by offering them concessions on police numbers and business rates. Salmond then announced that he was going to lead a minority administration, a new form of co-operative politics, a new politics for Scotland. Salmond made a series of speeches in May 2007 committing his administration to working for the good of Scotland rather than for party advantage. "Through the force of argument rather than force of numbers in Parliament." He intended, he said, to fulfill the original aspirations of the Consultative Steering Group of the Scottish Constitutional Convention, the founding fathers and mothers of the Scottish Parliament, who laid the ground rules for devolution in the 1990s. They had argued that minority government was preferable to elective dictatorship by one party and one leader, which had been the rule in Westminster. As it turned out, they were right – mostly.

The SNP's first concession to consensus was to accept Labour's plan for a £500m tram system in Edinburgh, which the Nationalists had opposed on the grounds that it was an expensive duplication of the rather efficient Lothian bus network. Under pressure from Labour and the Scottish Liberal Democrats, John Swinney, the new Scottish Finance Minister, reluctantly agreed to go with the "will of parliament" and allow the project to go ahead – though he said that Edinburgh Council would have to pay for any cost overruns. Edinburgh's trams ended up as an even bigger scandal than the Parliament building. At the time of writing, the cost has more than doubled, for a much-curtailed route, and the project is already four years late.

However, trams aside, the people of Scotland finally had a government they liked the look of. This was partly because it had the courage to call itself a "Government" instead of the bureaucratic and slightly apologetic "Executive". As the novelist Christopher Brookmyre put it, "'Scottish Executive' sounds like it could be just a bunch of six guys round a table whereas 'government' sounds like something far more powerful."[90] Scots seemed to like the sound of

Alex Salmond's policies even more, which was not surprising since they benefited from them financially. Swinney managed to find the cash from the fixed Barnett Formula to deliver a whole range of what came to be known as "Salmond freebies" by the opposition – the abolition of bridge tolls, the end of prescription charges and the scrapping of student fees.

Ambitious new targets were set for renewable energy, council house sales were curbed, and nuclear power ruled out. Salmond's administration hit the ground running, in a way his predecessors hadn't and the First Minister's popularity rating raced ahead of his rivals, and stayed there for the rest of the Parliament. The new SNP ministers' enthusiasm for governance – Nicola Sturgeon at Health and John Swinney as Finance Secretary – was undeniable. But Salmond's critics said he had bought public support with money he didn't have, and fully expected his administration to spend its way to disaster.

THE BANKS EXPLODE

The economic situation deteriorated almost as soon as Salmond entered Bute House. The collapse of Northern Rock in the summer of 2007 led to a chain reaction through the financial world and raised questions about the viability and the solvency of Scottish banks. Salmond promptly leapt to the defence of Halifax Bank of Scotland and Royal Bank of Scotland insisting that HBOS was a "well-capitalised and properly funded institution" – which it was not – and attacking the "spivs and speculators" who were trying to bring it down. He personally spoke out in defence of Sir Fred Goodwin, the indefensible boss of RBS – which soon became known as "the worst bank in the world". Remarkably, this advocacy for Fred the Shred – who became a national hate figure for leaving his bank in public hands while he departed with his pension rights intact and a substantial pay-off – did not appear to damage the SNP leader.

This may in part have been through Labour's inability to develop a coherent critique of Salmond's relations with the banks, since their own government's handling of the City of London had hardly been above criticism, It was Gordon Brown's "light touch" regulation in the City that had led to the banks behaving badly in the first place. Furthermore, Brown had made equally sycophantic remarks congratulating the City of London for creating "a new golden-age" only months before the entire system crashed, requiring a £1.3 trillion bailout from the taxpayers. It took a few years for Labour to develop the argument that, without the UK, an independent Scotland would have been buried under the bad debts of RBS.

Civic Scotland, and newspaper commentators, criticised the First Minister for having become a PR mouthpiece for the Scottish banks and becoming too close to RBS, especially during the bidding war for the Dutch bank ABN Ambro – the takeover that sank the Royal Bank. But the public didn't seem to mind. Perhaps they accepted the argument that as First Minister, he could not have refused to defend key institutions in a financial services sector employing nearly 100,000 Scots directly, and many more in support. Perhaps his very willingness to side with the arch exponents of finance capitalism persuaded some centre-right voters that the SNP really had changed and broadened the SNP's appeal. Salmond had moved a long way from his left wing, "penny for Scotland" nationalism of 1999. He had begun, imperceptibly at first, to adopt what might be called "Celtic neoliberalism", lauding small countries like Iceland and Ireland, who had achieved spectacular growth through low taxation, deregulation and an aggressive banking sector. Alex Salmond expressed no contrition for his flirtation with banker capitalism, even though it appeared to conflict with the SNP's rejection of New Labour and its appeal to the social democratic soul of Scotland. Where were Jock Tamson's bairns now, in the age of bonus culture?

However, the centre of gravity of the party has been and remains very markedly to the left. Throughout these years, Nicola Sturgeon continued to provide a Socialist counterpoint to Salmond's neoliberalism. The Deputy First Minister insisted on year-on-year increases in health spending, opposed any reintroduction of university tuition fees and argued for same-sex marriage against a number of members of her own party. The SNP, despite its recent pro-business rhetoric and its fundraising from businesspeople, remains an exceptionally radical party committed to unilateral nuclear disarmament, nationalisation, redistribution of wealth, council housing, free university tuition, free personal care and opposition to the Iraq War. Indeed, the SNP Government of 2007 was by far the most left-wing administration anywhere in Britain since the days of Attlee and Nye Bevan. And it was arguably the most popular.

WENDY ALEXANDER "BRINGS IT ON"

Meanwhile, Jack McConnell had finally tired of waiting for his peerage and resigned as leader in August 2007, allowing Wendy Alexander, Donald Dewar's former special adviser, to emerge as the leader of the Labour Group in Holyrood. Now, technically, Labour did not have a leader in Scotland – only a leader of the Labour Group of MSPs in Parliament. The party had only one leader, north and south, and that was the Prime Minister, Gordon Brown. But Alexander strained at the leash, without McConnell's caution or willingness to bow to Westminster.

Alexander was determined to seize the constitutional agenda once again, as Labour had in the 1990s, and her first act was to propose a cross-party Commission on Scottish Devolution to mark the first decade of devolution and set a course for the next. This would pre-empt Alex Salmond's own recently launched "National Conversation" – a consultation essentially on independence. She hoped in this way to seize the political initiative back from the Nationalists, and consolidate Labour's electoral support by giving Scottish voters what they kept saying they wanted: a Parliament with more powers within the UK.

The Commission was set up by a vote of the Scottish Parliament in December 2007 in face of opposition from the SNP Government which said it was a party political act, which of course it was. But like the Scottish Constitutional Convention in 1988, Wendy Alexander's commission derived its legitimacy from its cross-party support. It was difficult for the SNP to argue with that. It was the first time the opposition parties – Labour, Tory and Liberal Democrat – had got their political act together since the election – and it also turned out to be the last.

The Commission on Devolution was set up under the chairmanship of the former Chief Medical Officer for Scotland and Chancellor of Glasgow University, Sir Kenneth Calman, a highly respected figure in Scottish public life. Over the next two years he conducted the most exhaustive investigation of the constitution since the Kilbrandon Commission in 1973. Only Calman was very much more radical. His principal remit was to look at funding options for Holyrood. His conclusion: that a Parliament that spent £33bn a year could not be responsible and accountable unless it raised, through taxation, a substantial proportion of the money it spent on services. It was not sustainable, Calman concluded, for Holyrood to continue living on hand-outs from Barnett.

The significance of the Calman Commission is that it established beyond intellectual doubt the need for the Scottish Parliament to have tax-raising powers – proper ones, and not just the tokenistic 3p on the basic rate that had been proposed in 1998 and never used. In this sense, the commission was as significant, in its own way, as the 1998 devolution white paper, and the Scottish Constitutional Convention's Claim of Right in 1988. It was a milestone towards an essentially federal Scotland.

However, Calman's means of achieving this accountability did not quite match up to the ambition. His final report in June 2009 recommended reducing income tax by 10p and allowing Holyrood to make up the difference, by setting its own annual tax rate, which could be higher or lower than 10p. He also proposed that the Scottish Parliament be allowed to raise a primordial public debt, of £2.5bn a year, and that Holyrood should have the right to levy other minor taxes, like stamp duty, air passenger duty and landfill tax. The net result was that Holyrood would have control of 30% of its budget.

The main problem with the Calman scheme was that it was almost impossible to explain to voters how it would work. If a parliament is to be made accountable, why make it only 30% accountable? The tax-sharing sounded like an unnecessary compromise with the UK Treasury, which of course is jealous of its fiscal monopoly and doesn't like giving away power to tax. Nor does it like subordinate bodies being allowed to borrow – though why this is seen as unacceptable when every municipal authority in the world borrows money was never quite clear. In the Calman solution, the fiscal reins seemed still very much in the hands of the UK Treasury, and Nationalists attacked the Calman formula as inherently deflationary. They pointed out, after 2010, that moves such as the incoming Coalition government's proposal to increase tax thresholds to £10,000 would effectively diminish Scotland's spending budget by £800m to £1bn.

The other main problems with Calman, from a fiscal autonomy point of view, were that oil revenues, worth £11bn a year in 2011, and corporation taxes remained with Westminster, along with fuel duties, excise duties, National Insurance and VAT. But Calman at least established the principle of autonomy and broke the taboo on fiscal power for Holyrood. Before 2008, the idea of Scotland setting its own rate of income tax would have been seen as Nationalism. Similarly, the Treasury had been adamant that it could not allow constituent parts of the UK to start gaining borrowing powers because this might unbalance the UK national debt. Calman forged the way for other bodies to come up with what has become known as "Devolution Max" – the proposition that the Scottish Parliament should raise the vast majority of the revenue it spends.

This is where the constitutional story becomes highly technical, and one of the main problems with the whole debate as it progressed over 2010 and 2011 was that Scottish politics became a series of lists, as various versions of "Devolution Max" and "independence lite" were suggested by bodies like the STUC, churches and Scottish charitable foundations. The most coherent came, intriguingly, from the right-of-centre Reform Scotland think-tank. Its proposal for "Devolution Plus", submitted to the Scottish Parliament in September 2011, envisaged the Scottish Parliament raising 60% of its revenue. It called for income tax and corporation tax to be devolved in their entirety along with petroleum revenue tax, excise duties, stamp duty and various minor measures.

Only VAT and National Insurance would remain at Westminster under this model, proposed by the chairman of Reform Scotland, the former investment banker Ben Thomson. He also called for all major welfare benefits to be transferred to the Scottish Parliament, with Westminster retaining responsibility only for state pensions and sickness benefit. Had the Scottish people been offered a second option on the referendum ballot paper in 2014, as the First Minister Alex Salmond advised, then it would likely have been this option that would have been on the table. The fact that it came, not from the left or from the Nationalists, but from a Conservative-leaning think-tank, made it all the more remarkable.

The great virtue of Devolution Plus is that, in principle, it is easy to understand and relatively cheap and simple to implement. It has none of the traps and anomalies that arise out of the Calman proposals which, while sincere, had the fingerprints of the UK Treasury and Gordon Brown, who was Prime Minister at the time of publication in 2009, all over them. Devolution Plus was criticised by the Conservatives and Labour for going too far down the independence road, but in fact Ben Thomson's scheme would only have placed Scotland in line with many federal states like Victoria in Australia or Alberta in Canada, and with less fiscal autonomy than the Basque region of Spain. Only in such a grossly over-centralised country such as Britain would Devolution Plus be seen as a Scottish Nationalist ploy. It is the recommendation that the Calman Report should have made, had it been true to its own principles, which were that, to be truly accountable, a level of government should raise the majority of the money it spends. Calman's proposals were opaque, not transparent, unfair rather than equitable, and complex instead of being transparent. But Calman opened the door so that others could follow.

WHO KILLED WENDY?

Unfortunately, Wendy Alexander was not around long enough to see the publication of the Calman Commission Report in 2009 that she had inspired. Mad parliament disease struck again in 2008, and she became embroiled in yet another of those bizarre financial scandals that seemed to afflict the Labour Party in Scotland throughout the 2000s. She had been elected as Labour's Scottish group leader, replacing Jack McConnell in 2007, unopposed, but she had nevertheless had a fundraising campaign. Unfortunately, she failed to register donations made to this campaign because, she said, she had been advised by the clerks to the Holyrood Standards Committee that it was unnecessary to declare them.

Then it emerged that one of her supporters, Charlie Gordon the former leader of Glasgow City Council, had also accepted, on her behalf, a donation of £950 from a Jersey-based businessman, Paul Green, which also broke the rules because he was not a UK voter. It was a muddle and a fiddle.

The row in the press was, as in previous scandals, in inverse proportion to the seriousness of the offence. But after mild criticism from the parliamentary standards commissioner, Dr Jim Dyer, for these errors, she was suspended from parliament for one day. This was endorsed by the Parliament's Standards Committee after a vote which divided the committee on party lines. It was only a token punishment, but it was too much for Wendy Alexander, who resigned as Labour leader on the last day of June 2008, saying that the issue had become "too much of a distraction from the real issues that dominate our public life". She was replaced as temporary leader by her deputy, Cathy Jamieson. Ms Alexander had lasted an even shorter time as leader than Henry McLeish.

The departure of yet another Labour leader, in farcical circumstances revived the old public anxieties about whether the Scottish Parliament was a serious legislature or just a bunch of student politicians with salaries. Serious political leaders should not resign over taxi fares, small change donations, sub-let constituency offices. Every member of the Scottish Parliament felt damaged by yet another absurdist melodrama. It also raised questions about where these stories were coming from. "While Wendy Alexander has been the author of her own misfortune," remarked the SNP Deputy First Minister, Nicola Sturgeon, "there can be no doubt that the information on her illegal campaign donation could only have come from within the inner circles of the Labour Party." Incredibly, this is widely accepted as true. Wendy Alexander was brought down by someone in the Labour Party, who fed the information about the donations to the press. Only someone with intimate knowledge of the finances of this leadership campaign-that-never-actually-took-place, and was never made public, could have been in a position to leak the crucial information to the press.

Now, it seems hard to believe that a political party could be so riven by personal or political animosities that party members would seek to undermine its leader and deny it any chance of gaining power. Yet I have been told repeatedly by Labour insiders who were close to Wendy Alexander that she was indeed "fitted up". And one prominent Labour figure even told me he believed that it was Gordon Brown himself who authorised the black act, or one of his henchmen. Yet Brown had always been Wendy Alexander's political mentor and one of her closest friends. Not even the most cynical conspiracy theorist could seriously believe that he would have brought her down. Some have suggested the reason the finger of suspicion points at Brown is because Ms Alexander fell out with him when she called for a referendum on independence without getting his prior agreement.

In the early spring of 2008, in an inspired piece of political improvisation, Wendy Alexander decided to call Alex Salmond's bluff and accede, verbally at least, to his demands for a referendum on independence. "Bring it on," she said in a television interview. She calculated that with independence at a low ebb in the opinion polls, and the SNP leader running into difficulties over Royal Bank of Scotland and HBOS, that it would be a very good time to hold Salmond's referendum and lance the independence boil once and for all. What had Labour to lose?

Unfortunately, she hadn't quite got explicit approval for this course of action from her boss, Gordon Brown, the recently installed Prime Minister, whose authority had taken a severe knock after he "bottled" calling a snap General Election in October 2007. When the Leader of the Opposition, David Cameron, asked Gordon Brown at Prime Minister's Question Time in May whether he agreed with his Scottish leader that there should be a referendum on independence – a policy he had always opposed on the grounds that it would endanger the integrity of the UK – Brown flannelled and blustered and made clear that he did not support a referendum. Afterwards, tensions grew between Holyrood and Westminster, and mobile phones were abused. Ms Alexander believed that she had received Brown's "endorsement" for the policy during meetings with him and said so in a television interview, but the PM's recollection was slightly different. Wendy is a hard person to say no to, and he may have equivocated, but he had never authorised her to reverse policy. Clearly, there had been miscommunication. Either that, or Wendy Alexander was trying to deliberately create "clear tartan water" between herself and Labour in London and engineer a division that would demonstrate to Scotland that she was not simply "Gordon's woman" in Holyrood. Perhaps it was a bit of both.

This was clearly a mess, and did not enhance Labour's reputation for whelk stall management. However, to conclude from all this that Gordon Brown then went out of his way to destroy his own protégé by leaking details of her financial affairs to the press does seem, even to me, incredible. But the very fact that senior members of the Labour Party in Scotland genuinely believe this is insight enough into the state of politics in the party in Scotland. Such a degree of mistrust and paranoia can only be debilitating. In Westminster, a favourite saying of old parliamentary hands is "forget the opposition benches. Your real enemies are right behind you". In Holyrood they were on your right-hand side as well.

Looking back, it may well be that Henry McLeish's downfall was also brought about by disloyalty within his own party. Who else could have had knowledge of the multiple sub-letting policies of his constituency office in the mid-1990s? Journalists don't just stumble on that kind of story by accident. The former First Minister had antagonised many by his introduction of the policy of free personal care for the elderly, which was vehemently resisted by Labour in Westminster. It doesn't take Inspector Rebus to join up the dots and conclude that Henry too may have been "dealt with" by party insiders. Jack McConnell may also have been the victim of dirty tricks over his constituency accounts, an extramarital affair and the involvement of staff with commercial lobbyists in the so-called "Lobbygate" affair.

What could drive a political party to such self-destructive folly? Wendy Alexander was not a natural leader, but she was a highly intelligent woman who commanded respect and had a robust courage, summed up by the Scottish word "smeddum". She was Salmond's equal on economics and had an astute understanding of politics. Her sponsorship of the Calman Commission united the opposition in Holyrood and put the SNP on the defensive. Alex Salmond was left having to explain why, after all his promises of consensus and "working with not against Parliament", he was opposing cross-party plans to give Holyrood more of the economic powers he had been demanding for years.

The Calman Report continues to cause problems for the SNP to this day. The proposals were set before Westminster in a Scotland Bill in 2010 which, according to the new Coalition Scottish Secretary Michael Moore, would represent "the greatest transfer of financial power since the Act of Union in 1707". The Nationalists tried to block the measure, and then folded, realising that they couldn't be seen to reject more powers for Holyrood, even if they weren't the ones they wanted. Alex Salmond then demanded that the Scotland Bill should include devolution of broadcasting, the Crown Estate, corporation tax, excise duties and the right to lead delegations to the European Council of Ministers. He got none of them. Though the Scottish Government did win the right to borrow £5bn – twice the original Calman figure, and there was a broad commitment that Scotland should not lose out financially because of any unintended consequences of the new tax-sharing arrangements.

The Scotland Act was passed by a legislative consent measure of the Scottish Parliament on 18th April 2012, with the unanimous support of the SNP MSPs, who had had to swallow a bill they had promised to defeat. However, by then it had been overtaken by events, as attention had moved to the Independence Referendum, as David Cameron began talking about further powers for the Scottish Parliament if Scotland votes no: "I am open to looking at how the devolved settlement can be improved further." In February 2012, the chair of Better Together, Alistair Darling, said: "Most people think the present settlement does need to change and my view is that any parliament that can spend money, but doesn't have the pain of raising it, isn't satisfactory." The legislation had become obsolete before it gained the Royal Assent.

It is intriguing to speculate what might have happened if Wendy Alexander had got her way and managed to engineer a pre-emptive referendum on independence in 2008 or 2009. Jack McConnell now concedes that it "wasn't a bad thing to do". "She was seizing the initiative," he says. "Putting Alex Salmond on the spot, saying: you want it, let's have it."[91] Polling would probably have taken place in 2010, when the economy was in deep recession and the SNP was relatively unpopular.

Independence didn't seem like a very good idea in the middle of the worst financial crisis in 80 years. The idea of small countries going it alone had been severely damaged by the economic difficulties of Ireland and Iceland. Moreover, in 2008, Gordon Brown was still a figure of world renown, who had gathered the G20 in London and got the industrialised nations to launch a co-ordinated financial stimulus to head off an economic depression. Who knows? Had Brown not vetoed Wendy Alexander's referendum, she might have been in Bute House today, overseeing the implementation of the Calman recommendations.

But whoever was responsible for the downfall of Wendy Alexander, the result was devastating to Labour morale, fundraising and recruitment. Alexander was replaced by Iain Gray, a former finance spokesman, who was competent but profoundly uncharismatic, a politician who fully lived up to his name. Wendy Alexander was probably Labour's last chance in Scotland – the last link with the Labour Party of Smith and Dewar, powerful political intellects who had a clear idea of where they saw Scotland going. After she had fallen, there was nowhere for Labour to go.

MEATBALL MARINARA INCIDENT

In the 2010 Westminster Elections, Scotland again voted over-whelmingly for the Labour Party, hoping to forestall the election of the revived Tories under David Cameron. Labour won over a million votes in Scotland that May, winning 41 seats. It was a re-markable affirmation of Scotland's affinity with Labour, that so many Scottish voters were prepared to support the party despite scandals and misdemeanours in Holyrood. The SNP lost an MP in the General Election of 2010 and returned just six seats, fewer than the Scottish Liberal Democrats who secured 11. This was a deceptively easy victory for Labour and Iain Gray; his advisers persuaded themselves that they were back on the road to victory in Holyrood. Buoyed by positive opinion poll ratings throughout 2010, Gray thought his party could coast to victory. The line from Labour's political strategists was that they needed to do as little as possible, keep a low profile and avoid making any unforced errors that could damage their opinion poll lead, which was as solid as ten points over the SNP at the close of 2010. It was practically unheard of for a political party to lose a lead of ten points during a cam-paign, unless it was a complete disaster. It was.

Gray's low-profile approach exploded after a *Times*/Mori poll in February 2011 showed the SNP had nearly closed the gap with Labour. Most thought it was a rogue poll. It wasn't. Something had happened to public opinion over the New Year, as the effects of the UK General Election had worn off, and Scottish voters turned their attention to the forthcoming Holyrood elections in May 2011. Ed Miliband made matters worse by launching Labour's campaign at the Scottish party conference in March by calling on Scots to "send a message to Westminster that the fightback against the Tories has begun". All this did was send a message to the Scottish voters that Labour were fighting the wrong election. Iain Gray obediently echoed the slogan, "The Tories are back", ignoring the fact that they weren't – the Tories were politically irrelevant in Scotland. Many Scottish voters felt they were being patronised by a UK leader who seemed to believe that the purpose of the Holyrood election was to influence the climate of opinion in Westminster. A patronised voter is an angry voter.

On April Fool's Day, as the campaign got under way proper, Labour suddenly realised that they had been deluding themselves.

The low-profile approach had left them bereft of high-concept policies and saddled with an intentionally unambitious manifesto, focused on youth unemployment and knife crime. Iain Gray then belatedly adopted large chunks of the SNP manifesto.

Labour had made clear well before the campaign began that they intended to lift the freeze on council tax and restore university tuition fees through the introduction of a "graduate contribution". But on the very eve of the 2011 Scottish Parliamentary Election campaign, Gray – having looked at what the focus groups were saying – reversed both positions and insisted that Labour would continue to freeze council tax, at least for two years, and would not restore tuition fees. Gray also pledged to "abolish youth unemployment" by creating 250,000 apprenticeships, which sounded over-ambitious and strained credibility. From having a low profile, suddenly Labour's profile was all over the place. Labour's opinion poll lead continued to evaporate after Labour's manifesto launch. The crunch game in the second week of the campaign when Iain Gray, on walkabout in Glasgow, was chased by a group of anti-cuts campaigners into a branch of the Subway sandwich bar chain, pursued by TV cameras. It became known as the "meatball marinara incident" and remains the abiding image of the 2011 election campaign. Labour were cornered, besieged. The next week's *Times*/ Mori poll put the SNP ten points ahead of Labour.

Alex Salmond, needless to say, was enjoying all this immensely. Once again, the collective wisdom of the Scottish press – and I include myself in this – had been shown to be inaccurate and out of touch. Salmond had correctly interpreted the 2010 Westminster General Election as essentially a referendum against the Conservatives, rather than a positive endorsement of Labour in Scotland. He always believed the polls would turn in his favour, provided that the Nationalists could hold onto disillusioned Labour voters. The SNP manifesto was targeted directly at the heart of the Labour's core vote. It promised a further five-year freeze on council tax, no compulsory redundancies in the public sector, £1 billion more for the NHS, 130,000 jobs in the green economy, plus keeping Scottish Water and the Forestry Commission in public hands. Alex Salmond knew just how damaging had been Scottish Labour's suggestion that it intended to restore university tuition fees, now that fees had been set at £9,000 a year for students south of the border. He announced that "rocks would melt in the sun" (a quote from

Burns) before his party abandoned free education. A very attractive programme to Labour voters; Labour's attempt to pinch large parts of it only made it more attractive.

Why didn't Iain Gray go for the soft underbelly of the SNP – the crisis in the Celtic Tigers nations and the dangers of independence in the age of financial crisis? It did, but it failed to gain traction on this issue, probably because voters were not voting in this election on independence. They knew that there would be a referendum before any SNP Government could try to break up the UK. In 2011 Scots were voting, not on the constitution, but on who was best at running the devolved administration in Holyrood. Since the death of Donald Dewar, Labour's performance in Holyrood, in and out of office, had been mediocre when it wasn't dismal. Scots registered their discontent by delivering a message that Labour would never forget.

THE LANDSLIDE

For the first time, the SNP stormed Labour's west of Scotland citadel. Commentators and politicians in the BBC's election night studio could scarcely believe what they were hearing as seats such as Glasgow Cathcart, Kelvin, Shettleston, Southside were gained by the Nationalists. Even Glasgow Anniesland, Donald Dewar's old seat, fell to the SNP candidate, Bill Kidd. May 2011 was Labour's worst result in Scotland since 1931 – when Labour were split over Ramsay MacDonald's national government. The Scottish system of proportional representation was supposed to prevent any party gaining an absolute majority in the Holyrood Parliament. The SNP blew that theory by winning 69 seats out of 129.

This was an electoral rebuff almost as humiliating as that delivered to the Conservatives in Scotland in 1997. But to understand the scale of the SNP landslide victory in the 2011 you really need to look at the political map of Scotland. Before 6th May, the Highlands and much of the north-east of Scotland were Liberal Democrat orange; Glasgow and the west were the solid red of Labour; and Edinburgh and the east were red and blue. Now the map was almost uniformly SNP yellow, with only a few dots of red in the west, and a collar of Tory blue in the deep south.

The SNP could claim, after this result, to be the first political party in more than half a century to represent all corners of Scotland, and all social classes. All three opposition leaders – Labour's Iain Gray, the Liberal Democrats' Tavish Scott, and the Scottish Conservatives' Annabel Goldie – resigned before the night was out. Nearly all of the Labour front bench lost their seats. The Scottish Liberal Democrats were left with only five MSPs of the 16 they had before the election. Instead of going back to their constituencies to prepare for a return to government – as many had expected only two months before – they were reduced to a handful of inexperienced and relatively unknown faces. That decision not to discuss a coalition back in May 2007 had cost them dearly.

On the night of the disaster, I was in the BBC's Green Room in Pacific Quay, Glasgow. Some Labour luminaries arrived in tears. But there was little recrimination, more a sense of resignation. "It's over," shrugged one ex-minister. Others were saying – in effect – "I'm outta here." A number of prominent former Labour ministers, like Margaret Curran and Cathy Jamieson, subsequently took the long road to London, believing there was nothing left for them in Scotland. The Scottish political classes were still in a state of shock as MSPs assembled in Holyrood the next week to swear their oath of allegiance. Political journalists were bewildered by all the new faces. It was as if all the prominent non-Nationalist figures in Scottish politics had disappeared in a Waco-style collective suicide pact. The Scottish Parliament had turned into an Alex Salmond fan club, with the phalanx of beaming SNP faces eager to clap his every word. The Nationalist leader, Alex Salmond, now had unqualified power in a unicameral legislature. What would he do with it? Well, number one was to announce that there would be a referendum on independence in the autumn of 2014. The opposition parties were puzzled at first. Why wait? Why not call a snap referendum on the back of this massive victory? It was a clear sign that, despite the electoral landslide, the SNP leader realised that the Scots had yet to be convinced of the merits of independence.

The opposition parties hoped that Salmond might throw them a crumb of comfort by letting the elected Presiding Officer – equivalent to the Speaker – come from outwith the SNP. But no. The first act of the new Parliament was to install the SNP's Tricia Marwick as Presiding Officer. Holyrood does most of its serious work in the committees – but these all now acquired an SNP majority. There would be no more hectic late-night negotiations over the annual Scottish Budget, because the Finance Secretary, John Swinney, wouldn't need any opposition votes.

The age of consensus and minority government was over. This was not how the Scottish Parliament was meant to function, and Labour accused Salmond of electoral dictatorship. For some time, political journalists had jokingly referred to the First Minister as "El Presidente" because of his leadership cult in his party. Now the joke didn't seem quite so funny any more.

CHAPTER THIRTEEN
THE MOST DANGEROUS
MAN IN BRITAIN

" T H E   M O S T Dangerous Man in Britain" does not have a lean and hungry look. Alex Salmond is fat, some would say obese and is said to bear a disturbing resemblance to a bleached version of the cartoon ogre Shrek. But Salmond is widely regarded as one of the most gifted politicians of his age, with an extraordinary record of achievement, and remains immensely popular – in Scotland at least – even after six years as First Minister of Scotland. Salmond is the nearest Scotland has had to a truly national leader in the past 300 years. Indeed, his biographer, David Torrance, invited comparison with Robert the Bruce – though detractors say they'd never find a helmet big enough.

Historians don't much like talking about the role of personalities in history. The Great Man Theory of Politics has long been discredited. But it is hard to believe that Scotland and indeed Britain would be where it is today, facing this referendum on independence, had it not been for Alex Salmond. Certainly, the SNP would not be where it is. Salmond first became leader of the Scottish National Party in 1990, when they were on the margins of political life, having spent the previous decade wracked by divisions and electoral failure. He led this fractious organisation out of Nationalist fundamentalism and into an accommodation with devolution, which most of his party had regarded as a unionist trap. In the late-1990s, with Donald Dewar, he played a crucial role in restoring the Scottish Parliament after 300 years. Then, to everyone's surprise, he resigned in 2000 and went back to Westminster. The Scottish Parliament wasn't up to his high standards, it seemed.

The Scottish National Party went into a political tailspin under Salmond's successor, John Swinney, losing so badly in elections in that, in 2004, they practically begged Salmond to come back. He replied quoting the unionist General Sherman that "if

nominated I'll decline. If drafted I'll defer. And if elected I'll resign."
Salmond then broke all three promises at once, agreeing to stand
provided that a rival candidate, Nicola Sturgeon, now his deputy,
stood aside. Back in the saddle, in 2007 Salmond took the SNP to
its first election victory in its 80-year existence, and went on to run
a minority administration in Holyrood, which was so successful
that, in 2011, he was returned as First Minister of Scotland with a
landslide.

Now, "Eck" – as Unionists call him – faces his final challenge: a referendum on Scottish independence, to be held in 2014.
It is what he has worked for all his adult life, but it would require
a Herculean effort to persuade reluctant Scots voters, who oppose
independence by two to one, to vote Yes. It is a testament to Alex
Salmond's standing that no one is prepared to write off his chances.

CHANCER

So, why is he so popular? Why does he win elections? What is
the X-factor that has made Alex Salmond so successful? It isn't an
easy question to answer, because when you meet Alex Salmond
he doesn't come over as a Great Man, a towering presence, a commanding intellect or even, *a la* Tony Blair, an ordinary guy with the
"hand of history on his shoulder". He comes over as an ordinary
guy. A bright guy, certainly, but in no way a history man. Which
is one reason Alex Salmond has generally been underestimated
by his opponents and his colleagues. In the late-1970s, he was a
protégé of Jim Sillars, a charismatic left-wing orator in the mould of
Keir Hardie. Sillars didn't rate Alex Salmond at all, regarding him
as a political lightweight who couldn't deliver a speech or write a
decent pamphlet, and thought he would never win an election in
Scotland. Sillars crashed and burned in the 1992 General Election
and has been trying ever since to convince Scotland that he was
right, all evidence to the contrary.

Gordon Wilson, the leader of the SNP in the 1980s, also underestimated Alex Salmond. Wilson expelled him from the party
in 1982 for being a member of the republican socialist '79 Group.
He recalls thinking at the time that the young Salmond was a self-
publicist who thought highly of himself without having much to
back it up. "He had a tendency to bumptiousness and overconfi-

dence," Wilson says, "which didn't do him any good because it irritated people who might otherwise support him."[92] Within eight years, Salmond had replaced Wilson as leader of the SNP. Like the Decca Records executive who rejected The Beatles, Wilson had many years to reflect on his misjudgement. As have many of Salmond's political opponents, who simply cannot understand his popularity. Tony Blair didn't even telephone the First Minister to congratulate him on the 2007 election victory, a singular mark of disrespect. Salmond exploited this put-down by remarking at a press conference: "He doesn't write; he doesn't call ..." David Cameron is possibly the only major exception to this Salmophobia and seems to "get" the First Minister in a way his predecessors in Number Ten didn't .

Scottish Labour politicians have no time for the First Minister, regarding Salmond as a "con-merchant" who can't open his mouth without lying. The former Labour First Minister, Jack McConnell said that he was "not fit to be the First Minister of Scotland". The present leader, Johann Lamont, says he is "incapable of telling the truth". Tom Gallagher, an academic at Bradford University's Department of Peace Studies, has been waging a bitter personal war against Alex Salmond for the last decade, calling him "devious ... Machiavellian ... an accomplished political agitator" who has exploited "latent Anglophobia" to disguise his own economic incompetence.[93] He even compared the FM to the Italian populist Silvio Berlusconi as a product of anti-politics – though it is difficult to imagine anyone less likely to host bunga bunga parties than Alex Salmond. There are no butts in Bute House.

Salmond has been one of the most minutely scrutinised politicians in Britain, with unionists eager to find confirmation of his perfidy, and the press ever at the ready with its chequebook. Critics invariably cite Salmond's gambling – the First Minister is a dedicated aficionado of the turf who used to write racing columns for the Scottish press – as a confirmation he is a chancer. Before the 1999 Scottish parliamentary election, the BBC even sent a special unit up from London to explore Alex Salmond's alleged gambling debts. He was supposedly in a vice-like grip of professional money lenders and Irish bookies. They found nothing, but some journalists remained convinced he was hiding something. Scottish journalists regard it almost as a national disgrace that they have uncovered nothing seriously damaging about this "kenspeckle" politician, to use a useful Scottish word which means well-known and slightly dodgy with it. So far as we know, Salmond hasn't harassed female members of staff, been involved with private lobbyists, beaten his wife, had extramarital affairs, attended swingers bars, fiddled his taxi accounts, sublet his constituency offices, taken donations from foreign businessmen – in other words succumbed to any of the other temptations of office that have led to Scottish politicians resigning over the last tempestuous decade. At least not yet. His detractors believe it is only a matter of time.

WILY OPERATOR

In Westminster, politicians and journalists like Michael White of The Guardian invariably describe the SNP leader as "wily" and "slippery", as if he were some upstart demagogue leading an anti-colonial movement in the 1950s. This is perhaps as revealing of the attitudes of the metropolitan chateratti to Scotland as it is of the First Minister. It is Salmond's unapologetic provincialism that seems to cause resentment among the London intelligentsia – the impudence, the populism, the national attention seeking. There is almost nothing remarkable to say about Alex Salmond's background – no Oxbridge firsts, or Glasgow University debating honours, or rugby caps. He didn't take drugs, attend raves, go on gap years abroad, climb mountains or get locked up for refusing to pay the Poll Tax. He doesn't speak foreign languages or write novels in his spare time or do anything that might class as a "hinterland" – except perhaps golf. He must be a devious trickster, a svengali or live a double life. How could someone so ordinary threaten the integrity of the UK? Do you know he's only got a second class degree?

The one place Alex Salmond really did shine was in the debating chamber of the House of Commons. Salmond still says that he felt "at home" there, more so even than in Holyrood. He is a natural debater, and enjoyed the sense of being close to power – which in many ways is more intoxicating than being in office and discovering how little you can really achieve. One of the great strengths of the British Establishment has always been its ability to tame radical spirits by embracing them with parliamentary goodwill. However, Salmond was never a very convincing revolutionary, and though he was prominent in the republican Socialist '79

Group, he didn't go in much for civil disobedience or giving tacit support to Irish Republican groups like Sinn Fein. His disobedience was mainly parliamentary. The MP for Banff and Buchan studied Erskine May carefully before disrupting the Budget Speech in 1988 over the Chancellor Nigel Lawson's reduction of the top rate of income tax to 40%. "I had spent a lot of time in the parliamentary rule book," he says, "and there was nothing, absolutely nothing to stop you intervening in a Budget – it was just a statement like any statement."[94] But Salmond was suspended from Westminster for a week. It was the event that made his name.

As a unilateralist party that, until recently, rejected Nato, the SNP have been infiltrated by the British Security Service, MI5, and Special Branch. This was confirmed in declassified files released in 2007 and reported in the Scottish press. The files, placed in the National Archives in Kew, confirmed that through the 1950s, Special Branch officers posed as nationalist supporters as part of a campaign to undermine support for independence.[95] The SNP have been aware for many years of the attentions of spooks of various nationalities, including the Russians, before the collapse of the Soviet Union. The CIA has been watching closely also, which is only to be expected given Salmond's outspoken opposition to the Iraq War and his determination to remove Trident from the Clyde. There is no suggestion of dirty tricks, at least not recently. But easing the anxieties of the US State Department may be one reason the SNP leader was so determined to abandon, in 2012, the long-standing policy of opposition to Nato, even at the risk of splitting his party. Nicola Sturgeon, eager to crush suggestions that the SNP might be disloyal to the West, insisted that an independent Scotland would co-operate fully with MI5 and MI6 and would "share intelligence" with the various agencies – after all, wasn't James Bond a Scot? Labour's Margaret Curran responded that the SNP "had no idea what it would take to deliver security services in an independent Scotland".[96]

The Washington investigative blogger Wayne Madsen has recently claimed[97] that MI6 and the CIA have been "scenario planning" possible terrorist activity in an independent Scotland. "MI6 is secretly backing psychological warfare operations," he wrote in January 2013, "aimed at discrediting the leadership of the governing Scottish National Party". This was in the blowback from the controversy over the decision by the Scottish Government to release the

Lockerbie bomber, Abdelbaset Ali Mohmed al-Megrahi, in 2009, on compassionate grounds. There was widespread suspicion in America, not least among the Lockerbie relatives, that a deal had been struck between Salmond and the Libyan dictator, Muammar Gaddafi, to send al-Megrahi home. In fact, the deal had been made between Tony Blair and Gaddafi over prisoner transfer in a tent in the desert in 2007[98] and it actually had nothing to do with the Scottish decision. But it looked as if there had been collusion of some kind between the three governments, and many Americans were outraged at the release of al-Megrahi. It was one of the most damaging episodes of the 2007 to 2011 administration. Even the new American President, Barack Obama, criticised Scotland's actions. But Salmond has no regrets, and says that because earlier prisoners had been released on compassionate grounds, the Scottish Government had no choice but to release al-Megrahi when medical experts estimated that he had only three months to live. The man convicted of the worst terrorist atrocity in UK history hung on for two and a half years.

Salmond has since found himself under pressure to reject claims – by Professor Gallagher among others – that Scotland could be a soft underbelly for Islamic terrorists. Gallagher cites the First Minister's closeness to figures like Osama Saeed, the head of international relations at the al-Jazeera media network, who stood as an SNP candidate in Glasgow in 2011, as a sign that the SNP is close to "political Islam". Which it is – at least to the extent that it opposed the Iraq War, has an open immigration policy and a commitment to multiculturalism. When John Smeaton, the Glasgow baggage handler, staged his own war against terrorism at Glasgow Airport in 2007 against car bombers, the First Minister was unrestrained in his praise for "Smeato", and insisted that Scotland would co-operate fully with the UK in fighting Islamic or any other terrorism. He didn't try to make political capital, or appeal to the Muslim vote, by suggesting – as some others did – that British foreign policy and the Iraq War had "brought terrorism to Scotland".

THE LAIRD OF BUTE HOUSE

Let me take you on an imaginary dinner party from Hell with the wily manipulator, in his bunker, where his Machiavellian plots are hatched. This would be his official residence, Bute House, built in 1806 and occupying a commanding presence in Charlotte Square in Edinburgh's New Town. Salmond's real home is a converted mill in Strichen, Aberdeenshire, where he lives with his wife of over 30 years, Moira, who is 17 years older than Alex, childless, and keeps well away from politics. You know not to ask about Moira.

Bute House is much grander than Downing Street and the First Minister loves it. Recently, when it was suggested that he should move because upkeep was becoming too expensive – rent is £70,000 and utility bills top £90,000 – Salmond was horrified and insisted that this was a showcase for Scotland. The opposition parties said it was a showcase for Alex's ego. Inside, Bute House has that slightly spartan elegance you associate with Robert Adam and the Scottish Enlightenment. The rooms are big but not grand. The antique furnishings have a Presbyterian lack of ostentation and there is a faint smell of damp as you enter through security and up the flat stone staircase to the Cabinet and reception rooms. Bute House was so damp that when Salmond took up residence here, he developed chronic asthma and insisted on having the fireplaces opened to let the house breathe. He also says it was so filthy that Moira, his wife, spent all weekend on her knees trying to clean the place. Salmond is not what you would call a feminist – his excuse is that his acute back problems made participation in the makeover impossible.

In the evening, the First Minister will emerge, typically in a polo shirt, belly hanging perilously over a pair of crushed slacks and scuffed tan shoes. The smart suits and ties are dispensed with as soon as he gets off-grid. You realise that this is probably how he's been dressing since he was an economics and medieval history student at St Andrews University in the 1970s. Informality, in the Salmond circle, is almost a formality. When he worked as an oil economist after leaving university, first with the government service and then the Royal Bank of Scotland, he was invariably described as a "scruff" and censured for not wearing a tie.

For someone who is almost constantly in the media eye, Salmond is remarkably relaxed about his appearance and appears devoid of vanity. Unkind people might say he has a lot to be devoid about. He used to spend long hours watching recordings of his performances on television – he has tapes going back decades and has been known to show people his greatest hits. He is proud of his ability on the medium; it is something he has worked on. Having interviewed him countless times in my years as a television presenter, I have never come across any politician who is quite so adept at getting his message across on the box. He is careful always to have a pay-off soundbite for each answer, and has a knack of anticipating which soundbite is likely to find its way onto transmission. It isn't something he was born with; he just worked at it. Salmond realised through long experience of handling the local and regional media that you don't have to be a genius to sound good on television – just well prepared.

Salmond may be no oil painting, but he is a bit of an art collector, at least in Bute House, where he has surrounded himself with works on loan from the National Galleries of Scotland. Predictably there is one of the only two known oil portraits of Robert Burns, by Alexander Nasmyth, and Henry Raeburn's famous 1787 portrait of the fiddler, Niel Gow. More surprising is a large portrait of Thomas Johnston, the Labour MP and wartime Secretary of State for Scotland, which dominates the state room of Bute House. Salmond is particularly proud of this painting, by Gunn, and shows it to all his visitors. Why would the SNP leader want a politician who loathed Scottish Nationalists to be staring down at him as he hosts official engagements? Well, quite few reasons, all of them to do with Alex Salmond's political philosophy. Most pictures tell a story; this is a political manifesto.

Tom Johnston was Secretary of State during the high noon of Unionism, during and immediately after the Second World War, when the SNP was a speck of dust in the political wind. He was Labour's most successful Scottish politician, a radical journalist, a Red Clydesider and scourge of the privileged. Johnston wrote a polemic in the 1920s, *Our Scots Noble Families,* that excoriated the landed classes over their disregard for the welfare of the people during and after the Highland Clearances. Nevertheless, Winston Churchill appointed Tom Johnston, the Labour MP for Stirling and Clackmannan West, as Scottish Secretary in 1941 because he was simply the best politician around at a time of national emergency, when political divisions became irrelevant. Johnston turned the Scottish Office into a virtual government, with sweeping powers over industrial regeneration, health and housing.

This administrative devolution was intended to cement the Union, not break it apart. But Salmond is relaxed about this contradiction, and believes that devolution cuts both ways. As a gradualist, unlike rival Jim Sillars, Salmond has always regarded devolution as a necessary stage in the road to independence, rather than a Unionist roadblock on the way to it. In his praise for Tom Johnston, Salmond is sending a message to civic Scotland that his heart is consensual and he is not a separatist. The First Minister made clear in the aftermath of the 2011 election result that he would welcome a multi-option referendum on independence in which the "half-way house" of a parliament with greater economic powers was offered to voters as well as independence and the status quo. This was blocked by the UK Coalition on the grounds that Salmond shouldn't be allowed to have a "second best" option on the ballot. It is a gamble, to say the least, by Cameron.

Salmond also wants people to regard the SNP as part of a radical tradition that runs through from Red Clydeside, the Beveridge Report, the NHS and even to the social democratic Britain celebrated in Danny Boyle's Olympic Games opening ceremony in 2012. Salmond says he enjoyed the 2012 pageant even though it rather downplayed Scotland's participation in the Industrial Revolution and was regarded by most commentators as a celebration of Britishness – of what the New Statesman called a "New Patriotism". But Salmond's electoral success in Scotland has been based not on anti-Englishness and ethnic exceptionalism, but on assuming the mantle of enlightened social democracy that he believes was discarded by New Labour under Tony Blair.

Salmond outlined his philosophy of progressive universalism in a Hugo Young Lecture to *The Guardian* in January 2012 which remains the most comprehensive account of Salmond's concept of the "social wage":

"The Scottish government's policies attempt to protect many values which would be dear to any post-war social democrat in these isles. For example, we have promoted what we call a living wage – £7.20 an hour. And we have made a conscious decision to provide certain core universal services, rights or benefits, some of which are no longer prioritised by political leaders elsewhere – such as free university tuition, free prescriptions, free personal care for the elderly and a guarantee of no compulsory redundancies. We do this because we believe that such services benefit the common weal. They provide a sense of security, well-being and equity within communities. Such a sense of security is essential to a sense of confidence

– and as we have seen over the last three years, confidence is essential to economic growth."[99]

Salmond believes that this tradition of progressive universalism was started in Scotland by Tom Johnston during the war. After the war, Johnston became famous for another reason close to Alex Salmond's heart – renewable energy. Johnston set up the North of Scotland Hydro Electric Board, a kind of Caledonian version of the Tennessee Valley Authority, exploiting the original green energy: Scottish water. Salmond, formerly an oil economist with the Royal Bank, is almost as obsessed with renewable energy as he is with Robert the Bruce. The First Minister will tell you in exhaustive detail how Scotland can become a global leader in renewable energy, with one-quarter of Europe's offshore wind and wave energy. The Pentland Firth, he believes, will be the Saudi Arabia of tidal energy. Scotland has already surpassed its targets for CO_2 reductions and will have the capacity to be 100% carbon-free in electricity generation by 2020. Salmond sees this as another energy bonanza, like North Sea oil in the 1970s, and he doesn't want to see Scotland miss out. However, his rural MSPs are coming under intense pressure from objectors to the wind farms that have sprung up across Scotland's hills and glens. Mountaineers, ramblers, bird watchers and naturalists of all kinds have turned on Salmond for damaging what they call Scotland's greatest natural resource – its wild land.

In one portrait, you get the entire Salmond political philosophy. Tom Johnston's prominence is intended to demonstrate to everyone who visits Bute House that this is the official residence of Scotland's leader, and not just a here today, gone tomorrow politician. There is something very *West Wing* about the way Salmond talks of the role of First Minister and the importance of office. Salmond saw a large part of his job as being combating this "crabbit" Scottish mentality and demonstrating in the manner of his government that Scots are just as capable of running their own affairs as any other country. He believes the SNP restored the dignity of Scottish parliamentary democracy and have shown that Scots can govern themselves effectively if they work at it. Labour just think he has delusions of grandeur, and that instead of playing at being Prime Minister in Bute House, he should be sorting out problems on the ground in the NHS and schools.

Another of Salmond's political heroes, strangely enough, is Harold Wilson, who he insists is much underestimated and turned Labour into a party of government – which is what Salmond believes he has achieved for the SNP. Labour politicians, not surprisingly rather resent Salmond's attempt to co-opt their political figures to the cause of Nationalism, starting with Keir Hardie, and they accuse him of "political body snatching" and hypocrisy. They point out that this "Socialist" practically became a spokesperson for Scottish banks, RBS and HBOS, before the 2008 crash. Salmond even suggested that he would have an even lighter touch on financial regulation than Gordon Brown. They also criticise the First Minister for sucking up to Rupert Murdoch of *The Sun* – though this rebounds on Labour, since Tony Blair went half-way round the world to seek the support of the Sun King before he became PM.

REMEMBER BANNOCKBURN

Self-belief can become tiresome. Most politicians like the sound of their own voices and Alex Salmond is no exception. He will talk and talk. And talk. Just don't start on the Scottish Wars of Independence if you want to have an early night. Salmond likes to think of himself as an authority on the exploits of Wallace and Bruce, and certainly knows his history which he studied under the Scottish medievalist, GWS Barrow at St Andrews University. Salmond first became entranced by the Scottish story from his grandfather Sandy, the town plumber. Like most Scots, young Alex learned nothing about Wallace and Bruce at the local comprehensive in the West Lothian town of Linlithgow where he grew up in the 1960s. He likes to tell people that Sandy never made clear that Bruce's wars – he took over Linlithgow castle in 1313 – had taken place in the Middle Ages, and young Salmond believed it had all happened within living memory and not 700 years ago. And so, the old stories of Scotland, lying dormant like a seed in the desert, erupted into life again, making an indelible impression on the personality of the politician who would – possibly – lead Scotland to independence.

Salmond takes his history neat, but he doesn't rant about English domination, or insist that everyone sings *Scots Wha' Hae*. He is never seen in a kilt, and refuses to tolerate anti-English sentiment in the SNP – a ban that is rigidly enforced. Salmond insists that he is an "Anglophile". But he is fiercely protective of Scotland's history and Robert the Bruce's reputation. It may all be a long time ago, but for Salmond these are live issues – Scotland was, and is, a nation and the threat of extinction is as real as it was in the 13th century. The difference is that modern political battles are fought with opinion polls and ballots rather than swords and cannon.

Salmond eats heartily, as you might expect for someone of his size – no faddy diets despite his weight, which he apparently gained when he was on medication some years ago for a chronic bad back. He drinks too, and has a tendency to down a glass or two of wine late at night, which is probably bad for him. But I have never seen him drunk, even slightly, and I don't know anyone who has. Since he put on weight, his friends have worried about his health. This is Scotland after all – the country with the worst incidence of coronary heart disease in Europe. But like many fat men, Salmond seems to carry it well, and doesn't seem burdened by his flesh. In fact, he moves around like he was half his size, and is a manic worker, whether in his constituency or in St Andrew's House. People have thought of urging him to slow down, but as one of his colleagues once told me: "If Alex slowed down he would probably pop his clogs within the week. It's politics that keeps him going. It's his life."

Work is Salmond's real addiction. He prides himself on being one of the hardest-working politicians in the country and he tells long tales about how he managed to consolidate his hold on his Banff and Buchan seat by being "the best constituency MP ever". When he returned to Scottish politics in 2007, he chose to fight the safe Liberal Democrat seat of Gordon, where the SNP had come third and where he needed an 8% swing. It was a very risky bet, but he won comfortably.

Salmond is immensely practical, has little time for theorising and doesn't spend time with intellectuals, though he is not intimidated by professors. He does have a habit of letting his mouth run away with him, as in an interview with the *Sunday Politics* programme in March 2012, when he suggested to Andrew Neil that he had official legal advice to the effect that Scotland would remain in the European Union. He didn't. There was no formal legal opinion from the Lord Advocate, because one hadn't been asked for, and he only had the standard legal guidance from the Scottish Government's legal department. A minor solecism, perhaps, but one that caused him a great deal of trouble in the Scottish press, which focused relentlessly on the issue for the second half of 2012. Salmond doesn't "do" retractions though, and Nicola Sturgeon eventually had to unsay the remark for him.

He is interested in the arts, in a political sense at least, since like all Nationalists he realises how important writers and artists can be to any movement for national independence. Salmond can recite Burns, sometimes beyond the pain threshold, and claims to be an enthusiast for the writing of the "Scottish renaissance" of the 1920 and 1930s, which included Hugh MacDiarmid, Edwin Muir and Edwin Morgan, who became Scotland's first Makar, or national poet. His enthusiasm for Morgan may not be unconnected with the fact the poet left £1m to the SNP in his will when he died in 2010. He also says he is fond of the Welsh poet and Anglican priest, RS Thomas, who was a Nationalist and a dedicated supporter of the Campaign for Nuclear Disarmament. Salmond claims to be a great political friend of the Edinburgh Festival, still the largest arts festival in the world, which his government has supported financially since 2007. His favourite play is *Black Watch*, Gregory Burke's sensational account of the history of the Scottish soldier abroad as seen from the point of view of a squaddie in Iraq, produced for the National Theatre of Scotland in 2006.

Otherwise, Salmond's cultural taste is not what you would call highbrow. He is a great fan of Star Trek, or at least he claims to be, and says his favourite music is country and western. Mind you, Salmond's tastes sometimes seem carefully calibrated to appeal to the C1 and C2 voters that he needs to win over to the SNP. Golf, horse racing, football are subjects with which to break the ice with Scots of all classes and none. Salmond is a 24/7 politician and leisure time is put to the service of country. This doesn't mean he is insincere in his populism, or that he doesn't enjoy his passions. Quite the contrary – Salmond is one of the few people I have met in public life who doesn't mind if people think he is ordinary. He is what he is. Sometimes he isn't even that. Salmond's enthusiasm for the late Dusty Springfield arose because of a newspaper column ghosted by one of his aides who couldn't think of a subject and decided to invent Salmond's desolation at the demise of the peroxide chanteuse.

Salmond is provincial and lower-middle-class; his parents were junior civil servants, and he had a very conventional upbringing, going to church on Sunday and watching the football. His father, Robert, supported Labour, and his mother, Mary, was a Conservative. Salmond even has a slight speech impediment, and pronounces "th" as "f" – which means he says "growf" instead of "growth" and "boff" instead of "both". He used to worry about this in case it made him sound uneducated, but then he discovered that it was, if anything, an asset in his political work. It made him sound like an ordinary Scot.

He is the kind of industrious Scottish character who in times past would have made a name for himself in the British Empire – a Jardine or a Matheson perhaps, even a Campbell, running a colonial plantation. The Scots got by, not on wealth or connections, but because they were practical men, prepared to put in the hours, while their English superiors pursued a life of civilised indolence. You could imagine Alex Salmond doing business, meticulously ordering the accounts of the East India Company. Like William Paterson, the gambler who persuaded King William to set up the Bank of England, and then persuaded Scotland to invest in the Darien Scheme, there is an element of danger in the Salmond personality. His cockiness and his self-confidence, which so annoys his political opponents and makes him seem conceited, are very much a part of the Salmond package. If he seems like a bit of a chancer, that's because he is. If he has what Scots call a "guid conceit o' himself", that's because he wants to show that there is nothing wrong in self-belief. It is Salmond, the brand.

THE WINNER

People who have worked with Salmond say he is difficult, is given to angry outbursts and is a hard task-master. In the wake of a biography which referred obliquely to outbursts of anger, *Salmond Against the Odds*, by the journalist David Torrance, there were dark comparisons drawn in the press between Salmond and Gordon Brown. Both were said to be world champions in mobile phone hurling. From my soundings, this is exaggerated. I wouldn't say that his colleagues and underlings claim he is an easy person to work with, but they respect him. Salmond is not an easy person to be around, and people who have worked with him – while admiring his success – have not found it a particularly pleasurable experience. In the first Cabinet after his 2007 election victory, Salmond announced that he was not going to spare himself and anyone not prepared to do likewise should leave now. It was a rather ungenerous thing to say to politicians who had already devoted most of their lives to the cause. While he can be difficult and demanding, like all leaders in a hurry, he devotes his life to politics; Salmond can't quite understand why others choose not to do the same. Or even have relationships. There is sympathy for his special adviser, Geoff Aberdein, who has been described as "part special counsel, part Labrador".

For a politician who has been in front-line politics for two decades, Salmond seems to have relatively few real enemies, except for the "unforgiven" Jim Sillars. He has led a remarkably united party for 23 years, albeit with a Westminster sabbatical. Some regard his dominance of the Scottish National Party as sinister. Jim Sillars accuses Salmond of being a "totalitarian" who has dominated his party "like the old Communist Party" and subjected it to his personal control. But Salmond isn't a Stalinist and there is no reign of terror. He hasn't extinguished the democratic structures in the SNP – which bit back over the policy of remaining in Nato – and he has never expelled a party member, though the nationalist icon Margo MacDonald found she fell rapidly down the SNP candidates list when she fell out with him. She eventually decided to stand as an independent, which caused her automatic expulsion from the party.

Salmond has brought former enemies from the Sillars era, like Alex Neil and Kenny MacAskill, into the government and seems more interested in the effectiveness of politicians than what they have said about him in the past. The former chief executive of the SNP, Mike Russell, co-wrote a book in 2006 called *Grasping the Thistle* in which he described Alex Salmond as "a leader brilliantly suited to guerilla opposition but much less well attuned to the disciplines and demands of any new politics". Salmond was furious, not least because he was trying to win an election in just over a year. But Russell, too, was brought into the Cabinet in 2009, and is now Education Secretary. It's not that Salmond doesn't bear grudges, it's just that he doesn't see the point in letting personal differences get in the way of getting and holding power.

The main reason the party have been uncannily united under his guidance – and for those of us who reported on the SNP in times past, this unity is nothing short of miraculous – is simply because under Alex Salmond the SNP has become successful beyond all expectations. As recently as 2003, under John Swinney, the Nationalists were trailing Labour by 27 seats to 50 in the Scottish parliamentary elections, and going backwards. Salmond took them to their first-ever victory, and then to a landslide, and incredibly, at the time of writing in 2013, the SNP is still polling at the level of the 2011 election. In February 2013, Ipsos MORI put the SNP at 43% in terms of voting intention for Holyrood, only a few points short of their share of the constituency vote in the 2011 Scottish election.[100] It's hard to argue with results like these.

Despite sustained attacks on his probity in 2012, Salmond remains by far the most consistently popular leader in modern Scottish political history. At the close of 2012, after Salmond had been under sustained attack for months for allegedly "lying" over his legal advice on EU membership after independence, Ipsos MORI showed that more than half of Scots were still satisfied with the way the Scottish Government was running the country, against 39% who were not satisfied, giving a net satisfaction rating of +15%. This compared with the UK Coalition's satisfaction rating of -40%. Throughout almost his entire period in office, Alex Salmond has been more popular than all the other party leaders put together. The former Labour First Minister, Henry McLeish, thinks the secret of Salmond's success is simple. "Alex Salmond is not successful because he wants independence, but because he's distinctly Scottish," says McLeish, urging his own party to learn from Salmond. "He speaks up for Scotland, he is a national leader. It's all the pride, passion, patriotism issues that the people like".[101]

Salmond doesn't need to exercise totalitarian thought control on his party – they just like winning, and they realise that what has damaged the party in the past has been internal divisions. No one in the SNP group wants to sound like Jim Sillars, a remote figure who spends his time attacking the SNP leader from the pages of the press. Those who have remarked upon the success of Alex Salmond have been called his "cheerleaders", as if it is partisan to state the obvious. But Salmond really is a unique phenomenon, a politician who has been in political office and has had no "mid-term blues". He has seemed immune to the decline in popularity that has affected all political leaders, including Tony Blair and Margaret Thatcher. Journalists have been waiting impatiently for his fall and an opportunity to confirm the thesis that all political careers end in tears. They may indeed, but not yet. Even as the Scottish voters are saying, according to one recent poll[102], that they are not convinced with the case he has presented for independence, they still rate him as the best leader in Holyrood.

TEA WITH RUPERT

After you have had the full tour of Bute House, there is usually an invitation to sign up to the cause. Salmond genuinely feels that every Scot of whatever background living in Scotland should support the SNP. He can't see why people don't. Salmond is painfully aware that he has had this extraordinary success while receiving little support from the Scottish press – quite the reverse. The mass-circulation tabloids, the *Daily Record*, *Express*, *Mail* are intensely hostile to Nationalism and to Salmond personally. *The Scotsman* can hardly contain its dislike, and the explicitly unionist papers – *The Telegraph*, *The Guardian* – treat him as a devious manipulator. The SNP get fair treatment from the broadcasters, but as Salmond points out, the BBC tends to get its news agenda from reading the morning newspapers. The desperation to get at least one paper onside explains Salmond's willingness to associate with Rupert Murdoch, who he famously invited to Bute House for tea and Tunnock's (a uniquely Scottish delicacy) and to discuss how he could possibly help him in his attempts to gain control of BSkyB.

The *Sun* did briefly support the SNP in 1990, but not for very long. It was more of a sales stunt by its then editor, Kelvin MacKenzie, than a serious ideological commitment. The FM insists that his meetings with Murdoch were purely to promote Scotland's economic interests, which is the primary obligation of all political leaders. But offering to lobby the Culture Secretary, Jeremy Hunt, on behalf of News International, is carrying this responsibility just a little too far. Especially as the News International titles were in the dock for the phone-hacking scandal. Salmond gave evidence to the Leveson Inquiry and was roundly patronised by the judge who clearly didn't buy the FM's account of his transactions with the Dirty Digger, as Murdoch is called by *Private Eye*. He exonerated Salmond of any wrongdoing, but noted his "striking" willingness to lobby on Murdoch's behalf. Whether or not this is the case, his gesture to *The Sun* has been reciprocated, and *The Scottish Sun* is now much friendlier to the SNP. Alex Salmond allegedly leaked his original preferred referendum date of October 2014 to *The Sun* – shades of Tony Blair leaking the date of the 2001 General Election to Murdoch. But Salmond denies it.

The Murdoch affair was more than embarrassing, and gave valuable ammunition to his enemies. *The Guardian's* Michael White could hardly contain his glee: "So, the revelation that Wee Eck," he wrote, "was wining and dining with the Murdoch mafia and running errands may be the first and most untimely blow landed on him for a while. His more covert dealings with Donald Trump, the blow-dried American property man, has developed into a promising sub-plot." Labour only needed to say "if you can judge a man by the company he keeps ..."

Salmond has indeed been closer than he should have been to unsavoury souls like Fred Goodwin of RBS, Donald Trump, developer of the controversial Menie golf course in Aberdeenshire, and Rupert Murdoch, owner of the late and unlamented News of the World. It's not clear just how much damage Salmond's meetings with remarkable men have caused the SNP. The row may have contributed to the SNP's setback in the May 2012 local elections, where the SNP failed to take Glasgow. The bandwagon stalled just short of Labour's last bastion in the west. But like the banking crash, the odium hasn't lasted.

Salmond has a much more relaxed attitude to press hostility than he had, even a decade ago, perhaps because he feels their impact on public opinion has lessened. The press were universally hostile to Salmond, and yet he still won in 2007 and 2011 – over the heads of the editorials and the slanted profiles. On the morning of polling day in 2007, I remember seeing the front pages of the press at my local garage in their plastic bins. It was like an identity parade of a wanted criminal. Salmond was portrayed as a wrecker and an unreliable demagogue. "The most dangerous man in Scotland," said one tabloid, with one of those under-lit mugshots that made him look like a serial murderer. The front page of *The Scottish Sun* refashioned an SNP logo as a hangman's noose as a warning to Scots on the dangers of voting for the Nationalists. No truck with the Nats then. But Salmond went on to win the 2007 election. Somehow, Alex Salmond has been able to speak over the heads of the media to the Scottish voters. He has done this by speaking in a language the Scottish voters take note of – the language of example. It is his prodigious work rate, his conviction politics, and his determination to deliver on (most) of his key election pledges. Salmond has been able to neutralise his negative image by doing rather than by talking.

Salmond ran a highly successful minority administration from 2007 to 2011 after commentators like me were saying that his government wouldn't last six months. Despite lacking a working majority in Holyrood, Salmond managed to deliver a remarkably stable and effective administration, despite having no visible means of support – apart from his own personality. His administration delivered on a range of headline policies, from abolishing prescription charges to scrapping student fees; saving accident and emergency hospitals to introducing the most ambitious targets for CO_2 emissions in the world to freezing council tax – all this despite having no majority in Parliament. This is because, as the SNP Government quickly discovered, there is a great deal that can be done by executive order without bothering about Parliament. The opposition parties were divided and leaderless and lacked the will to bring down Salmond's government, even though they clearly had the numbers to do so.

Salmond avoided serious confrontations with the UK Government, even after the Conservative-led Coalition announced the deepest cuts in public spending in 80 years in the 2010 deficit-reduction programme. This was most unlike the Salmond of 1981, who would no doubt have launched a "Scottish resistance" of civil disobedience and refused to implement the cuts. But Salmond went along with the deficit-reduction programme, reluctantly, relying on his Finance Secretary, John Swinney, to somehow make the books balance – which he succeeded in doing. Swinney quietly achieved a great deal in 2007, delivering year-on-year increases in NHS spending and paying for all those "something for nothing" policies like free personal care and bus travel for pensioners. Salmond defied the combined might of the Scottish opposition parties who had threatened to extinguish his administration by voting down his budgets.

In 2009, it looked as if Salmond's luck had run out when the two Scottish Green MSPs, who had been supporting the SNP administration, withdrew their support in the Budget vote at the last minute over a failure by the Scottish Government to honour its commitment on insulation grants. The bill fell. Since this had never happened before, there was air of chaos in the garden lobby of the Parliament, because no one knew what happened next. Did this mean an early election? John Swinney announced that he was withdrawing the Budget and would resubmit it again in seven days. Labour waited for a desperate Salmond to come to them with a list of concessions, but he didn't. He simply said that if the Budget wasn't passed he would go to the country. It was a threat he had made before, and Labour laughed at him. But Salmond just sat in his office in St Andrew's House and waited. Within hours, the Liberal Democrats knocked on his door seeking terms. Labour's finance spokesman, Andy Kerr, was also reduced to knocking on Salmond's door, desperate to avoid an election, which Labour knew they would lose. There has never been a better political poker player than Salmond.

However, this was not the closest the SNP leader came to fighting an early election. In November 2009, his Education Secretary, Fiona Hyslop, came under fire after it emerged that Scotland had lost 2,000 teachers since the SNP had taken office. Class sizes were rising rapidly. Hyslop blamed Labour councils for this development, but Labour's new leader, Iain Gray, called for her resignation. SNP insiders say that Salmond fully expected to lose a confidence motion in Parliament, and was prepared for an election. However, Hyslop resigned on 1st December, and the crisis was over. She is the only Cabinet minister that Salmond has lost since 2007.

Salmond is adamant that the party's success in 2011 was because it delivered on all its election promises – that isn't quite true. He didn't scrap the council tax, as promised in the 2007 election manifesto, abolish student debt, replace PFI with public bond issues or repeal the Act of Settlement. But the record was enough to convince the Scottish voters, and showing that it was possible even within the confines of devolution, to run an administration that could make genuine improvements in people's lives. The Scots didn't vote for Salmond because they particularly liked him as a person, or because he bribed them with unaffordable policy giveaways, or because they supported independence for Scotland. They supported Salmond because he seemed the most capable person around to do the job. They also responded to his determination to emphasise the positive qualities of Scotland and talk up the prospects of the country at a time when the opposition were warning Scots that their country could not be economically viable without English subsidies. People don't like being told that they aren't fit to look after themselves, even if it's true.

Some commentators suspect that Salmond is no longer fully committed to independence anyway, and would prefer to carry on as he is now – First Minister of a devolved Parliament. After all, why did he appear to endorse a multi-option referendum with a Devolution Max option on the ballot paper? Since the vast majority of Scots say they want a Parliament with more powers, the independence vote would have been minimised, and independence might have been marginalised for a generation. He seems to be going to great lengths to persuade Scots that not much would change after independence, with Scotland keeping the Queen, the pound, MI6 and Nato. However, speaking to Salmond over many years, I have never heard him even hint that he has abandoned independence or would be happy to leave it to the never-ever. He insists that he is only in the politics business for one thing, and that is to make Scotland an independent country.

Salmond is supremely confident of his abilities to win the Independence Referendum in 2014. You never know with Salmond whether he truly believes what he says because he has become such a dedicated worshipper in the church of the positive. But it looks like a very tall order. At present, only around 34% of Scots, according to Ipsos MORI, say they will definitely vote for independence against more than 50% who say they will not. Yet Salmond is unshakeable in his conviction that he can reverse this position. He points to 2011, when he led his party to a landslide victory despite having been ten points behind Labour in most opinion polls, in the year before the campaign. He reminds you that the forecast was, when he returned as leader of the party in 2004, that he would win the 2007 Scottish parliamentary elections, and that no one believed him then. That's true – I certainly didn't.

But a constitutional referendum is very different from a parliamentary election. The stakes are higher. Voters in 2007 were comparing Salmond's people against a Labour Party that had been damaged by scandals and mediocrity. They weren't voting for a new country. Salmond's irrepressible self-confidence can look like complacency – as if he doesn't think he needs to go to the trouble of explaining about pensions and currencies, because people should just rely on him to get it right. There has been disquiet in the independence camp that there appears to be very little planning for the campaign and that too many people are relying on Salmond to make it alright on the night. The chairman of Yes Scotland, the former Labour MP Dennis Canavan, made an outspoken attack on Salmond's handling of the currency issue in May 2013, as the supporters of independence began to fear that they might be heading for defeat.

However, if Salmond loses in 2014, it may not be the last we will see of him. Labour is confident that he would be so discredited that he would be rejected by the Scottish voters at the 2016 Scottish Elections. I'm not so sure. In fact, a No vote could lead to the Scottish voters re-electing the SNP if only to guarantee that there is no back-sliding in Westminster over those extra powers that have been promised by the Unionist parties over the past year. Scots did not vote for Alex Salmond because of independence, but because the SNP seemed to be more competent than the opposition. Labour may well find that it is disappointed in 2016. Knowing Salmond, he could well be back in Bute House, perhaps handing most government functions over to Nicola Sturgeon, his inheritor, still showing visitors the Cabinet table and telling anecdotes about Ramsay MacDonald and Tom Johnston. Leave politics? They'd have to drag him out of Bute House with wild horses.

CHAPTER FOURTEEN
THE ARC OF INSOLVENCY

×

I N T H E spring of 2012, a rather annoying linguistic fashion hit Scottish politics. Suddenly, people were addressing each other as "Staatsminister", speaking in curious hurdy-gurdy accents and saying "Takk" instead of thanks. This outbreak of pseudo-Nordic was caused by the popular Danish television series, *Borgen*, which remade the American political drama, *The West Wing* in a small European country, Denmark, with a woman prime minister. When they showed the final two episodes at Edinburgh's Film House on 3rd February 2013, it packed the auditorium for three consecutive performances. The Deputy First Minister, Nicola Sturgeon, was not only in the audience, she interviewed the actress Sidse Babett Knudsen who played the fictional Staatsminister, Birgitte Nyborg.

Nationalists switched onto *Borgen* for two reasons. First of all, it showed that small countries could produce very good television. The state broadcaster in Denmark, DR, which made *Borgen*, and the internationally successful police thriller, *The Killing* was outpacing the BBC in the production of well-financed and highly acclaimed television drama. One of the Unionist arguments against independence had always been that Scotland would be denied the benefit of the BBC, the "best broadcaster in the world", and that a tiny country like Scotland would only be able to produce third-rate soap operas and boring political debate programmes.

But more relevant to the Nationalist case was the subject matter of *Borgen*. Week by week, it explored grown-up issues like military involvement in overseas conflict, trade union reform, welfare cuts, coalition politics and race relations, while following the disintegration of the Staatsminister's personal life. For the first time, Scottish viewers were able to see what political life might be like in a small country. It served as an antidote to the Unionist claims that an independent Scotland would be an impoverished and parochial statelet, without influence in the world and without cultural significance. Denmark has a population of just over five million, has an advanced welfare state, is independent in Europe, and has one of the highest living standards in the world. *Borgen* was like a two-hour party political broadcast every Saturday night.

This programme threatened to be for the referendum in 2014 what *Braveheart* was for the Devolution Referendum in 1997, and what *The Cheviot, the Stag and the Black Black Oil* was to 1979. By chance, another piece of popular culture had come along just at the moment when Scots were reconsidering their place in the Union. However, whereas *Braveheart* was patriotic Nationalist tosh, Borgen was both intelligent and extremely well-written, and didn't just play on Scotland's enduring sense of grievance at the behaviour of its powerful neighbour. Denmark doesn't look over its shoulder all the time, at anyone. It also reminded Scots that Nordic nations – Norway, Sweden, Denmark, Finland – have been much more successful, economically and socially, than Scotland.

According to the World Bank, Denmark has one of the lowest levels of inequality in the world, and was named the happiest country on the planet by Columbia University's Earth Institute. Social protection is generous. In Denmark, full-time childcare costs £300 a month, and unemployment benefit is £400 a week for two years – this compares with Britain's Job Seeker's Allowance of £71 for six months and then only for over-25s. They pay for it, of course, in tax rates ranging from 42% to 62%. Yet, Denmark is also regarded as one of the most competitive economies in the world and one of the easiest places to do business. It also has one of the most flexible labour markets in the world, according to the World Bank, which comes as a surprise to Labour "modernisers" in Britain, who assume that the economies of social democratic countries are overstaffed and inefficient. The flexibility comes from the social protections that allow people to move rapidly between jobs without losing too much income on the way.

Further north, Norway is number one in the United Nations Human Development Index of wellbeing in terms of life expectancy, income and education. Its geography, population, economy and social outlook is very similar to Scotland's. They are both cold, northern countries which have had to develop a collective spirit to cope with the rigours of the climate. I visited Norway and Denmark twice during the financial crisis to see how the "unaffordable" Nordic social model was faring. Norway, needless to say, doesn't need to worry about debt because of its oil. But even Denmark seemed to be experiencing relatively little financial stress. Its borrowing level has risen to 45% of GDP in 2013, according to *The Economist* magazine's public debt index, but this compares to the UK public debt to GDP level of 92% on the same measure. Denmark and Norway are two of the most stable economies in the world, according to the OECD. This is puzzling to politicians in Britain where there is an almost universal assumption that the European sovereign debt crisis has been caused by high levels of social protection. This is a myth. The most financially secure and economically dynamic economies in Europe, are actually the small Nordic nations – Denmark, Norway, Sweden and Finland.

Of course, these countries have been hit by the global slow-down, and Danish manufacturing exports are down. But at least it still is a formidable manufacturing nation. Denmark has its own currency, the krone, which is nominally pegged to the euro, and this has risen in value which doesn't help exports. Norway has recently developed an unsustainable property bubble, largely because of foreign investors looking for a safe-haven in a country with a petroleum-backed currency – something an independent Scotland might also have to face. This will have to unwind, eventually, and it will be painful. However, it was hard not to look with some envy at Norway in 2012, with its growth rate of 2.5%, unemployment at 3% and inflation at 1.5%. Britain, by contrast was experiencing near-zero growth, unemployment at 8% and inflation at nearly 4%. Whatever it is they're doing over there, it works.

The Unionist parties in the UK have taken it as self-evident that an independent Scotland would struggle because it lacked the support of the United Kingdom. That without subsidies from the Barnett Formula the Scottish economy would be something like one of the old Communist countries of Eastern Europe. The Scottish economic historian and Unionist, Niall Ferguson, in 2006, called Scotland "the Belarus of the west – a small, sparsely populated appendage of England". *The Economist* magazine dubbed Scotland "Skintland" in 2012 and declared it would be impoverished if it left the UK. There has never been any economic justification for these offensive appellations. It is also argued that tiny Scotland would be economically vulnerable to the vagaries of globalisation, where only big beasts rule. But it is the small and nimble European countries that seem to be doing better than Britain, France and Italy. Where would Scotland have been, say Better Together, without UK financial support during the banking crash? Well, the Nordic nations like Denmark and Norway actually did rather well during the financial crash of 2008, and demonstrated that not all small nations need end up like Iceland or Ireland. This dug the SNP leader Alex Salmond out of a hole of his own making.

CELTIC NEOLIBERALISM

Before 2008, the SNP had become enamoured of the nations of the "arc of prosperity" as the First Minister described the "Tiger" economies of Iceland and Ireland. Along with some of the newly independent Baltic countries like Latvia and Estonia, these small, neoliberal nations had been registering startling economic growth rates in the early years of the 21st century. Like Scotland, they had large and poorly regulated banking sectors, which was also their downfall. When Ireland's property bubble burst in 2008, the country was plunged into debt-deflation and the republic suffered mass unemployment, collapsing house prices and, for the first time in a quarter of a century, rising emigration.

Iceland, with only 300,000 inhabitants, seemed to be in even worse shape, since the debts of its banks were eight times national income. In 2008 to 2009, the value of the Icelandic krona fell by 90%, inflation rose to 18% and unemployment from 2% to 10%. House prices fell by 50% and there were street demonstrations in Reykjavik, as Icelanders, banging pots and pans, called for their political leaders to be brought to trial for their irresponsible economic policies. Amazingly, some were – including the then Prime Minister, Geir Haarde, who was tried in 2012 and found guilty of negligence, though he escaped imprisonment.

Across in the Baltic countries, matters were, if anything, even worse. In Latvia, which I visited in 2008, unemployment rose to 25% while the economy shrank by a quarter. Public sector pay was slashed by 30% as unemployment rose to 23% in December 2008. The car parks were filled with 4X4s that their owners could no longer afford to drive. Suddenly, being a small independent country in Europe didn't look like such a good idea. References to Celtic Tigers and arcs of prosperity disappeared from Nationalist speeches faster than tributes to Jimmy Savile in the BBC's Christmas schedules. It had become, rather embarrassingly, the "arc of insolvency", and Unionists pointed out that Scotland would have been bankrupt had it not been for the support of the United Kingdom and, in particular, the Bank of England. "Celtic neoliberalism", as it had been called, was discredited. The SNP's Thatcher moment had passed – but it left behind serious questions about the coherence of SNP economic policy.

It seemed obvious that Scotland – had it been independent in 2008 – would have suffered from an economic meltdown even greater than Iceland's, if only because two of the biggest and most insolvent banks in the world, HBOS and Royal Bank of Scotland, happened to be located in Edinburgh. If Scotland alone had been required to shoulder the colossal debts of RBS, which had a balance sheet running to £1.5 trillion in 2008, it would clearly have been in severe difficulties. Except that it almost certainly would not have had to. The point about RBS, Scotland's biggest bank, is that it is also England's biggest bank, with most of its activities taking place south of the border, where it is known as the National Westminster. Some 90% of RBS employees are English and most of its loss-making activities took place in the City of London.

Similarly, the Halifax Bank of Scotland was already a cross-border banking behemoth before it merged with Lloyds in 2008 to form what is now Britain's biggest bank, with nearly a quarter of all UK retail bank deposits. These delinquent institutions were simply too big to fail Had Scotland been independent when the banks became insolvent in 2008, the Bank of England would have had to mount a similar rescue operation on the nominally Scottish banks because the alternative would have been the collapse of the English financial system. The ATM machines would have shut down just as tightly in London as in Edinburgh if HBOS and RBS had been allowed to go under in that fateful weekend in October 2008, when the former Labour Chancellor, Alistair Darling, convened his famous "chicken tikka masala" summit at the Treasury with the bank bosses. RBS and HBOS are key City of London and global banks and their collapse would have caused a far greater economic shock than the collapse of the US investment bank, Lehman Brothers. This is why the US Federal Reserve put up several hundred billion dollars to underpin RBS and HBOS loans in America. Governments couldn't afford to let these banks go bust on either side of the Atlantic or on either side of the Scottish border.

It would have been uncomfortable, certainly, if Scotland had been independent when the banks crashed, but probably not much more uncomfortable than being part of the UK. Cross-border bail-outs are not unusual in Europe. The Belgian, Dutch and Luxembourg governments collectively bailed out Fortis and Dexis banks in 2008. By international convention, the bailout is shared in proportion to the sphere of activities of the banks. As Professor Andrew Hughes Hallett of St Andrews University has pointed out, since roughly 90% of RBS activities were in England, Scotland would have been liable for 10% of the bailout costs. He made this assessment in 2011 and it hasn't been disputed by the Bank of England or the Treasury.

Now, this doesn't mean that an independent Scottish ex-chequer would have been able to sail on regardless through the banking crash, or that there would have been no penalty for having Scotland's names on two of the biggest and baddest banks in the world. In submitting to the Bank of England bailout terms, the inde-pendent Scottish economy might well have lost much of its nominal autonomy. There might have been stringent conditions attached to capital injections in the Scottish banks, which amounted to some £76 billion in all. Scotland would not have been able to devalue its currency relative to England, because, of course, it remains in a currency union. However, it is almost inconceivable that the Bank of England, as has been suggested, would have refused to act as "lender of last resort" to the nominally Scottish banks, because to do so would have had catastrophic consequences for the financial stability of England.

A more serious risk for a small country with big banks is that the political classes will tend to be in the pockets of the finan-ciers because of their lobbying power and because of the size of finance relative to the rest of the economy. There is evidence that the Scottish Government was far too eager to exonerate the banks in 2008, merely because they were Scottish. As we saw earlier, the way that Alex Salmond leapt to the defence of banks like HBOS and RBS, as if they were national tennis champions being bad mouthed by London commentators, did not inspire confidence. And it is a curious argument for a Nationalist party to insist that, when push comes to shove, it would look to another country to sort out its financial affairs. But the reality is that British banking is organised on a UK-wide basis, and has been for decades, and it is now difficult to say any bank is either Scottish or English. Either way, they are just too big. They have long outgrown the limits of the national economy. The problem for advocates of Scottish independence is that this would appear to put significant limits on the extent to which Scotland ever could be financially independent of the UK.

However, while Scotland's dysfunctional banks were certainly a liability, there is no particular reason to suppose that Scotland, merely because of its small size, would be any more or less vulnerable to international financial distress than, say, Norway or Denmark. As a country with substantial oil wealth, an independent Scotland would have arguably been better placed to survive the current sovereign debt crisis alone than as part of the UK, especially if it had, like Norway, prudently invested oil revenues in an oil fund after the discovery of North Sea oil in 1970. Norway's sovereign wealth fund, now called the Government Pension Fund is now worth $684bn, and holds 1% of global equity markets. This is an asset that is worth more than just the sum of its deposits. Having this pool of wealth acts as a stabiliser for the economy and has insulated what was a very much less economically developed country from the vagaries of globalisation.

There is evidence that the smaller, social democratic countries – Finland, Denmark or Norway – where wealth differentials have been kept within limits, have coped with financial turbulence rather better than the larger neoliberal "Anglo-Saxon" countries like the UK. Certainly, they have been less prone to boom and bust. There is also evidence that small countries like Lativa have been able to recover from the crisis more rapidly. The Baltic state has been commended by the IMF for "taking the medicine", and getting on with restructuring its economy. Latvia grew by 5% in 2012. Similar claims have been made for Ireland, and though these should be taken with some scepticism, since unemployment is still high in both countries, there is an argument that smaller countries can cope rather better with crisis. This is because they tend to have greater social solidarity, flatter class divisions, and their businesses are more flexible.

The small Nordic nations certainly have a very much stronger record of business formation than Scotland.[103] In 2008, Scotland had 26 enterprises per 1,000 of population, while Denmark, Norway, Sweden and Finland had 43, 51, 67 and 61 respectively. According to the economist Professor David Bell of Stirling University, "high rates of tax do not deter Scandinavian entrepreneurship". Scotland has one of the lowest levels of new business formation in Europe, a problem that cannot be rectified simply by cutting spending, which seems to be the current government's solution. This "enterprise deficit", as it has been called by Ben Thomson of Reform Scotland, is arguably the biggest economic challenge facing Scotland, whether it remains in or out of the UK. Both economists argue that this is unlikely to be tackled without greater economic powers being devolved to Scotland. Something needs to be done to shake Scotland out of its dependency.

Scots have tended to see themselves as passive victims of the London political-industrial complex, which led to a culture of defeatism and negativity that may, only now, be coming under challenge. That post-neoclassical endogenous growth, that Gordon Brown used to talk about, did not happen in Scotland because the political power structures of Britain in the 20th century militated against it. The state that became such an important player in economic activity was firmly located in London and saw Scotland as provincial. It is only since the creation of the Scottish Parliament that there have been moves to develop a distinctive industrial economy in Scotland based on Scotland's universities with Labour's Wendy Alexander's "Smart, Successful Scotland" and Jack McConnell's "Fresh Start" initiatives trying to promote professional immigration. The Scottish National Party have sought to develop an industrial policy based on green energy.

THE ECONOMICS OF INDEPENDENCE

One of the unintended consequences of the independence debate has been the conversion of many on the political Left in Scotland to the economics of enterprise. Alex Salmond was a former leader of the avowedly socialist '79 Group in the 1980s, and the culture of the SNP has long been firmly on the Left. The SNP have been close to the public sector unions and tended to be unsympathetic to business – until, as we've seen, it started raising serious money from them after 2000. But, in facing up to the problems of justifying Scotland as an independent and viable economic entity, the Nationalists have had to address the lack of a developed business culture in Scotland.

However, if you'd believe Alex Salmond, Scotland's enterprise deficit is already being filled thanks to Scotland's "second energy bonanza" – renewables. With up to 25% of Europe's offshore wind and tidal energy potential, and around 10% of its wave power, the First Minster paints a picture of Scotland becoming the "Green Energy Capital of Europe", with companies like Pelamis, Wavegen, SgurrEnergy and Doosan leading the way. This isn't all Nationalist greenwash. The UK Energy Minister, Ed Davey, in a speech in March 2013, forecast that there could be 400,000 jobs supported by the renewables industry by 2020, and many of these will be in Scotland. Companies like Aveva, Gamesa, and Samsung Heavy Industries are piling into Scottish offshore wind generation.

Scotland is on course to generate 100% of its electricity demand through renewable sources by 2020, and, even taking this with a large dollop of Unionist scepticism, Scotland clearly has a comparative advantage in carbon-free energy – even if there is now significant local opposition building up in the Highlands over the proliferation of onshore wind farms. However, there can be no guarantees about the second energy revolution actually arriving on time, and even if that target of 100% electricity generation is met by 2020, nuclear power will still be providing a large chunk of it. And the SNP are opposed to nuclear power. Moreover, the present system of energy regulation and subsidies is organised on a UK-wide basis, which has led to the SNP having to argue that UK subsidies to Scottish renewables should continue after independence. This is not a comfortable place to be. But if the potential of Scottish green energy is to be realised, it will still need support from England. Like the banks, renewable energy is a UK-wide operation and will remain so for some time to come, whatever the result of the Independence Referendum.

The other inconvenient truth about the Scottish economy is that it is still heavily dependent on those unloved bankers. Scotland's financial services industry accounts directly for nearly 100,000 jobs and generates £7bn, or 7%, of Scottish GDP. Scotland's financial sector isn't just banks like RBS, of course, though you could be forgiven for believing when you arrive at Edinburgh Airport that you have arrived in a country called RBS, such is the extent of the bank's branding. Edinburgh is also a European centre for insurance and investment fund businesses that have been steadily making money throughout the lean years. According to the industry body Scottish

Financial Services, 24% of all UK life-and-pensions employment is in Scotland. There is much blue chip asset management and financial expertise in and around Edinburgh's New Town. And again, this sector is heavily integrated with the UK financial sector, though not to the same extent as the banks.

There is nothing necessarily to be ashamed of here. Scotland has a very long and rather illustrious tradition in banking, going back to the days when William Paterson set up the Bank of England. Scotland was the first country to have paper currency in wide circulation in the 18th century. In 1810, the Trustee Savings Bank movement was founded by Reverend Henry Duncan of Ruthwell in Dumfriesshire to make banking accessible to working people for the first time in British history. This was a hard-headed form of philanthropy, very much in keeping with the outlook of the Rev Thomas Chalmers and the evangelists. These friendly societies proliferated throughout the UK and there were more than 600 of them by the turn of the 20th century. Unfortunately, the mutual tradition was destroyed in the wave of flotations in the 1980s and 1990s, and the TSB is now a branch of Lloyds. But perhaps some of that tradition of socially responsible banking lives on in Scotland and could be revived.

What else does Scotland have to keep the wolf from the door? Well, the country also has five world-class universities and one of the most educated workforces in the world.[104] Scotland has more universities in the top 200 than many much larger countries like France; a legacy, perhaps, of the "democratic intellect" of the 19th century, though low percentages of students from working-class backgrounds rather confounds the notion that they are more egalitarian. Moreover, graduates tend to be attracted south to where the jobs are, or abroad. But that doesn't alter the fact that universities such as Edinburgh, of which I was Rector for three years, are significant economic players, with a turnover of £650m in 2012 and a staff of 10,000. Scotland's universities, St Andrews, Glasgow, Aberdeen, Dundee, are all attracting students from across the world in large numbers, indeed, up to one-third of their revenue now comes from the fees paid by international students. Scotland's industrial fabric was destroyed by the scorched-earth policies of Conservative governments in the 1980s, but Scotland does make things – very advanced things like Dolly the Sheep, the first animal to be cloned, and other scary things to do with genomes that I can barely understand. Silicon Glen may not be what it was, but Scotland is still a player in the electronics industry with 900 companies employing 55,000 people.

Scotland, of course, has a world-class tourism brand, though, in my experience, it has one of the most expensive and poor-quality tourist infrastructures on the planet. There can be few things more dispiriting in life than returning from a glorious day on the Scottish hills to inedible food and hostile service – though I'm sure that VisitScotland will take issue with that assessment. Scottish tourism is worth around £4bn a year and Scottish whisky earns around £4bn a year in exports. There is also a significant Scottish diaspora, the tens of millions of people in Canada, Australia, the USA who regard themselves as Scots and are favourably disposed to the old country. Scotland would not be alone as an independent country in Europe.

For a country of only five million people, this is a useful asset base. There is no reason to suppose Scotland would be unable to pay its way as an independent country. Scots have shown themselves to be adaptable and the country has 200 years of industrial experience. Before Norway discovered oil, all it had was trees and fish. Scotland, on the other hand, had been one of the most technologically advanced countries in the world – a cradle of the Industrial Revolution. Unfortunately, that tradition was largely destroyed in the 1980s recessions, as discussed in previous chapters.

Looking at all this, it seems surprising that Scotland was ever thought to be incapable of standing on its own. Yet, until very recently, this was the prevailing wisdom in Scotland and England. Even in the days of the great oil boom in the 1970s, few Scots took it as self-evident that Scotland could be a wealthy, independent country. Throughout the 1980s and 1990s, I recall English Tory MPs turning up regularly at Scottish Question Time in the Commons to jeer at the "subsidy junkies" of Scotland, who had a "begging bowl economy" and a "dependency culture", and were incapable of standing on their own two feet. This was a misrepresentation of the true situation since, the only thing that was keeping the British economy from the begging bowl during the early 1980s was Scottish oil revenue.[105] The UK Treasury has relied on hydrocarbon revenues for large periods over the past three decades to bolster the balance of payments. Westminster went to considerable lengths to underplay the significance of oil for political reasons. We learned in 2005, thanks to a Freedom of Information request, that a secret paper was produced for Whitehall in 1975 by the Scottish economist Gavin McCrone which argued that oil wealth was far greater than even the SNP realised and that it had the potential to make Scotland one of the strongest economies in Europe. Oil production is now past its peak, and there are worries about the cost of decommissioning many of the massive oil platforms in the North Sea.

However, there is still quite a lot of the black stuff under it. Oil and Gas UK, the industry body, says that there is about 40% of oil and gas reserves still to be extracted, worth around £1.5 trillion at present prices. PricewaterhouseCoopers, in November 2011, estimated that this would last for about 40 years. Much of it will be difficult to access, but that hasn't stopped the oil companies developing technologies for sucking the oil out in the past. There has been a spike in both the price of oil and the rate of extraction. In April 2013, *The Financial Times* reported record levels of investment flowing into the North Sea as 14 new oil fields came into production. Oil and Gas UK, expects production to rise to two million barrels a day by 2017, up from 1.5 million in 2012. Whether this constitutes a "second oil boom", as Alex Salmond claims, is debatable, but it seems that reports of the death of North Sea oil have been premature.

AN ACCIDENT OF GEOGRAPHY?

Nationalists often complain that Scotland remains the only nation, state, region or principality to have discovered oil and not benefited directly from it. In Alaska, one of the tasks performed by the former Governor Sarah Palin was to distribute a dividend to every citizen every year from oil revenues; in Alberta, Canada, a proportion of oil revenues are placed in a pension fund; and even in Shetland large amounts of oil money went directly to the local authority treasury. In Scotland, there has only been theoretical compensation through the Barnett Formula. Peak production has come and gone in Scotland without the locals being enriched.

But Scots never fully bought into the idea of Scotland as a cold Dubai. There always seemed to be something slightly unreal about the oil, as if it were the economic equivalent of fools gold that could distort an independent economy. And the Scots were right to be cautious. As McCrone himself noted, there is a risk that oil wealth can lead to an overvalued currency and a loss of competitiveness in non-oil export industries. Oil is sometimes called the "resource curse" for that very reason. Scots genuinely believed that oil was a UK resource and should be used for the benefit of all. Labour politicians insist that the oil wealth belongs to the UK, and not just to Scotland. An "accident of geography", it was argued, should not deprive the workers of Britain of their common inheritance. However, this argument really only applied so long as Scotland did benefit equally with the rest of the UK. Whether this promise of mutual benefit was actually delivered is highly questionable and many Scots feel a sense of injustice about this. Scotland gave up its oil in the sincere belief that it would be to the good of all, and found that its reward was the dole queue in the 1980s.

As I have argued above, there was no inevitability about the concentration of economic activity in the south-east of England. This was a direct result of the abolition of regional policy, and the anti-industrial policies of the 1980s, combined with the Lawson tax cuts which disproportionately benefited the south-east middle-classes. The privatisation of nationalised industries combined with the Big Bang of 1986 served to create the deregulated and dysfunctional City of London we have today – a financial services sector that gave us the Big Crash of 2008. Those policies, which neglected industry and accepted growing inequalities of wealth, were continued under New Labour after 1997. The great property bubble, which was Gordon Brown's principal economic legacy, again concentrated wealth in the south-east of England, both by enriching the finance houses who marketed the mortgages, and allowing the southern middle-classes to consolidate their wealth through property speculation. In the London borough of Kensington and Chelsea, the average house price is now £1.5 million. Mean net housing wealth in the south-east is more than twice that of Scotland.[106] Economic activity in Britain is now overwhelmingly in those sectors – finance, administration, defence – which disproportionately benefit the south-east of England – by which I mean London and the counties that make up the South-East England European Parliamentary Constituency.

Inequality is rising faster in Britain than any other developed country, according to the OECD.[107] The share of the top 1% of income earners increased from 7.1% in 1970 to 14.3% in 2005. On the eve of the financial crash, the 0.1% of highest earners accounted for no less than 5% of total pre-tax income. Wealth inequality in Britain has reached levels unseen since Edwardian times, and it is almost entirely a consequence of the housing market, tax cuts and the bonus culture which began in the banks, spread rapidly to CEOs in top companies, and thence to the public sector, where council bureaucrats can now command six-figure remuneration packages. The decline of Britain as a manufacturing nation has led to a striking concentration of wealth and economic activity in the south-east.

The OECD report was called *Divided We Stand*, and this division is increasingly a geographical one, with employment, income, investment, housing wealth and opportunity increasingly gravitating to the city state of London. By the turn of the century, viewed from Scotland, London had become an introverted and myopic city state, largely run by a financial kleptocracy who had not only captured the political elite, but had also been allowed almost unlimited access to public funds, in the banking bailouts of 2008 to 2012.

This over-centralisation in the south-east of England did not happen in France or Germany to the same degree, largely because those countries have effective regional polices, a manufacturing outlook and – most importantly – political decentralisation. Scotland has tended to be seen by both major UK parties as an awkward region that has to be bought off. As New Labour allowed public debt to reach levels unseen outside wartime, Barnett money continued to be sent north to boost public spending and cement the Labour vote, but without any coherent economic strategy behind it. Scotland's oil was once again enlisted to balance the UK books. Oil revenues spiked at £11bn in 2011/12, and were a vital component of Britain's public finances during the first post-crash recession. But this time there was no pretence that anyone was benefiting other than the financial plutocracy.

The economic case against independence depends almost entirely on the proposition that Scotland benefits, through the Barnett Formula, from redistribution of wealth from the south to the north. The argument, as put by the economist, John Kay – a former member of Alex Salmond's own council of economic advisers – is that, since Scotland spends 10-15% more per head of population than it raises in taxation, it has a pretty good deal from the Union.[108] This "Union dividend", as it used to be called by Labour, is said to be worth per head per annum more is received by England. Why bother going to the cost and expense of setting up the apparatus of an independent state, when you can get it all from Barnett? To maintain spending at current levels, an independent Scotland might be forced into increasing debt dramatically to finance public spending at this level in the future, argues Professor Kay. The Calman Commission in 2009 also argued against full fiscal autonomy on the grounds that the wealthy parts of the UK should not be allowed to ignore their responsibility to the poorest, and that this was best achieved by an integrated UK taxation system. "Income tax is a progressive tax: as well as raising revenue it is used as a tool of redistribution of resources across society. We believe this should remain a function of national government, because it is an aspect of the social Union to which Scotland belongs."[109]

These are powerful arguments. If the UK is to remain, as Alex Salmond wishes, a "social union", does that not imply there should be collective financial responsibility, a pooling of wealth through a progressive taxation system that ensures that the poorest areas of the country – by no means all in Scotland – also benefit from the wealth of all? Why should millionaires in the south-east be allowed to opt out of their responsibilities to poorer regions? Indeed, why should the rich in Scotland not have responsibility for the poor in the north of England, where income and wealth are less than in Scotland? The problem with the social union case is that it presupposes that this redistribution from rich to poor actually takes place. There is very little evidence that it does, either between regions or between social classes. The current government in Westminster doesn't appear to be much interested in social union anyway. And nor was the previous Labour administration under Tony Blair particularly enthusiastic about redistribution of wealth. The British taxation system ceased to be progressive, as the OECD argues, in the late 1980s. This argument for social union probably made sense in 1977 – the year that income inequalities in Britain were at their narrowest. But it is hard to sustain today.

Nor is it at all clear that Scotland benefits from any wealth "redistributed" from the UK. If you include oil revenues, there is little justification for thinking that Scotland gets any financial benefit from the union link. The "union dividend" argument assumes that Scotland does not and cannot "pay its way". Yet, at present this is very difficult to argue. On the current 2011/12 General Expenditure and Revenue Scotland (GERS) figures, Scotland more than pays its way. With 8% of the UK population, Scotland contributes 9.9% of UK revenues and receives 9.3% of UK public spending. The report also indicated that Scotland's notional deficit was considerably lower than that of the UK.[110] Oil prices may be volatile, and they were worth £11bn in the year in question, but oil wealth will be around for some time, and there seems no reason to suppose that Scotland would be any worse at managing its finances than the UK is at present.

There is an equally strong argument that Scotland stands in considerable financial peril from remaining within the UK, given the current level of debt, which is clearly unsustainable.[111] The UK has already lost its Triple A credit rating, the economy remains stuck in recession and the shadow of the IMF is never far from Britain's economic event horizon. Indeed, the IMF has been vocal in its recent criticism of UK economic management, claiming that the Chancellor George Osborne is "playing with fire" by persevering with austerity and low growth.[112] Indeed, if Scotland were to leave, the consequences could be rather serious for the continuing UK, since it would involve the loss of oil resources, 90% of which would fall to Scotland under accepted standards of international law. Britain's debt pile is not going away, and Mark Carney, the incoming Governor of the Bank of England, has described the UK as a "crisis economy". The United Kingdom economy is entering a period of great uncertainty. A combination of devaluation, public spending cuts, inflation and money printing has not solved Britain's debt problem. If there is a hard landing, those who sneer today at the eurozone's may have cause to regret their *schadenfreude*. Britain remains in a state of denial about its economic insignificance in the global economy. Scots may wonder why they didn't get out while they still could.

IT'S NOT THE ECONOMY, STUPID

Listening to BBC News bulletins has long been a frustrating experience for listeners north of the border. Stories about NHS scandals in England, hospital trusts going bust, free schools, Michael Gove's curriculum changes and the progress of UKIP have had little relevance in Scotland. Scottish listeners have to mentally disaggregate most of the domestic news bulletins because up to 40% of it is now from another country. Devolution has led to very different approaches to public sector provision north and south of the border. The growing divergence in social and economic philosophy between Scotland and England today is more likely to lead to the break up of Britain than the price of oil.

In Scotland, the comprehensive education system is unchallenged and retains public confidence. This is partly because of the minimal impact of private education in Scotland – the proportion of children attending private schools in Scotland, relative to population, is half that of England. There has not been the same pressure to create beacon schools, foundation schools, specialist schools, free schools or any of the other reforms which have dominated education in England for the last decade. Scotland seems content with the "bog standard" comprehensive as Alastair Campbell described them. In Higher Education, the difference is even more striking. Tuition fees were abolished in Scotland, and are unlikely to return since there is cross-party agreement to reject them. In England, by contrast, students now have to pay £9,000 per year for their tuition – even if they are studying at a Scottish university.

In health provision, the divergence is even more pronounced. Since the passing of the Health and Social Care Act in 2012, English doctors and hospitals are required to use market mechanisms to commission health services. English Foundation hospitals will be able to derive 49% of their income from non-NHS work. None of this will apply in Scotland, where market reforms have been rejected, and private collaboration with NHS hospitals is effectively outlawed. The former Labour First Minister, Jack McConnell, sought to increase the role of private hospitals to help clear waiting lists during his stewardship of the Scottish Executive, but it didn't lead to any significant changes in the pattern of hospital care and in 2007, the incoming SNP Health Secretary, Nicola Sturgeon, abolished the experiment. The only significant new private hospital to be built since the Second World War in Scotland, HCI in Clydebank, was nationalised by the Scottish Government in 2002 and is now called the "Golden Jubilee National Hospital". The "monolithic" public service provision, that Tony Blair so objected to in the NHS, remains intact in Scotland and there has been no diminution of public support for the service.

The SNP claim that Scotland is the only part of the UK where waiting times continue to fall. Under the latest standards for 2012/13, 90% of elective patients commence treatment in 18 weeks of referral and no patient is allowed to wait longer than 12 weeks for a new outpatient appointment at a consultant-led clinic. The results aren't quite as good as they appear. Audit Scotland has noted a significant increase in patients who are "socially unavailable" for their appointments, suggesting that there may be some manipulation of waiting lists going on – A&E waiting times are up. However, health has not been seen as a problem issue in Scotland for many years, and there is widespread support for the publicly run system. The main worry north of the border is that the developments in England could spill over into Scotland. If the English NHS increasingly seeks its income from private sources, this could mean that the resources in Scotland are cut back.

Public provision is not challenged in Scotland partly because there has been no consumer resistance to it. In 2007, the BBC conducted an exhaustive survey of Scottish political attitudes. It found that the number one priority of Scottish voters was "to ensure that all state schools and hospitals are built and run by public bodies rather than private companies". This came above things like more police on the beat or reducing council tax. The result was surprising because this was at the height of Labour's public sector reform programme in England, and there had been an assumption that Scots wanted to see reforms too, and Scottish newspapers had been urging the Scottish Government not to let Scotland "lose out" from improvements elsewhere in the UK.

The social ties of the Union have been further loosened by the UK Coalition's welfare reform agenda, which has caused profound disquiet in Scotland. Around one million homes in Scotland are likely to be affected by the real-terms cut in working-age benefits, cuts in child benefit and restrictions on housing benefit. Indeed, it has achieved what many believed impossible: a meeting of minds between the SNP and Labour, who joined together in the Scottish Parliament in December 2011 to withhold legislative consent from the UK Welfare Reform Bill – the first time that the Scottish Parliament has blocked consent to a major piece of UK legislation. Social Security is, of course, reserved to Westminster, so this did not impede the implementation of the Act. But it was an important episode that underlined the paucity of political support for the Work and Pensions Secretary Iain Duncan Smith's welfare reforms. These were supposedly inspired by his visits to Glasgow's Easterhouse estate in 2001, where he befriended the community activist Bob Holman, and saw for himself the consequences of the "benefits trap". Unfortunately, his proposals for reform have appalled Mr Holman, who now says Iain Duncan Smith should resign for introducing reforms that deprive the sick of adequate support and are forcing families into destitution.

The infamous "bedroom tax" reform, in which those on housing benefit lose money if they have an "extra" room, has reignited some of the moral anger of the Poll Tax in the 1980s – though the issue is rather more complex. The problem, according to the Scottish Government, is that only 26% of homes available for social rent in Scotland are one-bedroom properties, yet 60% of tenants affected will need one. This mismatch, it claims, will lead to an enforced cut in housing benefit for thousands of families. Some 3,000 people marched on Glasgow's George Square on 30th March 2013 to hear the former Scottish Socialist Party MSP Tommy Sheridan – the hero of the anti-Poll Tax campaign in the 1980s – demand Scottish resistance against the "tax". It wasn't quite the same as the Poll Tax glory days, and it felt a little like one of those post-retirement tours by a 1980s pop star. Nor is it clear just how many Scots actually oppose the welfare reform package – some polling by the Scottish Social Attitudes Survey suggests that Scots have, like many English voters, become less supportive of welfare over the past 30 years. There is probably support for the benefit cap of £26,000 because there are only a tiny handful of people – if any – receiving that amount in benefits in Scotland. However, the sense of history repeating itself is unmistakeable. The Scottish Government is unable to prevent the so-called bedroom tax being imposed and has urged Scottish councils not to evict tenants in arrears. But figures on the Scottish Left, like Mike Dailly of the Govan Law Centre, are demanding more. He has tabled a petition to the Scottish Parliament calling for the Scottish Government to use existing housing legislation to block implementation of the Act. This has placed the Nationalists in the curious position of being accused of not fighting hard enough against Westminster. Indeed, Alex Salmond has found himself in almost exactly the same predicament as the late Donald Dewar in 1988 – being urged to break the law. There is a widespread feeling in Scotland – as in the 1980s – that the country is being subjected to policies on health and welfare that have been rejected in successive elections.

Scots find themselves living in a country that thinks more like Denmark while England is beginning to look more like America. The divergence of political culture is most obvious in the collapse of the Conservative vote in Scotland. But it is equally apparent in New Labour. Modernisers like Tony Blair regard the kind of societies that exist in Denmark or Norway as essentially old Labour – high tax, high-spend welfare states, where trade unions still play too big a role in government and the public sector is too large. There is some dispute about just how social democratic the Scots actually are. They bought their council houses after all, and attitudes to redistribution of wealth in Scotland are not that different from those south of the border, according to some opinion polls. However, the assessment of Professor John Curtice, of Glasgow University, in 2005 was prophetic: "The advancement of social democratic values may be part of what it means to Scots voters to be Scottish," he said, commenting on one of the largest surveys yet undertaken of social and political differences. "And with Labour having moved to the ideological centre, voters might come to the view that the SNP is the best way of expressing both their Scottishness and their social democratic policy preferences at the same time." Labour ignored that warning to their cost. The Conservatives never heard it.

Margaret Thatcher's Poll Tax destroyed the old Tory Unionism, and her scorched-earth free-market policies destroyed the industrial communities that sustained Labour Unionism. Her corrosive policies rotted the moral and economic sinews of the old United Kingdom, until the two countries woke up to find that there was nothing holding them together any more.

Conservatism was destroyed as a political force in Scotland in 1997 when the party lost all its MPs. But the difference had been clear long before that as Scots continued to vote Labour in general elections in the 1980s when the party was increasingly rejected in England. Scots even voted in large numbers for the "longest suicide note in history" – Labour's 1983 UK Election Manifesto. Nearly one-quarter of the Parliamentary Labour Party after the 1983 General Election was Scottish, which is why, when Tony Blair started looking around for experienced Cabinet material, all he saw were Scots. In Scotland, even the most middle-class areas like Edinburgh continued to vote Labour – until they started to vote SNP in the Scottish

Parliament. After its narrow victory in 2007, the SNP stood on what they called the "social wage" – tuition fees, prescription charges and free care. The Scots had a chance to express their verdict on this social democratic agenda in 2011, and it was unequivocal. The Nationalists were returned with a landslide majority. There could be no greater demonstration of the divergence in domestic policy between Scotland and England. The question is whether these increasingly divergent political cultures can be accommodated within the broad constitutional framework of the United Kingdom.

THE OTHER REFERENDUM

And there is one final way in which the Scottish political culture appears to be diverging from that in England: Europe. David Cameron's promise of an in/out referendum on Britain's continued membership of the European Union has transformed the debate on the constitution in Scotland. The dramatic advance of UKIP, which won 25% of the vote in the English council elections of 2013 showed that England is no longer prepared to accept the UK's relationship with Brussels. A significant renegotiation of the terms of UK membership looks inevitable. And for the first time since 1975, there is a serious possibility that the UK may withdraw from the European Union altogether.

In Scotland, the debate is the other way round. There has been a presumption among Unionists that remaining in the UK also meant remaining in the EU. Indeed, one of the criticisms most frequently made of independence is that, after it, Scotland might be forced to leave the EU and re-apply as a new member state. It was assumed that Scottish membership of Europe is desirable and that the Nationalists have endangered it by proposing a referendum on independence. Now, the debate has been transformed. It is beginning to look as if Scotland is just as likely or more likely to end up leaving the EU if it sticks with the UK. Moreover, if Scotland remains in the UK, and is forced out of the EU, there will be no way in which it can reapply in future. It will be out for good.

In January 2013, David Cameron promised a fundamental and irreversible change in Britain's relationship with Europe, delighting his Eurosceptic backbenchers, but undermining the Unionist cause at home. Scotland has benefited from the social protections of the EU social policy such the working-time directive and doesn't feel the sense of alienation with Europe that is unmistakeable in many parts of England. The euro debt crisis has altered the dynamics of the Scottish Question, in much the same way as Britain's membership of Europe altered it in the 1970s. That was when the SNP began to come to terms with the idea of Scotland being "independent in Europe". If the United Kingdom is on its way to the outer fringes of Europe, then what is left of the argument that only by remaining in the UK can Scotland be assured of representation at the "top table of Europe"? The charge against the SNP has always been that they are "separatists", who seek to divide nation from nation, and risk leaving Scotland alone and isolated from the mainstream of Europe. Now it appears as if David Cameron is the separatist and that Britain is now isolating itself from the other 26 members of the European Union.

Danny Boyle's pageant of social history opening the 2012 Olympic Games was a remarkable tribute to the achievements of Great Britain. Dancing NHS nurses, workers forging the Industrial Revolution, the 10,000 volunteers. The land, the people, the multicultural community. It was watched with as much unexpected joy in Scotland as in England, perhaps even more so, given the success of Scots such as Sir Chris Hoy. But there was an air of nostalgia too. This was the Britain that Scotland signed up to after the war, that propelled Scotland and England into the 1960s in the great communion of popular culture. But it is hard to reconcile this vision with the reality of Great Britain today. It's not Scotland that has changed but England. The old social democratic certainties are gone, the NHS is facing commercialisation, the welfare state is being reformed. Even Britain's place in Europe is under question in England in a way that is inconceivable in Scotland, where the Conservatives are nowhere and UKIP is non-existent. Increasingly, Scots are looking around and wondering, How did we get here?

CHAPTER FIFTEEN
TOO WEE, TOO POOR, TOO STUPID

×

A POLL for the Scottish Social Attitudes Survey in December 2011, indicated that 65% of Scots would support independence if they were £500 better off as a result, but only 21% said that they would vote for it if they were made £500 worse off.[113]

The deputy leader of the Scottish National Party, Nicola Sturgeon, said that this "demonstrated conclusively that the people of Scotland want to continue the positive, optimistic journey our nation is on". But equally it suggested that for the price of a week in Benidorm, Scots would happily remain in the UK. What would Wallace have made of that?

If nothing else, this poll illustrates the increasingly instrumental attitude Scots have towards a Union in which they no longer have a strong emotional investment. It is essentially an economic question for most Scottish voters, rather than about national freedom or about imperial greatness. So, if they have a viable economy as both sides more or less accept, why don't the Scots just go for it? If the Union is seen as an anachronism, if Scotland is committed to a social democratic consensus that has been abandoned in England, and if the Tories are now threatening to take Scotland out of Europe, why wait? Why doesn't Scotland just vote to become Denmark? Even the television is better.

It isn't as simple as that, of course. In the end, nationhood is about community and family. You don't leave your family behind simply because you could be better off on your own. There is also the institutional momentum that has been generated by 300 years in which Scotland has been governed as part of England. What no Nationalist can dispute is that there would be, initially at least, disruption and cost as Scotland had to detach itself from UK institutions like the Treasury, the Revenue, the Diplomatic Corps. The Finance Secretary, John Swinney, in a leaked Cabinet memo in 2012 suggested that it would cost £600m to set up a Scottish Revenue alone – but that would only be the start.[114] These costs might well be worth the investment if Scotland were to recover some of its lost national dynamism. But the greatest obstacle to radical change is fear of the unknown. And there are a lot of known unknowns about independence, let alone Donald Rumsfeld's unknown unknowns. These are troubled times. Britain has been through a double-dip economic recession; the eurozone has been in chaos over the sovereign debt crisis, with countries like Greece going bankrupt; world trade is slowing; and there is increasing competition from low-wage countries in Asia. Is this the right moment for Scotland to consider going it alone? Independence is a hard sell at the best of times to a country that doesn't feel it is under foreign domination.

We live in an era, moreover, in which politicians in general are mistrusted, their promises disbelieved. Labour in Scotland have been playing on this mistrust by attacking the credibility of Alex Salmond over issues like the legal advice he said he had on EU membership, but didn't. "You can't believe a word he says," they jeer. "He's making it up as he goes along." Doubt is a difficult thing to dispel, and with a Scottish media that is prone to hyperbolic negativity, fears about independence are never far from the front pages. This has become known in Nationalist circles as the "too wee, too poor, too stupid" agenda. The SNP lack the formal support of any of the Scottish or UK newspapers and independence tends to be portrayed as a reckless gamble.

According to front page stories during 2012, an independent Scotland would be thrown out of the European Union[115] and would have to reapply for membership; the Bank of England would refuse to let Scotland use the pound[116] or impose draconian terms;[117] Scotland would be left undefended as military co-operation ceased;[118] border posts would be set up to keep immigrants out of England.[119] Scotland would then be plunged into penury, as the Scottish Treasury was forced to take on the multi-billion-pound debts of the Scottish banks as well as the £120 billion of the national debt;[120] Scotland would lose its Triple A credit rating (even though it has already been lost by the UK).[121] Businesses might depart Scotland overnight to escape left-wing Nationalist tax policies and Scots might lose their pensions.[122] Scotland's oil would dry up, after collapsing in value,[123] and investment in the "windmills" dry up as UK carbon subsidies are axed.[124] As the lights went out all over Scotland[125] because of the SNP's anti-nuclear policies[126], Scotland would be given a bill for decommissioning and nuclear waste.[127] Up to 19,000 jobs would be lost on the Clyde as Trident was removed,[128] and Scotland would be presented with another multi-billion-pound bill for relocation of Britain's nuclear deterrent to England.[129] Scotland's universities would lose their best staff and students and go into irreversible decline;[130] and there would be a new exodus of Scots escaping the turmoil by emigrating.

And it doesn't end there. Scotland could even become a target for English bombing,[131] according to a former Scottish Lord Advocate; MI6 might treat Scotland as an enemy power according to Teresa May, the UK Home Secretary;[132] Scotland might become a haven for Islamic terrorists, according to Professor Tom Gallagher.[133] British embassies abroad would boycott Scottish whisky, according to the Foreign Secretary, William Hague.[134] Even Scotland's pandas, Sunshine and Sweetie, loaned by the Chinese Wildlife Conservation Organisation, might have to be sent back to China if Scotland became independent, according to one press report.[135] These stories play on the uncertainties of independence and the predisposition of many Scots to look on the negative. The only one that can be categorically denied is the panda threat, since they were given directly to Edinburgh Zoo and not the UK. It is very difficult to give definitive rebuttals to the other warnings about independence because no one can predict the future.

There are legitimate questions about financial arrangements, such as pension entitlements. The Institute for Chartered Accountancy in Scotland has said that, under new EU directives, pension schemes that are unfunded cannot be held across borders. Since many private pension schemes currently have deficits, and the UK government has around £1 trillion in unfunded pension liabilities to public sector workers, there is clearly a question here about how things would work if Scotland were a separate country. This is not an insoluble problem, given good will, as even the ICAS accepts. The Scottish Government points that such cross-border pension schemes exist already in Europe, and there is currently one with the Irish Republic. But since most voters are vague and fearful about their pensions at the best of times, all Better Together need to do is raise questions to sow doubt. There can be no definitive answer to this pension issue unless and until the Scottish and UK Governments get together, as advocated by ICAS, to work out a transitional arrangement. And, of course, the UK Government isn't going to do that because it would look as if it was accepting that independence was actually going to happen. The UK has refused to enter into "prenegotiation" on independence. Good will is not there.

In March 2013, Better Together published a leaked cabinet discussion paper drafted by the Scottish Finance Secretary, John Swinney, from the previous year, which suggested that the Scottish Government would have to reckon on volatility in the oil price in the early years of independence. This could put pressure on social spending like pensions, given Scotland's ageing population. This was billed as "Swinney's Secret Bombshell", and was published by the Unionist campaign to coincide with the annual GERS report, which showed Scotland's deficit to be significantly less onerous than the UK's. It was "Swinney's secret dossier" that dominated the press coverage. It showed, according to the *Daily Record,* "that the SNP was saying one thing in public and another in private". It was even suggested the SNP was planning to cut pensions in an independent Scotland.

However, there was nothing particularly secret about the fact that the oil price rises and falls. Swinney's bombshell was essentially saying what the UK Office of Budgetary Responsibility had also said around the same time – but about the rest of the UK. In July 2012, the OBR remarked that "the public finances are likely to come under pressure over the longer time, primarily as a result of the ageing population … the [UK] government would end up having to spend more as a share of national income on age-related items such as pensions and health care … non-demographic trends are likely to reduce the revenue from sources such as North Sea oil."[136] The situation is no worse in Scotland, in fact is significantly better because of Scotland's asset base. There has been a significant upturn recently. According to Oil and Gas UK's chief executive, Malcolm Webb, "record investment is forecast this year to search for and produce UK oil and gas. This will be followed by an upturn in production from 2014". Beyond that, who knows?

There are numerous examples of issues not unique to Scotland being presented as "independence warnings". A headline in the *Daily Mail* that read "Break Up Will Cost Scots £140bn" (from 12th January 2012) claimed that this would be the bill for voting Yes in 2014. The figure was generated by assuming that Scotland would take on a population-based share of the UK national debt, which was at the time forecast at £1.4 trillion for 2014. The point here is that if this is "crippling", as the *Mail* suggests, then surely it is also crippling to the rest of the UK. In fact, as explained in the previous chapter, on the basis of the GERS figures, Scotland is running up debts rather more slowly than the UK, largely because of oil. Of course, if the UK decides not to allow Scotland to use sterling, as has been suggested, there is a very simple and obvious solution to the "£140bn independence bill" – that is not to pay it. If Scotland is not to be recognised as a successor state, and is forced to secede, then there is no particular reason why Scotland should feel bound to pay any of the UK national debt. When the Irish Republic left the UK in the 1930s, it didn't pay its nominal share of the UK national debt. Under the terms of the Edinburgh Agreement in 2012, the Scottish Government has accepted that it will take a share of the debts, but that could change.

There is not a lot of goodwill, at the moment, in the UK Treasury, which has been encouraging the press to run stories to the effect that Scotland would not be able to use sterling. "Scotland warned," said *Metro* "gain independence and you might not be able to keep the pound". These stories have been attributed to George Osborne, the Chancellor, though he has never stated categorically that Scotland could be denied access to sterling, only that Scotland could face "significant policy constraints". This is because sterling is a convertible currency – in theory, anyone can use it. Scotland could also peg its own currency to the pound, much as Norway and Denmark do with the euro, if it wanted. Even the chairman of Better Together, the former Chancellor, Alastair Darling, conceded in a BBC interview in January 2013 that a currency union would be "desirable" and "logical". Which, of course, is the case: companies and banks in England would not want to have to pay the cost of switching currencies every time they deal with a subsidiary in Scotland. The Bank of England wants stability above all, and it would be opposed to the idea of deploying punitive measures against Scotland for continuing to use the currency that the two countries have shared for 300 years.

Prominent figures in the Yes campaign, like its chairman, former Labour MP Dennis Canavan, argue that remaining in sterling might leave too much power with the Bank of England. Salmond has said he favours remaining in a sterling zone for pragmatic reasons, and only for the time being. He doesn't rule out a different arrangement in future. After the "velvet divorce" between Slovakia and the Czech Republic, the countries initially opted for a currency union, but then decided later to have separate currencies while they waited to join the euro. Most European countries, in and out of the euro, are treading water, currency-wise, until they see what happens to the sovereign debt crisis.

However, it has also been claimed that Scotland might not only be denied the pound, but could be forced to adopt the euro as a condition of membership of the EU – even though Britain has an opt-out, and countries like Denmark are also outside European Monetary Union.[137] This is another of those vexatious hypotheticals. Other authorities, like the fabulously named Fabian Zuleeg, chief economist of the European Policy Centre, disagree and say that because Scotland is already part of the European Union, its negotiating position would be *sui generis*. Anyway, a country has to be in the Exchange Rate Mechanism for at least two years before it can join the euro. You pays your money ...

For the latter half of 2012, the Unionist campaign against independence was largely based on the claim, not that Scotland would be forced into the euro, but that it might be forced out of the European Union. The claim is that Scotland could be ejected from Europe if Scots vote Yes in the 2014 Independence Referendum and would have to go through a lengthy and uncertain process of re-negotiation in order to return. No one seriously believes, not even the Scottish Labour Party, that Scotland would be denied membership of the EU eventually, since it fulfils all the conditions set out in the Copenhagen criteria for membership – democracy, rule of law, human rights and a market economy. Nevertheless, the press coverage suggested that ejection was a real possibility. "EU tells Scotland: independence would force you out," said *The Independent* in December 2012.

There would of course have to be renegotiation of the terms of membership. What would Scotland's contribution be to the EU budget? What about the membership of the single currency? What about the Schengen rules on free movement of citizens? "Legal experts in warning over Scots Independence," read the front page of one leading Scottish newspaper in February 2013, explaining that "14,000 treaties" would have to be negotiated. Scotland would be regarded as a "new state" outside the EU. However, on the BBC *Today* programme the next day, Professor John Crawford was asked by presenter John Humphrys how long this would take. He replied that 18 months "looked about right" – which also happens to be the timescale for renegotiation proposed by the SNP Government. Which rather killed the story. As discussed in the last chapter, Scotland's departure from the EU looks just as likely if Scotland stays in the UK as it does out of it.

As for nuclear weapons, the Scots are overwhelmingly opposed to the presence of weapons of mass destruction on the Clyde and frequently make their views known in opinion surveys.[138] These weapons, which have been in Scotland since the 1960s and contributed greatly to the rise of the SNP in the 60s and 70s, are arguably illegal under international law because they target civilian populations – specifically Russian cities. Trident has no conceivable use against any of our known enemies, and the boats that carry them go out on patrol without any target. However, an independent Scotland could not dictate defence policy to England, and there is no way that Scots could force England to give up their nuclear deterrent. If the rest of the UK chooses to retain weapons of mass destruction, they should be located somewhere suitable in England, like Devonport. That's if any community in England can be found that would want to have them. The idea that Scotland would have to pay for the relocation is one of the more absurd of the scares that have graced the front pages in the past year. One solution might be for the nuclear warheads, which anyway have to be moved on an annual basis to the Atomic Weapons Establishment at Aldermaston in Berkshire for maintenance, to remain in the south. The Vanguard submarines could remain in Scotland, but unarmed.

If Scotland became independent, there would almost certainly be some reasonable arrangement between Scotland and the rest of the UK to phase out nuclear weapons on the Clyde. This is the subtext to the SNP's decision to remain in Nato, which is, of course, a nuclear alliance, and Faslane is part of Nato's strategic defence formation. A Nationalist government, if such is elected in an independent Scotland, would retain the non-nuclear activities at HM Naval Base Clyde, while honouring Scotland's moral commitment to remove nuclear weapons. No purpose would be served by Scotland and England falling out over this. There is, anyway, a significant body of military opinion in England which believes that nuclear weapons are an anachronism and that the UK should use its limited defence budget more imaginatively than in renewing a weapons system that is obsolete before it is built. Fears that 19,000 jobs would go after independence assume that the UK, out of spite, would throw away its huge investment in the Clyde and would relocate its main base for conventional submarines. That might happen, but it would not happen overnight.

The SNP get very annoyed at the way the Scottish press appears to favour negative stories about independence, and there has been no shortage of them in the past couple of years. But this is not simply because the Scottish media has been "bought and sold" by the Unionists. These stories resonate with their readers. The Better Together campaign and the UK Government know from their internal polling and focus groups, as does the SNP, that these are the issues which Scots worry about. Scotland has spent too long regarding itself as an economic backwater, which in many ways it has been in the past 30 years, to take seriously the notion that it could be a dynamic and prosperous independent country overnight. The experience of generations weighs heavily on the Scots, and the habit of outmigration mitigates against economic optimism. Scotland has exported its optimism with every generation that departs to find a better life in London, Montreal, Melbourne, and which leaves behind a disempowered population predisposed to a sense of national inferiority.

However, the Nationalists' case has not gone by default, and the days when the SNP could be accused of trying to turn the UK into war-torn former Yugoslavia are gone. In the 1990s, the former Shadow Scottish Secretary, George Robertson, famously accused the SNP of promoting "the dark side of nationalism". He would not be able to do that today. Nor can Unionists simply take the worst-case scenarios of international relations and map them directly onto Scotland – as with Greece and Portugal during the sovereign debt crisis, Iceland and Ireland during the banking crash, or Croatia and Bosnia during the Balkans crisis. The SNP hopes and believes that this negativism will ultimately prove to be counterproductive for the Unionists. By remaining positive, and by talking Scotland up rather than down, Alex Salmond is confident he will eventually win the argument. However, time is getting short, and there is every indication that the Better Together campaign is hitting home. Over the past two years, the opinion polls have hardly moved, and pollsters like Peter Kellner of YouGov believe that the Yes campaign has "a huge mountain to climb. More Everest than Ben Nevis."

WHAT IF ENGLAND SAYS YES

If the Scots are becoming less enthusiastic about the Union, the feeling is shared by an increasing number of English voters, according to opinion polls. In fact, there is evidence that support for Scottish independence might even be higher among English voters than it is among Scots. In January 2012 a cross-border poll of 2000 people by Survation suggested that 29% of English votes thought Scotland should leave the UK against 26% of Scottish respondents.[139] Other polls have said "gertcha", in similar spirit. The Institute for Public Policy Research in the north has been conducting research on English attitudes to the Union for the past five years. The conclusion it has reached is that England has had enough and wants a new deal. In *The Dog that Finally Barked* in 2012, the IPPR traced the emergence of what it called "a new Anglo-British identity in which the English component is increasingly the primary attachment for English people". Their research also indicates that "English identity is becoming more politicised" and that there is an increasing feeling that the present arrangements in the UK are "unfair". The number of voters in England who believe that Scottish devolution has made Britain worse has doubled since 2007 from 17% to 35%. The number believing Scotland "gets more than its fair share of public spending" has also doubled to 45%.

It has been evident, since the European Football Championships in 1996, that there has been a growth in the number of English people identifying themselves as "English" rather than "British". However, the English Question has been around politics for many years and has never quite ignited. The UK press has long complained about the alleged unfairness in English taxes being used to finance Scottish policies like free higher education, which are not available to English taxpayers. But most people now realise that the argument that Scotland pays for free elderly care and for free higher education from English taxes is also unfounded, since Scotland receives a fixed block grant from the UK Treasury. Increased spending on things like free prescriptions have to be paid from elsewhere in the Scottish budget. It is a tribute to John Swinney's budgetary management that he has managed to pay for all these "social wage" policies – elderly care, tuition fees, prescription charges – while running balanced budgets, year on year, even as the Scottish finances have been squeezed by the UK deficit-reduction programme. Commentators, like me, kept saying that he couldn't do it, that he would bust the budget. But he never did. The fact he worries about keeping the books in order in future, with the ageing population, in his "secret bombshell report" is probably rather a good thing.

The final answer to English anxieties about "subsidised Scots" is of course fiscal autonomy – or Devolution Max or any of the other proposals for making the Scottish Parliament fund its spending from taxation. One of the reasons that we hear less of the subsidy argument today is that, with a Scottish National Party Government actually in Holyrood, the possibility of Scotland abandoning the Barnett Formula and seizing control of its finances is very much greater than before. The UK Government is worried that Scotland might well call England's bluff, and it doesn't want shouty Tory MPs to be seen encouraging separation by telling Scots they should "pay their own way". But really, the solution to all these problems, and to the English Question, are readily to hand in the various formulas for turning Scotland into a quasi-federal state.

But Barnett bickering aside, the reality, increasingly, is not so much that England resents Scotland, as that England has no feelings either way. Scotland is becoming largely irrelevant to politics south of the border. The Barnett Formula and the West Lothian Question have been raised many times, and proposals have been made to address them in Westminster. The idea of setting up an English Parliament, using the House of Lords as a regional chamber, even setting up an English Grand Committee in Westminster to process specifically English legislation – all these have been suggested, but they never seem to get anywhere. This is because, when it comes down to it, England is not sufficiently concerned about the anomalies and unfairnesses in the present arrangements to go to all the trouble of creating new constitutional machinery to address them. England does not want an English Parliament, because it already has a Parliament – Westminster – and it's quite happy with it. English regions do not want to set up their own regional parliaments either – they were offered to the north of England in 2004 and decisively rejected in referendums. Scotland may get a little bit more in public spending per head than most areas of England, but Scotland with only five million people is only one-twelfth of the UK, and the sums involved are really not that worth bothering about. Five or perhaps six billion pounds going north is easily outweighed by oil revenues going south.

Not only are the English nationalist grievances rather artificial, there is increasing indifference to the Scottish dimension of the UK. Scotland figures less and less in the affairs of England – or rather in the affairs of the city state called London. Looking back over the centuries that these two countries have been in union, at the contribution Scotland made to the Empire, the Industrial Revolution, to the foreign wars, to the World Wars and post-war welfare state, one can appreciate how Scotland really mattered to England in the past. It was a source of manpower, ideas, blood and latterly energy in the form of hydrocarbons. What does it provide today? A wet holiday destination perhaps, but little else. Scottish soldiers aren't English heroes any more, fighting British wars in hot countries. England doesn't depend on the products of Scottish universities to run colonial administrations or plantations. Scottish bankers aren't so welcome in the City of London any more as they were in the days when "Scottish" and "prudent" were almost synonymous. The greatest involvement English middle-classes have in Scotland is sending their children to study in St Andrews and Edinburgh.

After the war, when Scotland and England were united by social democracy and nationalised industries, something like the HS2 high-speed rail link would have been used as a great unifying project to bring Britain together. You can almost visualise the black-and-white newsreels and stirring commentary about how Britain was becoming smaller. Now, it is almost casually announced that the biggest rail project of the new millennium will get to Manchester and not very much further. The Coalition Government didn't even bother making a pretence that HS2 will start at both ends of the Union, the better to bring England and Scotland closer together. Also, the debate about Britain's continued membership of Europe, that has been raging in England, takes no account of Scotland whatever. Not once has any Conservative or Labour politician, when discussing the future renegotiation of the EU treaties, or the proposed referendum, said: "Wait a minute. What about Scotland?"

In 2006, the former Tory Defence Secretary, Michael Portillo, spoke for many Conservatives when he remarked that "from the point of view of political advantage, the Conservatives have a much better chance of being in government if Scotland is not part of the affair". The Union is no longer sacrosanct for Conservatives. For Labour, it is merely regarded as a useful source of MPs rather as William Pitt the Elder saw Scotland as a useful repository of military manpower. Scotland is increasingly falling off the map as far as Westminster politics is concerned. Neither the Conservatives nor, increasingly, the Liberal Democrats have much political investment in Scotland, since the Scots have decisively rejected them at elections. The Conservatives have only one MP in Scotland. One sometimes wonders, if Scotland went off on its own, quietly and without fuss, would England even notice?

CHAPTER SIXTEEN
INDEPENDENCE IN THE UK

H I S T O R Y   M A Y   judge that the Scottish National Party has been a victim of its own success. It was doing rather well after 2007, running the Scottish Parliament on its own terms, receiving plaudits from the press and the approval of the Scottish voters. It could have quite happily continued for another parliament or two until the Scots became more reconciled to the idea of national autonomy. But Alex Salmond had to go and win a landslide in 2011. That meant having to ask the Scots to vote for independence – a proposition they have only just begun to think about, and which involves scary issues like currencies and armies; new taxation systems and split pensions. For a country which has never felt itself actually under foreign oppression, it's a lot to take.

The theme of this book has been the rise, as if from nowhere, of Scottish Nationalism. I hope if nothing else, I have made clear that Scotland is not Ireland, has come to political Nationalism very late in the day, and still doesn't quite know what to do with it. But nor is Scotland simply the Labour country it is often characterised as, despite the myth of Red Clydeside. The Scots were never really Tory, as the Conservatives discovered after 1965 when they stopped being the Unionist Party. What dominated Scottish public life until the 20th century, was the Presbyterian Kirk, which had combined a kind of congregational democracy, with Calvinist theocracy that crowded out radical politics and Nationalism. Scotland lost its parliament after 1707 but gained an Empire – or at least the illusion of one. Through the Kirk, colonial business and the British Army, Scotland endeavoured to colonise the colonisers. But now, these pillars of Scottish public life are gone: the Kirk is a lost world, the Empire a distant memory and the Scottish Unionist Party forgotten. The Scots don't need a referendum – they need therapy.

Margaret Thatcher made the break with the old Britain, destroying her own party in Scotland in the process. England has less economic interest in Scotland now that North Sea oil is less important to the balance of payments. Some Conservatives give the impression that if they could be rid of Scotland tomorrow, they would be rather relieved. It would certainly consolidate their political hold on England, because Labour can only govern in Westminster, generally speaking, on the strength of Scottish Labour MPs making up the parliamentary majority. However, David Cameron does not share this attitude and understands that the UK would be significantly lessened if Scotland departed, rejecting nuclear weapons on the way.

In the deepest recession since the 1930s, the UK Government's priority has been to cut taxes on the highest earners in the land and clamp down on welfare. Britain's very future in Europe is now in serious doubt because of the increasingly anti-European politics of the south of England. For many Scottish voters, the scary prospect right now isn't just Scotland being independent; it is Scotland staying in a UK that is increasingly dancing to the tune of UKIP. Scottish voters have registered their disapproval of these developments at successive UK general elections and have ensured that very different policies are pursued in the Scottish Parliament. Over the past 20 years, Scotland has acquired many of the political characteristics of the Nordic countries, like Norway and Denmark. The question is whether this divergence can be contained within the confines of a United Kingdom state.

The decisive moment in Scottish history was 1997, when Scotland voted to restore the Scottish Parliament after 300 years. Scotland now has a directly elected legislature responsible, with a few notable exceptions, for domestic affairs. It seems likely that the Scottish Parliament will acquire powers over taxation, broadcasting, the Crown Estate lands, and energy transmission. Under the Scotland Act, passed last year, the Scottish Parliament will assume the power to levy up to 10p on the basic rate of tax, and the ability to borrow up to £5bn a year, thus creating a primitive Scottish national debt. The Scots have been comfortable with the present constitutional arrangement and have come to regard the Parliament as a positive contribution to Scottish society, despite their initial disillusion with devolution in the early 2000s. But now, the Scots have to decide at very short notice whether or not to become independent, with only the vaguest concept of what independence might actually mean in practice.

Independence in the UK

The choice is particularly difficult because it's not clear what No means. As the referendum draws near, the Unionist parties are offering ever more radical alternatives to independence. The Scottish Labour Party is now suggesting that it might even back full tax-raising powers for Holyrood – a policy that used to be dismissed by Labour as Nationalism by another name. The Scottish Conservatives, too, are bearing gifts. The Scottish Conservative leader, Ruth Davidson, executed an abrupt U-turn in 2013 and is now proposing lots of extra powers, despite having said only two years ago that it was time to "draw a line in the sand" under constitutional change. What are Scots to make of all this? Do they believe them, after what happened in 1979, when the "better devolution" promised by Lord Home never materialised? What Scotland does not need is another divisive referendum, as in 1979, after which Scotland lapses into another 20 years of morbid introspection and economic decline.

In an ideal world, all the parties in Scotland would get together and work out a form of federalism, based on Devolution Plus (or minus, or whatever), which would provide a workable way forward. We know that the default position of the Scots is for a Scottish Parliament which makes all or most decisions on taxes,public spending, pensions and welfare, leaving defence, foreign affairs and monetary policy with England. But this is the one option that isn't on offer in the 2014 referendum. And it may be that its moment has passed. The Scots may be deluding themselves that there are any more halfway houses between the Union and independence for them to occupy. There appear to be limits to which the UK is prepared to contemplate constitutional change, as evidenced by the failure to use House of Lords reform and the debate over a Bill of Rights as a basis for federalism. Instead, the only constitutional change that appears on the horizon is renegotiation of Britain's relationship to Europe and possible abolition of the Human Rights Act, neither of which are of interest to many Scots. In England, there is a growing body of opinion that Scotland should go and do its own thing, if only to stop Scots absorbing English taxpayers' money – a fallacy, but a persistent one.

The Scottish political parties are incapable of forming a common front as they did in 1997 for the Scottish Devolution Referendum. Labour wants Scotland to vote for no change, out of fear of the unknown; the SNP wants Scots to vote for independence because it is the only way of getting Devolution Max. I have always argued, in the past, that home rule within the UK was the only plausible constitutional destination for Scotland. Of course, I accepted the right of the Scottish people to leave the UK – but I just thought it would never happen. Independence seemed too dramatic, too disruptive, too revolutionary for this small "c"conservative country which, contrary to its popular image, avoids confrontation whenever possible. Now I am not so sure. It seems that the political cultures of Scotland and England are departing so rapidly that it is going to take a formidable effort of will on both sides to make the Union work. Is that will still there?

It is not clear to me that, in its present state, the Labour Party has the will or the vision to seize the political agenda in Scotland, as has been urged by figures like the shadow Foreign Secretary Douglas Alexander. The attempts by Johann Lamont to break out of the Unionist corner by proposing a tax-raising parliament have already been criticised by Labour MPs in Westminster who warn against "being more nationalist than the Nationalists". It will be very hard for the Conservative leader Ruth Davidson to get a hearing in Scotland for her party's amorphous agenda of further constitutional change. The Scottish Liberal Democrats, who actually propose federalism, have become largely irrelevant because of their coalition with the Conservatives. In Scotland, Tory is still a four-letter word.

Scots say they don't want to "break up Britain" even as they vote in huge numbers for a party dedicated to precisely that. However, the SNP has not managed to convince Scots that independence will be in their interests because the word seems to have been emptied of any meaning. The Nationalists say they want to form a new United Kingdom – indeed, that the existing one is largely a Scottish creation. But many Scots see that as a reason for reforming the existing Union rather than creating a new one. The SNP believes that Scotland's economic dynamism can only be reborn by becoming independent in Europe, but at the same time, wants to remain in a currency union with England that will inevitably leave a lot of economic decision-making where it is right now – in London. One could equally raise an argument that the SNP should be demanding better representation in Westminster, rather than pulling out of it altogether.

Given the animosity between the two tribes of Scotland – the SNP and Labour – there is surprising unanimity on the need for further change. Here is the former Labour First Minister, Jack McConnell:

"On the one side, there are those that believe Scotland's future is better if we are entirely independent from the UK. Even if that is within the framework of accepting the pound and being part of the European Union and so on – and that Scotland's potential will be better realised in that circumstance. There are others who believe that the voluntary union of nations that is the United Kingdom has, by and large, helped Scotland develop and grow over the last 300 years, and that it can continue to offer that function. These are two positive points of view and I don't denigrate either of them." [140]

The only other living former Labour First Minister, Henry McLeish, agrees with this sentiment:

"The Unionists are not offering, in my view, anything. And you cannot go into an independence poll in 2014 saying we have been together since 1707, let's be together for the next 300 years. For a lot of young Scots, in particular, that's not an attractive proposition ... I want Scotland to be just the best, and I believe as a country, a nation, as part of the UK we can do that if the Union changes. If no, then I think eventually we will head towards independence, and why not be like Scandinavia, Norway, Sweden Denmark?" [141]

For his part, the SNP leader Alex Salmond is also calling for a new United Kingdom in which would retain the best of the old Union and promote future partnership:

"And when you consider our shared economic relationships, our cultural ties, our many friendships and family relationships, one thought becomes clear. After Scotland becomes independent, we will share more than a monarch and a currency. We will share a social union. It just won't be the same as a restrictive state which no longer serves the interests of either Scotland or England." [142]

Alex Salmond is convinced that Scotland is on the road to independence because the timeline of constitutional history appears to be moving in that direction – Union, devolution, Nationalist Government, independence. But there is no inevitability about Scotland becoming independent, any more than there was anything inevitable about Scotland being extinguished and becoming a region of England. History doesn't move in straight lines, and Scots have yet to be persuaded that independence would be much different to what happens now.

Scots seem to know what they want – which is a continuation of the incremental home rule that has been happening for the past 20 years. However, they find no mechanism by which they can ensure that this is continued. The Independence Referendum is an unsatisfactory either/or decision on a choice most Scots do not want to make. They aren't sure about independence and they do not want the status quo. However, they realise that a No vote in 2014 could lead to unpleasant consequences, as was the case after 1979. The pressure would be off Westminster to respond to Scottish issues, and Scots should brace themselves for changes to the Barnett Formula and UK subsidies that they will not like. There will likely be further changes to Scottish representation in Westminster to address the West Lothian Question following a No vote in 2014. Scots will have even less influence on the character of government in the UK.

There are many of reasons why the Scots are reluctant to take the ultimate step of leaving the United Kingdom. The Empire was a common project for which Scots fought and died until the 1940s, after which Scots thought they were creating a new social commonwealth. You don't give up that kind of history overnight. It may well have become redundant. It may even become something of an anachronism. But Britain was a great idea while it lasted. The greatest achievement of the Union, and the one everyone forgets about, was that Scotland and England stopped fighting each other. The 1707 Treaty of Union brought to an end 400 years of border warfare. It did so, by offering a common economic project to keep the "animal spirits" of both sides harnessed in the pursuit of economic gain rather than at each other's throats. And it worked. But the Empire is no more, and there is nothing obviously to replace it.

There clearly have been powerful forces at work in the United Kingdom over the past three decades that have led us to something of a crossroads in the history of Great Britain and a fundamental renegotiation of Scotland's place in it. In time, Scotland and England may decide that they have no particular reason to remain in the one political state any longer. The Union was always a bit of an anomaly anyway, a marriage of convenience. It was two sovereign states who elected to become one Great Britain, while holding their fingers crossed behind their backs. England did not sink its identity into Great Britain and neither did Scotland, which retained many of its distinctive institutions – the Kirk, education and law. The Union was an alliance of convenience, useful for strategic and economic purposes. It was an instrumental union and as such should always measured on a criterion of continued usefulness.

So, perhaps instead of talking about the end of Union we should be turning this argument on its head, and talking about its regeneration. The Scottish parties are reluctant to admit it, but there is something like a consensus that we need a new Union – even the SNP is now talking about a new "social union", a revived UK. One that will be more flexible, and will not maintain the pretence that the two have become one. Perhaps, in the end, it doesn't really matter whether this is called independence or Devolution Max or federalism – it is still a union. It will require a degree of economic and, in particular, fiscal disengagement, because the present arrangements of the Barnett Formula do not retain the confidence of either side. But it will not lead to the end of co-operation across the border. Once the anomalies of the Union, and the perceived inequities – at least from the English point of view – are resolved, we will still be left with two English-speaking countries, with very similar democratic histories who share a relatively small island, off the coast of Continental Europe and have a very great deal in common, not least families and businesses which straddle the border. After the trial separation, the two countries would probably be closer than ever.

This could even come about through incremental acquisition of new powers by the Scottish Parliament. Donald Dewar's great legacy to Scotland was the Scotland Act of 1998, as Alex Salmond has always recognised. Dewar always said that devolution was a process and not an event, and there is no formal limit to this process. By only specifying those powers that are retained in Westminster, rather than those which are ceded to Holyrood, Dewar began a open-ended process of constitutional revision which could lead to Scotland exercising most economic powers, while still remaining nominally in the British state. Given Britain's history of constitutional improvisation, or "muddling through" as it is often called, this could be a way of achieving the new Union. Equally, some will argue, it is better to adopt the SNP's policy – stop muddling, face up to reality and make a new start. Formally constitute Scotland as an autonomous entity before reconnecting it with the other elements in the British Isles, Wales, England, Northern Ireland.

Alex Salmond was one of the few people in his party who really "got" what the Scotland Act was about in 1998. Between them in the discussions over the sovereignty of the Scottish Parliament, Donald Dewar and Alex Salmond may unconsciously have devised a mechanism through which Scotland could become progessively disengaged from the UK, and set in motion a process which could lead to the best outcome for both Scotland and England. A contradictory constitutional settlement: Independence in the UK. Living apart, together.

REFERENCES

1 'The Caledonian Antisyzygy and the Gaelic Ideal' in *Selected Essays of High MacDiarmid*, ed. Duncan Glen. California. 1969, 70.

2 Poll - 35 years of Scottish attitudes towards independence | ipsos-MORI.com (bit.ly/17oW9Sv)

3 David Maddox, SNP wins no friends by snubbing the underdogs | *The Scotsman* (bit.ly/13uQfMp)

4 Anti-English Artists are fanning the flames of bigotry | *The Scotsman* (bit.ly/18LlyF1)

5 Murray Watson, *Being English in Scotland: A Guide*. Edinburgh. 2003, 146.

6 Attacks on Minorities | Newsnet Scotland (bit.ly/WhW26t)

7 Currency Union questions | BBC News (bbc.in/16wEiss)

8 Electoral Commission forces the pace on possible paths for Scotland | *The Guardian* (bit.ly/12rnGy5)

9 New setback for SNP over EU membership | *The Scotsman* (bit.ly/YGAhwI)

10 Interview: Mel Gibson | *The Scotsman* (bit.ly/1285Oql)

11 Michael Penman, *The Scottish Civil War: The Bruces and the Balliols and the War for Control of Scotland, 1286-1356*. Gloucestershire, 2002.

12 G.W.S. Barrow, *Robert Bruce and the Community of the Realm*. Edinburgh. 2005, 116.

13 Alastair Campbell, *A History of Clan Campbell: From The Restoration to the Present Day*. Edinburgh. 2000, 214.

14 Scottish independence: it'll cost you | *The Economist* (econ. st/12wRbxg)

15 HoL Economic Affairs Committee Report. 10/4/13

16 Allan I. Macinnes, *Union and Empire: The Making of the United Kingdom in 1707*. Cambridge University Press. 2007.

17 I. J. Gentles, *The English Revolution and the wars in the three kingdoms: 1638-1652*. Pearson/ Longman. 2007.

18 *The Herald* 12/2/13

19 The hidden Scots victims of the slave trade | *Caledonian Mercury* (bit. ly/169ySUP)

20 David Hume, *Essays and Treatises on Several Subjects, V. 1*. London. 1758.

21 Adam Smith on Slavery | paecon.net (bit.ly/10UKWjM)

22 Richard J. Finlay, *A Partnership for Good? Scottish Politics and the Union Since 1880*. Edinburgh. 1997.

23 'Missing faces': Jackie Kay on Scotland's role in the slave trade | *The Guardian* (bit.ly/14juyOf)

24 T. C. Smout, *A History of the Scottish People: 1560-1830*. London. 2011 [1969], 204.

25 Tim Jeal, *Livingstone*. Yale. 2001.

26 Tom Devine, *Scotland's Empire: 1600-1815*. London. 2003, 233.

27 Ibid.

28 Jeremy Paxman, *Empire: What Ruling the World Did to the British*. London. 2011.

29 J. Symington, *The Working Man's Home*. Edinburgh. 1866, pp. 158-9.

30 James Millar, *Swords for Hire: the Scottish Mercenary*. Edinburgh. 2007.

31 Tim Newark, Highlander: *The History of the Legendary Highland Soldier*. London. 2010.

32 Lawrence James, *Warrior Race: A History of the British at War*. London. 2002.

33 Tom Devine, *The Scottish Nation: 1700-2000*. London. 1999.

34 Gerald Parsons, *Religion in Victorian Britain: Controversies*. Manchester University Press. 1988.

35 Callum G Brown, *Religion and society in Scotland since 1707*. Edinburgh University Press. 1997. pp185-6

36 Duncan B. Forrester, *Truthful Action: Explorations in Practical Theology*. Edinburgh. 200, 177

37 Scotland's Census: An Interactive History (bit.ly/fM8uTq)

38 Tom Devine, *The Scottish Nation: 1700-2000*. London. 1999

39 'The Caledonian Antisyzygy and the Gaelic Ideal' in Selected Essays of High MacDiarmid, ed. Duncan Glen. California. 1969, 70.

40 *Sunday Times* 6/11/2005

41 *Road to Referendum*, STV Productions. 5/6/13

42 Quoted in David Torrance, *The Scottish Secretaries*. Edinburgh. 2006, 170

43 *Road to Referendum*, STV Productions. 5/6/13

44 Ibid

45 Ibid

46 *Road to Referendum*, STV Productions. 5/6/13

47 Ibid

48 T. C. Smout, *A History of the Scottish People: 1560-1830*. London. 2011 [1969], 186.

49 *Road to Referendum*, STV Productions. 5/6/13

50 Carol Craig, *The Scots Crisis of Confidence*. Edinburgh. 2003.

51 *Road to Referendum*, STV Productions. 5/6/13

52 Ibid

53 Ibid

54 David Torrance, *Whatever Happened to Tory Scotland?* Edinburgh. 2012, 5.

55 Richard J. Finlay in *Whatever Happened to Tory Scotland?* Edinburgh. 2012, pp. 29-43

56 *Road to Referendum*, STV Productions. 5/6/13

57 Ibid

58 Ibid

59 Ed. J. Bochel, D. Denver and A. Macartney, *The Referendum Experience: Scotland 1971*. Aberdeen. 1981

60 Ibid

61 *Road to Referendum*, STV Productions. 5/6/13

62 Ibid

63 Ibid

64 Ibid

65 *Road to Referendum,* STV Productions. 5/6/13

66 Warning over oil production drop | BBC News (bbc.in/OI8zK5)

67 Scots need to put some spark into the economy | reformscotland. com (bit.ly/13ED4bl)

68 How Britain changed under Margaret Thatcher | *The Guardian* (bit. ly/17mMFpb)

69 Could this study at last tell us why Glasgow is the sick man of Europe? | *The Sunday Herald* (bit.ly/y8RaZA)

70 *Road to Referendum,* STV Productions. 5/6/13

71 Ibid

72 Ibid

73 Ibid

74 Ibid

75 Ibid

76 Council urged to write off £32m Poll Tax debt | *Hamilton Advertiser* (bit.ly/18VMimj)

77 *Road to Referendum,* STV Productions. 5/6/13

78 Ibid

79 D. Denver, 'The 1997 General Election in Scotland: an analysis of the results', *Scottish Affairs* 20. Edinburgh. 1997.
80 *Road to Referendum,* STV Productions. 5/6/13

81 Ibid

82 *The Blair Years: Extracts from the Alastair Campbell Diaries.* London. 2008, 49

83 *Road to Referendum,* STV Productions. 5/6/13

84 *The Blair Years: Extracts from the Alastair Campbell Diaries.* London. 2008, 474

85 Peter Jones, 'Labour's Referendum Plan: Sell-out or Act of Faith?' *Scottish Affairs* 18. Edinburgh. 1997 (bit.ly/Z6i2Dr)

86 *Road to Referendum,* STV Productions. 5/6/13

87 Ibid

88 Ibid

89 *Road to Referendum,* STV Productions. Transcripts

90 *Road to Referendum,* STV Productions. 5/6/13

91 Ibid

92 *Road to Referendum,* STV Productions. Transcripts

93 The Rapid and Unlikely Rise of Scotland's Independence Movement | *The Atlantic* (bit.ly/INIMKG)

94 *Road to Referendum,* STV Productions. Transcripts

95 Files prove that MI5 spied on SNP | *The Scotsman* (bit.ly/124X6MZ)

96 SNP 'has not thought through' Scottish MI5 and MI6 | *The Telegraph* (bit.ly/XOto88)

97 MI6 working covertly to scuttle Scottish independence | intrepidreport.com (bit.ly/VQThqn)

98 Brian Barder: Megrahi at centre of transfer deal mystery | *The Scotsman* (bit.ly/Z6j6qI)

99 Hugo Young Lecture: Scotland's place in the world | snp.org (bit.ly/xGkKcg)

100 Support for independence bounces back | ipsos-MORI.com (bit.ly/Z9J7oC)

101 *Road to Referendum*, STV Productions. Transcripts

102 *The Herald* 28/4/13

103 Scots need to put some spark into the economy | reformscotland.com (bit.ly/13ED4bI)

104 Scottish universities appear in world's elite top 200 | BBC News (bbc.in/rsc25v)

105 Britain has squandered golden opportunity North Sea oil promised | *The Guardian* (bit.ly/HrUg90)

106 Policy Commission on the Distribution of Wealth | birmingham.ac.uk (bit.ly/SU7dBD)

107 Divided We Stand: Why Inequality Keeps Rising | OECD.org (bit.ly/XVchE4)

108 Scotland would gain few benefits from going it alone that it cannot already get as part of the United Kingdom | johnkay.com (bit.ly/lUTlZK)

109 Serving Scotland Better: Scotland and the United Kingdom in the 21st Century (bit.ly/yk2pLt)

110 Annual finance figures show Scotland pays its way, says Swinney | publicfinance.co.uk (bit.ly/13FfkoY)

111 Independence: own currency will protect Scots against looming run on pound, warns expert | scottishtimes.com (bit.ly/11ORKCn)

112 Blanchard: UK economic policy is "playing with fire" | edmundconway.com (bit.ly/11n3rRs)

113 Scots count price of independence | BBC News (bbc.in/txxNDj)

114 Leaked Swinney document makes devastating reading | *Evening Times* (bit.ly/10HOxlw)

115 SNP anger as EU says a breakaway Scotland will have to reapply to join | *Daily Mail* (bit.ly/VlwkI4)

116 An independent Scotland would end up like Panama without control of the pound, George Osborne warns | *Daily Mail* (bit.ly/XSF4uP)

117 Osborne scorns Scottish independence camp's plan for currency union | *The Guardian* (bit.ly/12FSUSY)

118 How would an independent Scotland defend itself? | *The Guardian* (bit.ly/xAiiMH)

119 'Hadrian's Wall' customs if Scotland goes it alone to stop illegal migrants flooding into England | *Daily Mail* (bit.ly/zwxWw1)

120 Britons run up £ 120bn of debt on their credit cards | *The Herald* (bit.ly/12GwFf0)

121 Scots 'risk loss of top credit rating if they quit the UK', says leading agency | *Daily Mail* (bit.ly/Io4aJw)

122 Scottish independence: 'Havoc' warning from pensions firm | BBC News (bbc.in/UgfXO2)

123 Scotland 'faces bill of £30bn' after North Sea oil runs out | *The Scotsman* (bit.ly/17Z8kmK)

124 Could Scottish independence spell problems for UK renewables? | businessgreen.com (bit.ly/vZqoEM)

125 Independence warning: the lights will go out if Scotland votes yes | iainmacwhirter2.blogspot.co.uk (bit.ly/ZszEFj)

126 Scotland's nuclear stations could stay open | BBC News (bbc.in/ym7vGj)

127 £25bn to remove Trident from Scotland | *Daily Express* (bit.ly/13FCjiv)

128 Labour claims 19,000 Scottish jobs depend on Faslane | *The Herald* (bit.ly/VcRzA5)

129 £25bn to remove Trident from Scotland | *Daily Express* (bit.ly/13FCjiv)

130 Universities lose out as fees charged for non-Scots | *The Herald* (bit.ly/UwM93N)

131 England could bomb Scottish airports | presstv.com (bit.ly/12oKywD)

132 May criticises nationalists over security plans after 2014 vote | *The Herald* (bit.ly/V5T171)

133 The Rapid and Unlikely Rise of Scotland's Independence Movement | *The Atlantic* (bit.ly/INIMKG)

134 'We won't back your whisky if you break away,' Hague tells Scotland | *Daily Mail* (bit.ly/zuTbkb)

135 Independent Scotland could be banned from using the pound - and lose its pandas | *Daily Mirror* (bit.ly/10EWDMP)

136 Investment by oil and gas sector 'to reach £13bn' | *The Courier* (bit.ly/18a6ZcF)

137 Independent Scotland could be forced to join euro, say SNP ex-leaders | *The Herald* (bit.ly/SpEs9T)

138 *The Herald* 13 /3/13

139 Independent Scotland could be forced to join euro, say SNP ex-leaders | *The Herald* (bit.ly/xQERhO)

140 *Road to Referendum,* STV Productions. Transcripts

141 Ibid

142 Hugo Young Lecture: Scotland's place in the world | snp.org (bit.ly/xGkKcg)

FURTHER READING

Lynn Abrams, Callum G Brown. *A History of Everyday Life in Scotland in the 20th Century*. Edinburgh. 2010

Neal Ascherson, *Stone Voices: Search for Scotland*. London. 2002

R.D. Anderson, *Scottish Education Since the Reformation*. Edinburgh. 2000

G.W.S. Barrow, *Robert the Bruce and the Community of the Realm of Scotland*. Edinburgh. 2005

D. W. Bebbington, *Evangelism in Modern Britain*. London. 1989

Caroline Bingham, *Robert the Bruce*. London. 1998

Jack Brand, *The National Movement in Scotland*. London. 1978

Callum G. Brown, *Religion and Society in Scotland since 1707*. Edinburgh. 1997

Stewart J. Brown, *Thomas Chalmers and the Godley Commonwealth*. Oxford. 1982

Alistair Campbell, *Diaries, Volume 1 Prelude to Power*. London. 2010

Alistair Campbell, *Diaries, Volume 2 Power and the People*. London. 2011

Alastair Campbell, *History of the Clan Campbell: from Restoration to the Present Day*. Edinburgh. 2004

S.B. Checkland, *The Upas Tree: Glasgow 1875-1975*. Aberdeen. 1985

Linda Colley, *Britons: Forging the Nation*. Yale. 1992

Carol Craig, *The Scots Crisis of Confidence*. Edinburgh. 2003

Tam Dalyell, *Devolution, The End of Britain?* London. 1977

Norman Davies, *The Isles*. London. 1999

George E Davie. *The Democratic Intellect*. London. 1961.

Tom M. Devine, *The Scottish Nation 1700-2000*. London. 2000

Tom M. Devine, *Scotland's Empire 1600-1815*. London. 2008

Ed. Tom M. Devine, *Scotland and the Union 1707-2007*. Edinburgh. 2009

Tom M. Devine, *The Tobacco Lords*. Edinburgh. 1975.

R. J. Finlay, *Modern Scotland 1914-2000*. London. 2004

R. J. Finlay, *Independent and Free - Scotland and the Origins of the SNP*. Edinburgh. 1994

R. J. Finlay, *A Partnership for Good: Scottish Politics and the Union since 1880*. Edinburgh. 1997

Michael Fry, *Patronage and Principle*. Aberdeen. 1987

Iain J. Gentles, *The English Revolution and The Wars in The Three Kingdoms*. London. 2007

Tim Harris, *Restoration - King Charles II and his Kingdoms 1660-85*. London. 2005

Christopher Harvie, *Scotland and Nationalism*. London. 1994

Christopher Harvie, *No Gods and Precious Few Heroes*. Edinburgh. 2000

Gerry Hassan and Eric Shaw, *The Strange Death of Labour Scotland*. Edinburgh. 2012

Arthur Herman, *The Scottish Enlightenment: The Scots' Invention of the Modern World*. London. 2002

R.A. Houston and W. Knox, *The New Penguin History of Scotland*. London. 2002

J. Hunter, *The Making of the Crofting Community*. Edinburgh. 1979

James Hunter, *Scottish Exodus*. Edinburgh. 2007

Tim Jeal, *Livingstone*. Yale. 2001

Michael Keating and David Bleiman, *Labour and Scottish Nationalism*. London. 1979

J. Kellas, *The Scottish Political System*. Cambridge. 1993

Colin Kidd. *Union And Unionisms*. Glasgow. 2008

W.W. Knox. *Industrial Nation: Work, Culture and Society in Scotland 1800 to the Present*. Edinburgh. 1999

Michael Lynch, *Scotland: A New History*. London. 1991

J. D. Mackie. *A History of Scotland*. London. 1964

Allan MacInness, *Union and Empire*. Cambridge. 2007

Andrew Marr, *The Battle for Scotland*. London. 1992

David McCrone, *Understanding Scotland: The Sociology of a Stateless Nation*. London. 1992

Nicola McEwen, *Nationalism and the State: Welfare and Identity in Scoland and Quebec*. London. 2006

Rosalind Mitchieson, *A History of Scotland*. London. 1991

James Mitchell, *Conservatives and the Union*. Edinburgh. 1990

James Mitchell, *Devolution in the UK*. Manchester. 2012

Tom Nairn, *The Break Up of Britain*. London. 1977

Neil Oliver, *A History of Scotland*. London. 2009

Michael Penman, *The Scottish Civil War*. London. 2002

N.T. Phillipson and Rosalind Mitchison, *Scotland in the Age of Improvement*. Edinburgh. 1970

Murray G. Pittock, *The Invention of Scotland*. London. 1991

John Prebble, *The Darien Disaster*. London. 1969

John Prebble, *The Highland Clearances*. London. 1963

John Prebble, *Culloden*. London. 1961

P.H. Scott, *1707: The Union of England and Scotland*. Edinburgh. 1979

T.C. Smout, *History of the Scottish People 1560-1830*. London. 1969

T.C. Smout, *Century of the Scottish People 1830-1950*. London. 1997

Edward Spiers, *The Scottish Soldier and Empire*. Edinburgh. 2006

David Stevenson. *Revolution and Counter Revolution in Scotland 1644-51*. London. 2003

Ed. David Torrance, *Whatever Happened to Tory Scotland?* Edinburgh. 2012

David Torrance, *Salmond: Against the Odds*. Edinburgh. 2011

Murray Watson, *Being English in Scotland*. Edinburgh. 2004

Iain Whyte, *Scotland and the Abolition of Black Slavery*. Edinburgh. 2006

Andy Wightman, *Who Owns Scotland*. Edinburgh. 1996

ACKNOWLEDGEMENTS

Thanks to Mark Buckland, Craig Lamont and David Flood at Cargo for their patience and support. Tom Thomson of Herald and Times and Alan Clements at STV for making the project happen. The brilliant Brendan O'Hara who produced the documentary series. Barclay McBain of *The Herald* and Susan Flockhart of the *Sunday Herald* for putting up with my many absences. My partner Tiffany Jenkins for always being there.

X